COMMUNITY ORIENTED POLICING

COP Talk

Essential Communication Skills for Community Policing

DR. VIRGINIA KIDD
California State University, Sacramento

CAPT. RICK BRAZIEL
Sacramento Police Department

Acada Books
San Francisco

Copyeditor: Helen Walden
Proofreader: David Sweet
Indexer: Paul Kish
Cover and Interior Design: Desktop Miracles

Acada Books
1850 Union Street, Suite 1236
San Francisco, California 94123
Tel. 415.776.2325
acada@ix.netcom.com

Publisher's Cataloging-in-Publication
(Provided by Quality Books, Inc.)

Kidd, Virginia V.
COP talk : essential communication skills for community policing / Virginia Kidd, Rick Braziel. – 1st ed.
p. cm.
Includes bibliographic references and index.
ISBN: 978-0-9655029-3-1
1. Police-community relations—United States.
2. Community policing. 3. Communication in police administration. 4. Interpersonal communication.
I. Braziel, Richard A. II. Title. III. Title: Cop talk
HV7936.P8K54 1998 363.2'0973
QBI98-1530

Printed in the United States of America

1 2 3 4 5 — 03 02 01 00 99

Contents

Preface

One day a few years ago, the authors sat in Rick's Dessert Diner discussing the latest police-community forums we had attended. A common theme kept creeping into the conversation. The police officers and their managers, who organized and led the forums, were not completely prepared to handle the many communication issues involved in this type of event. As we discussed the problem, we realized it was larger than just community forums. Many officers assigned to community policing projects throughout the United States struggle with their new roles within the community. The field of communication studies teaches practical skills that could help the police, but the two fields are virtually isolated. Over cheesecake and chocolate almond torte, a vision for this book was born.

A review of literature on communication issues related to community policing and problem solving turned up little direct research. Officers and supervisors have been forced to translate their policing skills into techniques suited to such issues as community mobilization, public speaking, group meeting leadership, and ways to deal with hostile audiences, without much help from research literature. Most officers are succeeding but not without much trial and error.

COP Talk: Essential Communication Skills for Community Policing presents communication information to help community officers become more successful. We envisioned a text that would be fun to read at the same time that it was practical. We wanted officers faced with giving a speech to turn to the public speaking chapter and immediately find help, officers planning a work meeting to quickly find advice on how to lead it, and so on.

This is not a book of hard-and-fast rules. Even though the advice in the following chapters reflects many years of communication research, both scholars and police officers daily find new ways to communicate, solve problems, and achieve goals. Modify the advice in this book to fit your needs. Let it be a springboard to new techniques that work for you.

Features

COP Talk includes several pedagogical features designed to help enhance learning and recall. *COP Talk* includes the following features:

- **Composite Stories.** Throughout the text you will be introduced to a group of fictional characters in the River Heights Police Department and the community it serves. These stories are designed to illustrate communication principles in action. Although the cases are fictional, they are composites of actual officers' experiences.
- **Action Clips.** Each chapter includes several Action Clips, which show how specific communication techniques and strategies have been used successfully in community interactions. Action Clips confirm the importance of a

topic and often provide related information, practical advice, and additional insights into its real-life application.

- **Pocket Guides.** These sidebars expand on the topic at hand, introduce helpful related information, and summarize complex processes. The Pocket Guides offer practical advice, proven strategies, resource references, and ancillary information.
- **Activities.** Each chapter includes five to seven exercises designed to help you apply the concepts and to practice implementing the techniques introduced in the chapter. In addition to furthering your own understanding, many of these activities are appropriate for real-world application.
- **Glossary.** The definition of each boldfaced term introduced in the chapters is included in the glossary. This list provides a convenient way to review terms and vocabulary.

Acknowledgments

Many people either directly or indirectly helped make *COP Talk* a reality. Our thanks to Sacramento Police Chief Arturo Venegas, Jr., for allowing unlimited access to community meetings, department meetings, and interviews with employees; to Sacramento Officers Harold Bickel and Greg Dieckmann for the honest assessment of their award-winning community policing project, including the pitfalls; and to the many community officers throughout the United States and Canada who posted their success stories on the Web so that others could benefit from their experiences. We also thank Anne Richards, California Highway Patrol Public Information Officer; Ann Reed, Assistant Vice President for Public Affairs at California State University, Sacramento; and Michele Quattrin, Sacramento Police Department Public Information Officer; for their technical advice for Chapter 8.

We are indebted to Betsy Wackernagel Bach, Ph.D., The University of Montana; Ronald J. Cristando, Cristando House, Inc.; Sergeant Marc V. DeLuca, In-Service Training Supervisor, Charlotte-Mecklenburg Police Department Training Academy; Detective Pat Heine, Pueblo Police Department; Captain Blaine Koops, Holland Police Department; Mark M. Lanier, Ph.D., University of Central Florida; Captain Lesli Lord, Ph.D., San Diego Police Department, Regional Community Policing Institute San Diego; Nicholas P. Lovrich, Jr., Washington State University; Ann McIntosh, Ph.D., Communication Connection; Director Nancy McPherson, Community Policing Bureau, Seattle Police Department; and Len Silvey, Department of Justice Advance Training Center for their reviews and comments that offered perspectives to add to the text, and to Robin and Brian Romer, Acada Books, for their faith in this project and their guidance.

Lastly, and most importantly, Rick thanks his daughters, Megan and Christine, who kept him focused through their patience, understanding, and concern.

Community Oriented Policing and Communication

Introduction

"Community policing emphasizes the development of close communication between citizens and police. This communication helps police gather information for both preventing and solving crime."

MARK H. MOORE,
ROBERT C. TROJANOWICZ,
AND GEORGE L. KELLING (46)

Officer Alan Richards hears muffled voices as he slowly pushes open the door. He hesitates slightly as he tries to scan the large room without being seen. He is concerned that he's alone; he should have requested backup. With sweaty palms and a pounding heart, he weighs the options of slipping in slowly and quietly in the hope of being undetected or rushing forward in a dynamic thrust and putting them on the defensive. All of the training and experience of his eleven years in law enforcement provide little help or comfort right now. Longingly, he remembers the days when his canine partner would bound into danger ahead of him. Taking a deep breath, Richards pushes open the door all the way. The room is long and well lit. All eyes turn toward him.

This is not a gang fight, a drug deal going down, or burglars caught in the act. It's a crowd of fifty community members waiting to hear him speak about problems in their neighborhood.

PUBLIC PRESENTATIONS, ALONG WITH OTHER COMMUNICATION SITUATIONS such as interpersonal conversations, work group meetings, team-building sessions, and community events, are becoming more important to policing agencies as they move swiftly into community oriented policing (COP).

Philosophy of Community Policing

Community oriented policing (or **community policing**) is a philosophy that promotes police-community partnerships. It is a way of doing business that focuses on the community's identified quality-of-life issues. In their text *Community Policing: How to Get Started*, Robert Trojanowicz and Bonnie Bucqueroux describe community policing as

> . . . a philosophy and an organizational strategy that promotes a new partnership between people and their police. It is based on the premise that both the police and the community must work together to identify, prioritize, and solve contemporary problems such as crime, drugs, fear of crime, social and physical disorder, and neighborhood decay, with the goal of improving the overall quality of life in the area. (2)

A "new" partnership implies that the community and police have been working apart. To now work together requires "a breed of line officer who acts as a direct link between the police and the people in the community" (Trojanowicz and Bucqueroux 5). In other words, community policing requires increased and improved communication between the police officer and the community, which includes area residents, businesses, schools, churches, medical facilities, community-based organizations, and visitors to the area.

Community policing has changed the working relationship between officers, their supervisors, the police administration, the community, business, the government, and elected officials. Before community policing, most jurisdictions operated within a hierarchy of government and law enforcement officials, as shown in Figure I-1. Communication flowed up and down this hierarchical chain of command structure in a well-defined path. Any deviations from the accepted structure usually met with negative consequences in the form of discipline. This linear path of communication often prevented effective and efficient information exchange and problem solving because police officers communicated mostly with their supervisors, and little information flowed down or back up the chain of command. The flow was structured with established rules and roles that did not encourage open communication.

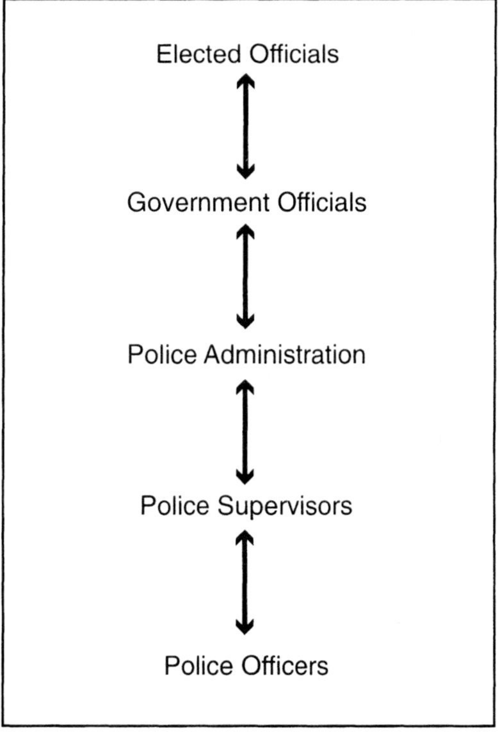

Figure I-1: Linear path of communication

Today officers communicate directly with the community, businesses, government agencies, and elected officials, as shown in Figure I-2. This very dynamic pattern of communication exchange has replaced the old linear model. Community policing has changed not only the way policing works with the community but also the way local governments do business.

As policing agencies work more closely with communities, the rest of local government is following closely behind in a change that can truly be called **community oriented government (COG)**. This new type of government and policing provides a different way for officers to communicate. With such a dynamic pattern comes a need for officers to understand the communication process.

Increased Community Expectations

As communication opportunities increase between the police officer and the community, so does the community members' expectation that they will be included in

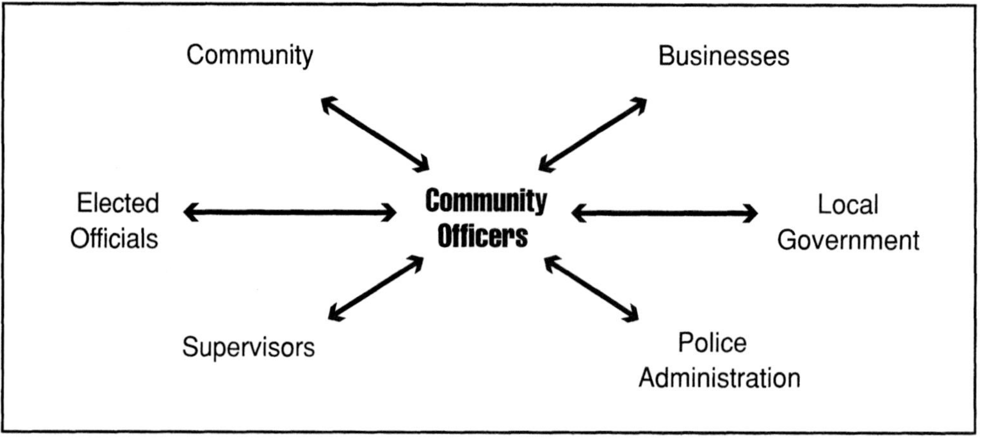

Figure I-2: Dynamic pattern of communication

decisions that affect them. The community wants to be part of such decisions as staffing, spending, and policing priorities. The increased community demand to be involved necessitates a change in the way police interact with the community. No longer can police assume they know what a community's problems are and what the solutions should be. Such an attitude will only serve to isolate policing agencies from the community. This increased communication exposure has both benefits and challenges, which are listed in Figure I-3.

Effective Communication

Officer Richards' apprehension about public speaking is not uncommon. Why would a seasoned veteran suffer so much anxiety? As departments nationwide move into COP, training in communication skills has not kept pace. The explanation for this depends on whom you ask. A police manager might say, "Communication is a skill learned through experience and exposure to a wide variety of community interactions." A street cop might respond, "We know how to communicate; it's just like handling a call." And a community member might answer, "Cops should already know how to communicate well simply because they are cops."

> "Communication is the foundation for cooperation, coordination, collaboration and change. It is important to start communication early in the community policing implementation process."
>
> —Community Policing Consortium, "About Community Policing"

But can officers transfer the skills honed on the streets into those needed to mobilize a community? Look at Officer Richards. This is his first community meeting, and he is starting off on the wrong foot. He is anxious and fears the audience will be against him. Can he use his crisis intervention training to control the group? *Should* he control the group? How does he handle an angry or frustrated audience? Richards needs answers, suggestions,

Benefits	Challenges
▪ Officers receive firsthand information about most community issues—the concerns, ideas, and proposed solutions—rather than information passed down through the organization. ▪ Officers and government agencies better understand each other's demands, needs, and limitations. Frequently, the problems associated with community policing are also problems for federal, state, and local governments. ▪ Community members recognize officers as *their* officers. An extreme attachment often develops between community officers and the community. This attachment can create new lines of communication. ▪ Officers have direct access to the decisionmakers within government. They can "tell it like it is" out in the community and show them what it's like to be on the front lines.	▪ More chances exist for misunderstanding. COP increases the amount of communication, which in turn increases the potential for misunderstanding. ▪ Officers must keep an entire network of people informed about their activities. ▪ Officers can be misled and used by others to accomplish their hidden agendas. The hierarchical form of communication shelters officers from self-serving individuals trying to manipulate the governmental and private processes to their advantage. ▪ The community expects quicker responses to their problems and interprets delayed responses as disinterest or politics. Yet officers do not always have the power to move quickly. Their increased responsibility as problem-solvers does not come with an increased decision-making authority. The phrase "I need to check with my supervisor" can strain an officer's relationship with the community.

Figure I-3: Increased communication with the community

and strategies. So do thousands of other officers who are taking their first steps as community officers.

This text provides officers moving into community policing concrete ways to improve their communication skills by describing such subjects as how to build relationships, how to conduct meetings, how to give talks, how to stage community meetings, how to involve the community in crime prevention projects, and how to avoid some common pitfalls experienced by others. The text is designed for officers who want to successfully apply the principles of COP, department leaders who want to help their officers succeed, students who hope to become community officers, people who work with community officers, and anyone who wishes to understand the importance of communication to the COP process.

Throughout the text you will be introduced to a group of fictional characters in the River Heights Police Department and the community it serves. Any resemblance to real individuals is coincidental. However, the stories are composites of actual experiences of officers in various parts of the United States. Through the experiences of Officers Alan Richards, Diedra Holland, and Randy Washington, their supervisors, and the people in their community, you will learn ways to improve your communication skills.

To facilitate a smooth flow of the text, common terms are used to identify agencies and individuals. *Police officer* includes everyone who is involved in the community policing effort regardless of the type of agency in which he or she works. This term stands for sheriff's deputies, troopers, highway patrol officers, probation officers, federal and state agents, police officers, and a host of others whose titles identify them as working in the policing field. *Policing agency* includes all local, county, state, and federal agencies working in the dynamic area of community policing.

The chapters are structured to allow easy access to the information you may need for a given situation.

Turn to	To find out more about
Chapter 1	The basic communication principles that explain how a message is sent and received. Examine the content and relational message components, communication context, verbal and nonverbal codes, channel, and feedback.
Chapter 2	Improving your interpersonal communization. Community policing dramatically increases the number of interactions between an officer and the community. Understanding and practicing quality interpersonal communication will help you in all your interactions.
Chapter 3	The dynamics of work groups. Follow these step-by-step instructions for planning and leading a small, task-oriented group meeting.
Chapter 4	Americans' greatest fear—public speaking. Learn how to prepare and deliver a talk.
Chapter 5	Preparing for and leading a community meeting. Topics cover selecting a presentation format, planning the details of your meeting, and dealing with a hostile audience.
Chapter 6	Creative problem-solving techniques that supplement the SARA model.
Chapter 7	Ways to convince others to support your creative solution and how to involve them in an action plan for change.
Chapter 8	Ways to publicize your program via the media and let others, including fellow officers, know what you are doing.

The success of community policing rests largely on the shoulders of officers like Alan Richards, who are out on the front lines, and on the supervisors who allow them to spend time problem solving. This text will help make that effort more successful by explaining ways to interact more effectively. Communication skills are a powerful, effective, and essential tool in the ever-increasing bag of tools used in policing.

Works Cited

Community Policing Consortium. "About Community Policing." www.communitypolicing.org. 20 Oct. 1997.

Moore, Mark H., Robert C. Trojanowicz, and George L. Kelling. "Crime and Policing." *Police Practice in the '90s*. Washington, D.C.: International City Management Assoc., 1989.

Trojanowicz, Robert, and Bonnie Bucqueroux. *Community Policing: How to Get Started.* Cincinnati: Anderson Publishing, 1994.

Chapter One

Why They Still Don't Understand When You Told Them So Clearly

The Communication Process

"When you get up in front
of a crowd in a uniform,
people will listen,
right up to the point where
you say something stupid."

HAROLD BICKEL
COMMUNITY OFFICER

Officer Diedra Holland listens intently as the radio picks up Alan Richards' voice. "Where can we go?" she hears him say. The wire taped to his chest under his shirt crackles. Through the static she hears a woman's soft voice finish, "—urant over in the shopping center."

Ridding the neighborhood of prostitutes is a high priority for the community. Holland and Richards and their partner, Randy Washington, are part of an undercover sting operation. Richards, driving a Bronco, is wired and broadcasting to officers in waiting patrol cars and unmarked vans. The patrol cars cruise nearby, listening to the pickups and waiting for the code phrase "Well, here's your money" that signals an illegal act: the exchange of money for sex. Within seconds, police cars will rush up with lights flashing.

"Where are they?" Randy Washington asks over the radio.

Holland answers, "I can't hear him."

Another voice chimes in, "She said behind the Chinese restaurant in the strip mall."

"Where is that?"

"Next to K-Mart."

Holland spies Washington's van across the K-Mart parking lot. As she turns into it, she hears Richards offer the money. She flips on her overhead lights, shifts into low, and speeds around behind the China Dragon on Washington's tail.

No one is there.

A third car zooms up. The radio sputters. "Where the hell are they?"

Holland gasps, "There's another Chinese restaurant in the mall over on 24th!" She throws her car into gear as she hears Richards choking out, "I don't know about this. It's so public here. I don't feel comfortable. Don't you think there's too much light? A car's really uncomfortable, isn't it? Do you think this is safe?" followed by the annoyed reassurances of the prostitute.

DESPITE THE POTENTIAL CONSEQUENCES, Alan Richards' communication problems were simple compared to many. Communication difficulties can involve much more than misinterpretation of words. Problems can occur at any point in the communication process: in words, the nonverbal tone, the style in which a message is sent, the distractions grabbing a listener's attention, or the channels conveying the message. This communication process underlies all the specific skills discussed in this book. Understanding the whole communication process helps you prepare for the multiple communication situations you will encounter as a community officer.

A Message Sent Is Not a Message Received

A message is not a concrete thing like a cup of coffee, to be handed over to another person. Our language creates this illusion that a message is a material item. Because the word "message" is a noun, we think of a message as a solid substance composed of words with specific meanings. We picture "sending a message" as being much like dropping a letter into a mailbox or transmitting e-mail over the Internet.

In reality, a message is constructed of **message cues**—sounds, symbols, and behavior the listener recognizes as words or meaningful action, and assigns meaning to. The speaker tosses out message cues like puzzle pieces in the hope that the listener can reassemble them. The puzzle pieces "Chinese restaurant in the shopping center" may wind up as "China Dragon in the strip mall" for the person who receives the pieces. That the message must be put together by the listener is obvious when someone speaks to you in a language you don't know: *Le bountee ak dah remanelle*. Got it? Not if you don't understand the message cues.

Even seemingly simple statements in a language you do understand can be confusing. Consider some examples:

- *"Take four of these a day."*

  Four at once? Four spread out through the day? Is this a 24-hour day or day as opposed to night? Do you have to get up in the middle of the night and take one?

- *"Take the first left after the river and drive for a half a mile. You can't miss it."*

  Is this the river? Or was it that dry ravine where a river obviously runs sometimes? Turn left and follow the freeway or turn left under the freeway?

- *"I want a red apple."*

  Easy, until you stand in front of your supermarket's produce section staring at Fuji, Gala, Delicious, and Macintosh apples.

- *"We're concerned about safety in your neighborhood."*

  You are referring to new prevention efforts you know the department is planning. The listener, remembering the low priority assigned to the case when his car was broken into, translates your sentence as: "We're not doing anything for you, but we want you to think we are."

Each listener supplies meaning for a message based on what meaning he or she assigns to words and actions. This is why you never can be entirely sure someone understands what you intended or that your interpretation of their words matches what they said.

Content and Relational Components

Messages communicate at two levels at the same time through two components. The **content component** is the topic or subject of the message, what the speaker talked about. The **relational component** conveys the relationship between the speaker and the listener. "Close the door" spoken as an order and "Close the door" spoken as a request both convey the same content, but the relational component of each is quite different. Simply understanding the content of the words does not fully explain the communication that occurs when the words are spoken. You also must take the relational component into account.

These dual components explain some responses you may encounter in policing. The simple fact that a message comes from an officer changes the relational component. Some people interpret your comments through the veil of all the biases they carry about police. You say, "Nice car"; they hear, "I'm parked wrong. I'm going to get a ticket." Or you say to a child, "Hello. How are you?" and he thinks, "I'm very special. When I grow up, I want to be a cop, too." Neither is the message you intended to send or suggested in any way in your content, but the relational message of an officer speaking carried additional meaning.

A listener can misinterpret the message cues in both the content and the relational component, but because the relational component is less often discussed, people are less aware of misinterpretations in this area. People often give meaning to others' behavior without even realizing that alternative interpretations exist.

One- and Two-Way Communication

Communication flows in two ways. Either the speaker can send a message to the listener or the speaker and listener can interact so that information goes back and forth. Each option vastly impacts the message process.

One-way communication occurs when the speaker sends a message and the listener has no avenue to respond. Public speeches, video recordings, and even books such as this use one-way communication. This format is typical of traditional police department messages. Orders are sent out—and often "down"—and the source of the message never realizes the message is not received, not understood, not believed, or simply ignored. For example, in River Heights, Capt. John Trader used one-way communication to order department substations to post Management Board committee minutes. He never knew that the orders slipped under Sgt. Emilio Fritz's desk at the South Station, that Lt. Stefan Ivancic at the North Station went on vacation without passing the order to his sergeant, or that a secretary at Central Station posted the wrong committee minutes.

The advantage of one-way communication is that it is time efficient. Information can be given to many listeners at once. The disadvantages are that the speaker does not know if the listener understands the message and the listener has no recourse for clarification.

Two-way communication occurs when the speaker and listener interact about the message. Two-way communication provides an opportunity to get and give additional information: Holland speaks, Washington answers, then Holland speaks again.

If either person doesn't understand the other, he or she can ask for clarification. Two-way communication also can occur simultaneously: while Holland speaks, Washington nods, frowns, takes notes, or laughs, and in response, Holland changes her message. The visual model in Figure 1-1 highlights the difference between one- and two-way communication. An arrow from the speaker to the listener represents one-way communication, while an infinity sign, continually looping back on itself, represents two-way communication.

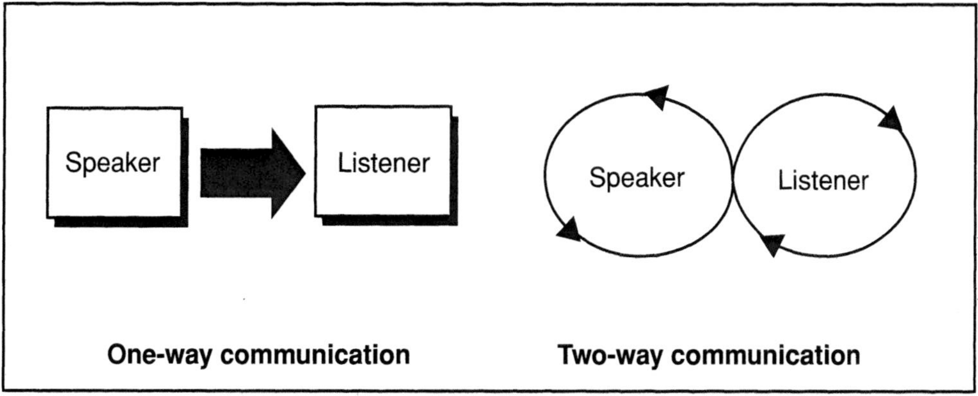

Figure 1-1: One- and two-way communication

Two-way communication doesn't automatically prevent all misunderstandings but it does increase the likelihood that people will understand one another. Unfortunately, two-way communication takes much more time than one-way communication.

Communication Context

One weapon we have against total communication chaos is that messages occur in some context. The **context** is the totality of the situation in which communication occurs: the setting, the roles of the participants, the standards for normal behavior in that situation, the reason for the gathering. The context prescribes what is appropriate for one person to say to another given the positions they hold and the situation they are in, and thus heavily influences what meaning a listener gives to message cues. For example, the simple phrase, "How are you?" has vastly different meanings when asked of a person on the street, in the hospital, after a funeral, or before a speech.

> "Whether a raised arm is a greeting or a sign of impending attack can only be decided by its context."
>
> —Sarah Trenholm (124)

You might think of the context as the rules of the game. You cannot play soccer by the rules of ice hockey or cricket by the rules of baseball. If you are the pitcher, you don't wear the catcher's mask. When you step out onto the field, people assume you know the rules. They will assign meaning to any violations of those rules.

In *Crazy Talk, Stupid Talk*, New York University professor Neil Postman calls the context a semantic environment that includes people, their purposes, "the general rules of discourse" that tell them how to talk, and the words they use. This environment or context is part of the process by which words take on meaning. Consider a man saying, "Father, I have sinned":

> [This] can be judged perfectly reasonable when uttered inside a box that is inside a church to a man who wears a special garment and is pledged to secrecy. But the same words come out *stupid talk* when uttered inside an office-building elevator to a man who is reading *Popular Mechanics* and is on his way to the dentist. (10)

Essentially, the context decrees what sort of communication is appropriate as well as "who talks when and to whom and, especially, in what sort of way" (43).

When you attend a community meeting as a police officer, the context determines much about what kind of communication you will experience. You will be the recipient of much information because you are an officer. You may receive complaints meant for the department or for police in general, not you personally. People will treat you deferentially to some degree. You will be expected to discuss neighborhood safety, not your problems with your lawn or your new car.

The context and your role do not determine, however, exactly what you will say or how you will say it. If you interact cheerfully, and enthusiastically share your ideas for the neighborhood during National Night Out On Crime, people will hear a much different message than if you stand stiffly against the wall.

Codes

All communication occurs in code. Some codes are obvious, such as Morse code, sign language, and musical notes. Language also is a code, as are nonverbal signs. Both of these form the message cues we rely on to try to tell another person what we think and feel.

Verbal Codes

Verbal codes involve communication exchanges in words. No matter how a dictionary defines a word, words have meaning based on how we've heard them used before. *Concert*—a public performance of music or dancing. That's the **denotative meaning** of concert, the dictionary definition of the word. Words also carry **connotative meanings**, definitions people assign to words based on their own emotional baggage. To you, the very word *concert* may evoke images of extra shifts, crowd control, youth problems, and fights. To a concert goer, the word connotes pure delight, loud music, light shows, and beer.

For an instant understanding of the difference between denotative meaning and connotative meaning think of any highly controversial person in the last few years: Rodney King, Bill Clinton, Janet Reno, your favorite (or least favorite) politician. The denotative meaning is who the person is, but the connotative meaning is the emotional response the name arouses. Simple words do this too: *family, football, written report, promotion, salary increase, Christmas*. The difficulty with connotative meanings is that a word does not necessarily have the same connotative meaning for everyone involved in a conversation, and no dictionary can tell you what the word "means" to others.

> "You cannot *not* communicate."
>
> —Paul Watzlawick, Janel Helmick Beavin, and Don D. Jackson (49)

Nonverbal Codes

Nonverbal codes involve communication exchanges that are in a form other than speech. Some nonverbal elements are used together with words, some in place of words, and some appear unrelated to the words. Officers have learned to look for obvious signs of guilt when interviewing suspects, such as pupil dilation, increased respiration, diverted eye contact, fidgeting. Nonverbal codes include such signs, but also involve many other elements—physical appearance, body stance and posture, facial expression, tone of voice, eye contact, touch, personal space, territoriality, artifacts, and time.

Giving meaning to nonverbal behavior occurs at an almost unconscious level. We see a frown and hear a loud voice, and assign the code "angry." Often, we give little consideration to how we reached the meaning we assigned. Only when an alternate meaning is offered do we really think about what led to our conclusions. Nonverbal codes are among the most ambiguous ways to communicate, especially as their meaning tends to vary by culture. As you consider various types of nonverbal codes, remember that their meaning is always an interpretation.

> "In many cases, when police interact with the public, all the public sees is the badge on the chest and the gun at the side. These officers took steps to minimize this phenomenon. . . . For example, they . . . put on shorts and high-tops to play basketball with neighborhood teenagers, and got dressed up to go to the neighborhood dances. These actions helped break down the barriers between the community and the officers, and facilitated communication."
>
> —Harold Bickel and Gregory Dieckmann (5)

- **Physical appearance.** People make a personal statement or project an image by their appearance. You give meaning to the red suit a woman wears, her curly hair, her jaunty walk across the room. You ascribe qualities to the young man with pants hung too low on his hips, an oversized shirt, a tattoo of a striking cobra up his arm, a head with hair a quarter inch long. When he turns his head and you discover Mickey Mouse has been shaved into his hair,

POCKET GUIDE

The Police Uniform: To Wear or Not Wear?

The police uniform with its attendant gun and badge is like a neon sign. When you walk into a room wearing a uniform, attention is immediately drawn to you. The uniform communicates an immediate and powerful message: authority, security, integrity, trust, safety—and to some, a threat. For some people the uniform has a very positive effect, which allows you to establish an immediate rapport with many groups. Wearing your uniform sends a dual message that you are serious about your topic and that your department supports you. It conveys to an audience that you know what the options are and how best to handle a situation.

For others, the uniform can be intimidating. Some people are uncomfortable in the presence of authority, and the uniform is a symbol of authority. A hostile audience has a tendency to talk to the uniform and not to the person in the uniform. In such situations you might want to wear street clothes, which can convey several meanings. You can be all business, wearing a suit. You can convey a more relaxed message with casual attire. (The Strategic Dressing chart provides some general guidelines for using clothing to set a tone.) Each article of clothing worn for a specific situation conveys a unique message about you as an officer and as a person. Repeated contact will let the community come to know you more as a person who wears a uniform and less as a uniform with a person in it.

Strategic Dressing

To appear	Wear
Formal	Uniform or suit
Relaxed professional	Sport coat, no tie, sweater, slacks or dress
Casual	Golf shirt, button shirt, or blouse and slacks or skirt
Ready to pitch in on community projects	Jeans and tee shirt
Ready to play	Athletic clothes

you might be confused. The confusion exists only because Mickey Mouse doesn't fit the meaning already assigned to the young man. One of the most powerful of these appearance messages is the police uniform.

Officer Alan Richards is a regular volunteer at the local grammar school where his daughter is a third grader. He understands the nonverbal message of his uniform and asks the teachers not to share with the class that he is a police officer. His goal is to allow the children to get to know him first as a concerned parent who cares about kids. Only after the children accept him as a regular dad does he come to class in uniform to talk about safety. The reaction from the kids is exactly as he expected: "Wow, we didn't know you were a cop! How cool! Megan's dad is a cop!" Richards has used a very strong nonverbal communication tool to teach the children that police officers are people.

- **Body stance and posture (kinesics).** The way you stand and hold yourself conveys a strong nonverbal message. A vast difference exists between the person with head up and shoulders back and the one drooping like a wilted flower after a banquet. You are probably skilled at reading body movement from your police work. Remember that community members, too, read messages from the way you stand and move. Standing in a strong stance as you would with a suspect will not send a message of approachability at a community meeting.
- **Facial expression.** Your facial expression is one of the most obvious ways you convey nonverbal relational messages. A frown, even if it's due to a headache, can be interpreted as a negative police reaction to the community, while a smile sets an amiable tone. Similarly, you can read other people's faces. Listeners' facial expressions provide instant information about how people are responding to your message. You can glance at faces as you speak to judge whether you are being understood.
- **Tone of voice (paralinguistics).** Whether your voice is gentle, loud, harsh, firm, tentative, certain, or teasing affects how people perceive your message. Often facial expression and tone of voice together carry your relational message while your words convey your content.
- **Eye contact.** Your eye contact with others sends a strong nonverbal message. Whether you look people directly in the eye, glance at your watch, gaze out a window, or observe what's happening across the room, you send a message about your concern, or lack of it, for them and the topic. The amount of eye contact often conveys status. In a group, for example, the person who receives the most eye contact is generally the one with the most power. However, interpreting what eye contact means depends on cultural backgrounds. Some cultures believe that looking another person in the eye is rude and looking down is a sign of respect. As you work with people from cultures different from your own, be careful not to judge them based solely on your values. Assuming that people are dishonest because they won't look you in the eye may be a false inference.
- **Touch (haptics).** Police officers, in certain situations, have license to touch strangers to a degree equaled only by the medical profession. Unfortunately, the police touch is not perceived as quite so healing. Furthermore, in an era of harassment issues, touching can be quite a risk. Nonetheless, little has as much power

"Eye contact seems to be a particularly difficult barrier between some African Americans and non-African Americans. According to a communications expert, Dr. Bob Mexzoff, most non-African Americans look away when speaking but look at an individual when listening. African Americans do the exact opposite."

—Community Policing Consortium

as a gentle pat on the back, and a firm handshake is a symbol of trust, friendship, and an openness to partnership. For kids, in particular, shaking hands with an officer in uniform is a thrilling experience.

> *It had been one of those days for Capt. Patrick O'Malley. Reports to write. Meetings to attend. Phone calls to return. Budgets to draw up. He could have been in middle management at IBM for all the police work he did these days. With a sigh he slipped his papers into his briefcase and then smoothed his uniform shirt tight. On impulse he decided to walk to his next meeting at City Hall.*
>
> *At the corner of 8th and Elm he stopped for a red light. Beside him, a girl of about five held her mother's hand. She tilted her head to look up at him, her eyes wide. He smiled and watched her shyly smile back. "How do you do," he said and stuck out his hand to shake. With a quick intake of breath, the girl reached out. He watched the mother step back slightly so two children on the other side could be included. He shook their hands, too, and watched grins break out on their faces.*
>
> *After they crossed the street, he turned left toward City Hall, his step brisk, his head high. It wasn't such a bad day after all.*

- **Personal space (proxemics).** Have you ever found yourself stepping backward when someone was talking to you, only to watch him or her step closer? We all have a sense of our **personal space**, how close we can comfortably stand to people when conversing. Renowned anthropologist Edward T. Hall found that Americans tend to be most comfortable carrying on personal conversations between eighteen inches and four feet away from someone. Essentially, this distance is about how far the voice will carry with no effort. Closer than eighteen inches is reserved for intimate conversations, which explains why we become uncomfortable when someone steps within that space, even in a very legitimate situation like a crowded elevator. Figure 1-2 lists standard distances for communication in the United States.

  These mainstream American expectations about distance do not apply to everyone. Some ethnic groups are accustomed to a much smaller space. Space preferences also vary with gender, age, status, degree of acquaintance, and personality.
- **Territoriality.** A variation of space as a relational message is the territoriality or "turf" issue. Where do you hold the meeting—the council member's office or yours? Do you get to sit at the head of the table or does the community leader? Who is seated closest to the podium or in front of the TV camera? These kinds of issues, petty as they seem at times, can undercut a community effort. Offering to meet at someone else's preferred location or finding a neutral space and a round table can go a long way toward helping groups get off on the right foot.
- **Artifacts.** When you go into someone's office, do you look around to get a feel for who he or she is? The use of physical space and the artifacts or objects within it

Type of communication	Distance between people	Type of interaction
Intimate	0–18 inches	Loving, comforting, protecting, fighting, arresting, helping victims
Personal	18 inches–4 feet	Conversations with friends and acquaintances
Social	4 feet–12 feet	Business and social gatherings
Public	12 feet +	Public speeches, ceremonies

Figure 1-2: Standard distances for interaction in the United States

convey messages. The photographs of the white-water rafting trip make a different statement than the wall of official plaques and framed degrees. The leather briefcase conveys one message, the canvas book bag another. The Lincoln says something different than the Harley, and neither causes people to slow down on the freeway like the sight of a Highway Patrol car in the rearview mirror. Sometimes these are deliberate, staged messages, sometimes they are inadvertent, but they are always messages.

- **Time (chronemics).** How a person uses time is an unspoken message. A man who is fifteen minutes late to a meeting makes a statement, but what is it? That you're less important than he is? That he's disorganized? That time is not important in his culture? That he answered an emergency call before the meeting? This nonverbal code has very different meanings in different cultures and for different individuals.

  Understanding that people interpret their time use differently is critical because of the tendency to judge people negatively for being "late," for "wasting" time, or for not proceeding efficiently.

> "There are many possible breakdowns in verbal communication that can cause difficulties for police officers and those of different cultures. For instance, a Nigerian who is stopped for a traffic violation will quickly exit his vehicle (as a sign of respect and humility, by not troubling the officer to exit his patrol car); the Nigerian may ignore that command to 'step back', because most likely, in his view, he is not even close to the officer."
>
> —KENNETH J. PEAK AND RONALD W. GLENSOR (216)

All of these nonverbal cues are filtered through your personal history with the listener. The listener will give meaning to your nonverbal cues based in part on your

POCKET GUIDE

Clues to Nonverbal Meanings

- Hesitation and discomfort shown at the approach of one person to another indicate status and dominance differences.
- Body relaxation is one very important indicator of status. A small (but not excessive) amount of tension can be a sign of respect and interest.
- People move closer to those they like than to those they dislike.
- Looking at a person and establishing eye contact is a way to start a conversation.
- The amount of conversation you have with someone indicates your involvement and liking.
- People who sit close together and orient themselves so they can have eye contact are far more likely to converse than those who sit far apart or turn to provide little possibility of eye contact.

(cf. Merabian)

shared past experiences. If you have a long history of trust, both parties have a stronger sense of what nonverbal cues mean to one another. A friend, for example, does not harass with a touch because you know what the touch means. A friend can stand closer, frown more, and be sloppier than a stranger without changing your assessment. He can pull on his earlobe continuously, and you'll still take his ideas seriously, and even though his office is a mess, you'll trust him to organize the next community meeting. A long assignment among the same community group enables you to develop such understanding.

The Communication Model

The complex web of meaning-giving called communication can be demonstrated with the use of a model. As Figure 1-3 shows, communication involves multiple elements. Realizing the role of each element helps you understand the communication process.

Encoding

The communication process starts with a **source**, the person who creates a message to send. Sgt. Emilio Fritz thinks, "I need to tell those new community officers to do something about the violence in the high school. Those counselors over there are driving me nuts." The source creates the message by **encoding**, or translating thoughts into verbal and nonverbal codes for a particular audience in a specific context. The encoded message contains an intended content component and an intended relational component. Sgt. Fritz tells Officer Richards, "Get together with people over at the school. Find out what the problems are and do something about them." The content component is that Richards should deal with the school; the relational component is that Fritz has authority to order Richards to do this.

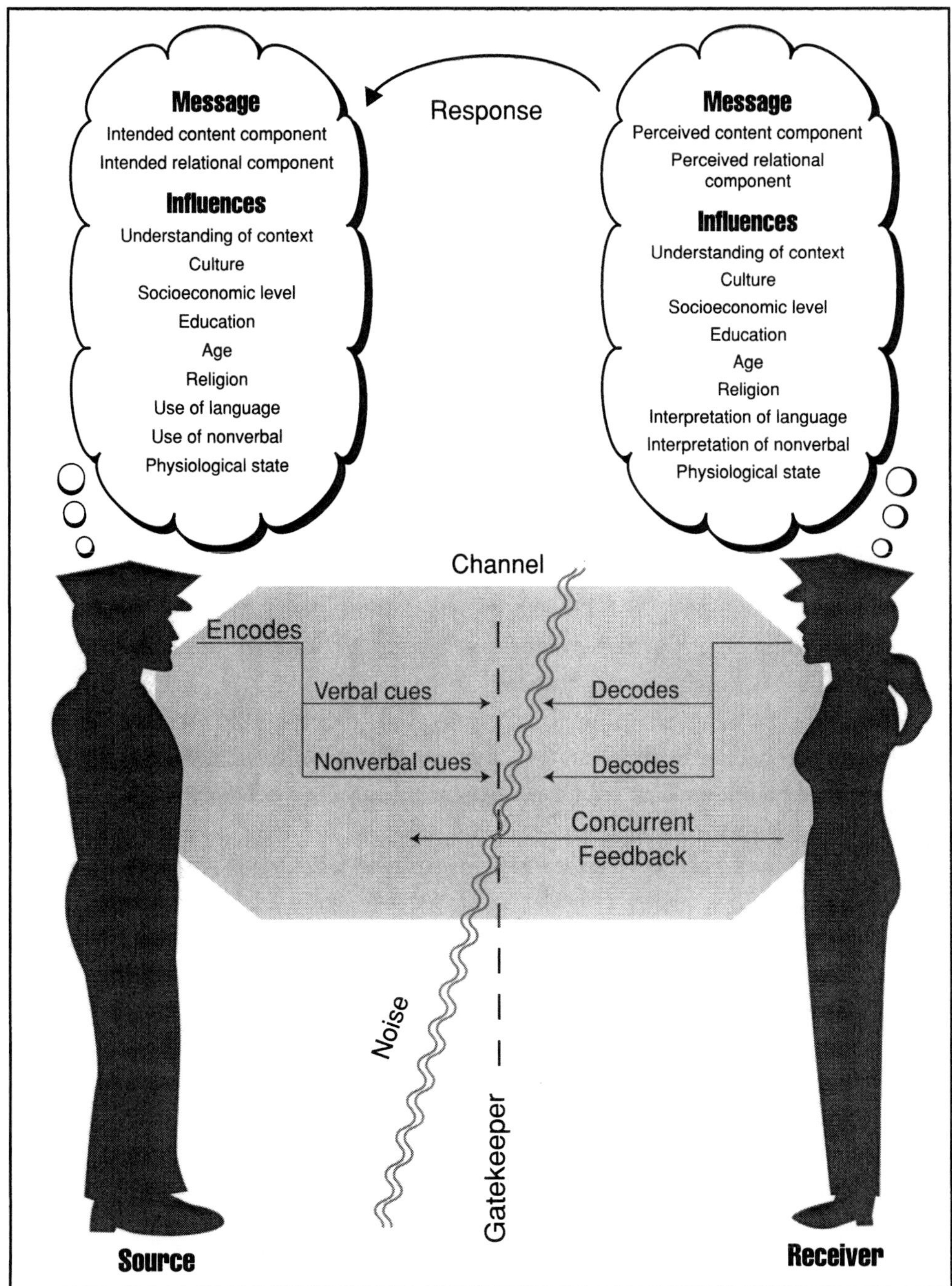

Figure 1-3: The communication model

People encode their thoughts based on their perceptions of the situation, knowledge of language, understanding of the context, education, social level, ethnic background, religious or moral beliefs, physical and emotional state, attitude, and purpose for speaking. People do not consciously think about all these influences every time they speak. It is just that their backgrounds have taught them to say A-B-C rather than X-Y-Z in certain circumstances, because A is more polite, more effective, or more suited to the situation. Encoding is easiest to see when the way the speaker encodes is unique to him or her. Four-year-old Claire has learned that it is "not nice" to call people "stupid" or to shout "shut up." Claire has encoded these as "bad words." When confronted by situations she does not like, such as getting a shot in the doctor's office, she "curses" by yelling her bad words: "Stupid! Stupid! Shut up! Shut up!"

Decoding

Before message cues have meaning, a **receiver**, or person to whom the message is sent, must **decode** them—turn them from random sounds and sights into a meaning. Officer Richards hears Sgt. Fritz's order, decodes both the perceived content message and the perceived relational message, and leaps into action. He and Diedra Holland work with school officials at Mark Twain Elementary to set up an after-school reading program for at-risk kids from the local housing project. They gradually involve parents in the program, enabling the officers not only to help the kids but also to win the parents' trust.

Richards is shocked to find Fritz apoplectic. "You did what? Where? What the hell for? What's going on at the high school, you blockhead? I've had five calls from those lunatics in the principal's office over there!"

The same factors that influence the encoding process influence the decoding process except that the listener draws on alternate perceptions and a different lifetime of experiences than the speaker, which can twist a message into new meanings.

Officer Randy Washington has information about events in his community that Capt. Patrick O'Malley should know before he addresses the public hearing, but the captain is talking with Councilwoman Grace Chan. Washington steps forward as Chan leaves and the captain begins to review his notes. Lt. Stefan Ivancic stops him, saying, "Leave O'Malley alone. He has five minutes to get ready for his presentation. If he wants to talk to you, he'll ask for you." O'Malley sees Washington talking with Ivancic and figures the conversation is unrelated to the business at hand.

The three officers decode the communication in the situation differently. Ivancic decodes it as his having been efficient, saving the captain work. O'Malley decodes it as a time when he has done a good job schmoozing the councilwoman and handling her issues. Washington decodes the interaction as the brass seeing officers as unimportant; he vows never to approach the captain again.

Channel

The encoded message is conveyed through a **channel**, the medium used to convey messages. For Officer Richards on the prostitute roundup, the channel was a thin wire transmitting information to a receiver. For Sgt. Fritz, telling officers to curb violence in the high school, the channel was oral words and nonverbal cues. Government bureaucracies, including some police departments, commonly demand a "paper trail," where even the simplest messages must be sent in writing. With the plethora of new media available, the number of communication channels today can be overwhelming: e-mail, voice mail, videotape, audio cassette, pager, fax, photographs, synchronous computers, audio conferences, video conferences, speaker phones, and Internet sites. A pot of chicken soup can be a channel to convey concern when someone is sick. Gifts and greeting cards are channels for sending messages of love, friendship, or gratitude.

The chain of command in a typical policing agency is also a channel. Sources expect information to move systematically and unchanged through numerous people. A problem with the chain of command as a channel is that there is an assumption by those initiating the message that the message was delivered completely and accurately. Many times this is not the case.

Noise

A message may be affected by noise as it passes through a channel. **Noise** is anything that interferes with a listener's attention to a message. Noise can exist in the channel, in the message, and even in the sender or receiver. Three kinds of noise interfere with communication.

- **Physical noise** is something external that interferes with receiving the message. Physical noise is the static that blocked Diedra Holland's reception of Alan Richards' words during the prostitution operation. It's the leaf blower outside

ACTION CLIP

Lines of Communication

When the Alexandria, Virginia, Police Department took on five open-air drug markets, their effort needed multiple lines of communication. Former Chief Gary Leonard reports that they relied on "jump-out" units and spotters with telescopes to identify drug dealers. Coordinated with that effort, uniformed officers stopped and talked with everyone possible in the problem areas to get to know the community and to find out who the troublemakers were.

The department also used the printed word for communication. To prevent misunderstandings and possible confrontations, brochures were handed out to let the helpful community members know what the officers were doing and to tell them how to handle being stopped by the police. At the same time, police spokespersons presented slide shows of officers working in the community to introduce Community Policing to neighborhood groups. The department relied on an array of communication channels: interpersonal exchanges, community meetings, printed documents, public speaking, and visual aids. Ultimately, they reported the results on the Internet (McLanus).

POCKET GUIDE

Redundancy

Redundancy is the practice of repeating your message in a number of ways. Research has shown that people not only better understand information when they hear *and* see it, they also are more likely to recall it later. Say your message in person, write it, e-mail it, phone it. If you are giving a speech, speak orally, repeat on an overhead, give an example that makes the point another way, and summarize at the end. If you are dealing with a community issue, talk to a group and then give the story to a neighborhood newspaper. If you are demonstrating a technique, show it and make a video. The more times you repeat a message and the more forms you repeat it in, the more likely your listeners are to re-create the message you intended to send.

and the baby crying. It occurs when a speaker uses an overhead transparency that looks as if mice got into the ink and ran across the film.

- **Physiological noise** is created by your own physical condition. When you can hear a speaker perfectly well but you are distracted by your discomfort in the meeting room, you have physiological noise in the channel. When you have been sitting too long, the room is too hot, your stomach is growling, and your head is starting to ache, physiological noise is distracting you.
- **Psychological noise** is a distraction caused by your own thoughts. Psychological noise occurs when you are daydreaming about your vacation to Hawaii or worried about the kids at daycare, when you don't like the speaker or you like the speaker too much. When you are biased against the speaker's race or religion or profession, you don't hear the message as the speaker means it because of psychological noise. When you discount the message because the speaker is ugly, overweight, old, a teenager, a journalist, has missing teeth or spiked maroon hair, or drives a rusty Volkswagen bus emblazoned with peace signs, noise in the channel is blotting out part of the message.

  Speaking with an officer causes psychological noise for some people. They cannot hear your message because you are a cop. To understand such a reaction, reverse the situation. How often do you awake in great anticipation because this is the day you get to go to the dentist? The dentist may be a perfectly nice person who studied for years to help you today, but when she explains patiently and kindly about the tooth repair procedure, and you don't hear anything after the phrase "drill into the bone," there's noise in the channel.

Gatekeeper

A message may have to pass through a gatekeeper before it gets to its intended receiver. A **gatekeeper** is the person who receives a message from a source and determines its distribution to others. Not every communication situation has a gatekeeper. Gatekeepers filter or limit the amount of information that gets through the channel.

In today's information-overloaded world, gatekeepers are information guards who must make decisions about ever growing mounds of messages.

The very process of selecting information to share puts everyone in the gatekeeper role at one time or another. Each person in a police chain of command is a gatekeeper. Richards and Holland decide to describe their neighborhood efforts in briefings so the patrol officers know what is happening in their district. Out of fifteen projects, they select two to share. Washington attends a leadership training program. He shares highlights with Richards and Holland, condensing a two-day workshop into fifteen minutes.

Every time a message goes through a gatekeeper, it gets changed. Capt. O'Malley gives written information to Lt. Ivancic who skims it and passes on the highlights to Sgt. Fritz. Out of this, Fritz announces what he thinks is important at briefings. That's all he tells the officers about; the rest of the message doesn't reach them.

Feedback

Feedback is information that is fed back to the source from the receiver; it is the receiver's responses to the messages of the source. Feedback is your weapon against the distortion and misunderstanding that constantly threaten clear communication. You can help clarify messages when you feed information back to people by asking probing questions, summarizing, and restating their thoughts, opinions, and feelings to be sure you understand. Sometimes feedback is immediate, such as the nonverbal responses people give as you talk. Sometimes it is delayed and even formal, coming in written notes or later conversations. The key to good feedback is to create an atmosphere in which information, both verbal and nonverbal, flows freely.

> "Communication is something that surrounds people and holds their world together. Through communication, social groups create collective ideas of themselves, of one another, and of the world they inhabit."
>
> —Sarah Trenholm (37)

Verbal feedback. Verbal feedback may be formal or informal, spoken or written, positive or negative, or a blend. Set a norm that feedback is helpful information. People don't feel comfortable telling you what's wrong with your ideas or your work if they like you or if they fear you, so keep the communication environment upbeat to help information flow more freely. You may need to probe a bit or set up systems for getting feedback rather than just hope it comes. You can gather feedback formally from the community through surveys, suggestion forms, or focus groups. You can also get verbal feedback informally through personal conversations. For the informal channel to work, you must spend time with people, making yourself available. When you stand around chatting casually, you often get good information you would not get otherwise. Chapter 3 discusses techniques for giving feedback.

Nonverbal feedback. Nonverbal feedback is expressed behaviorally. For example, when you speak to a group, are your listeners frowning, yawning, whispering to one another, nodding, staring at you intently with a look of excitement? When you talk to community members one-on-one, do they cross their arms and lean away? All of this is feedback from your listeners. In two-way communication, nonverbal feedback occurs concurrently with your message; it is ongoing and continuous. It relies on many of the nonverbal codes at one time and some sounds, such as "um-hum" or "unh-uh," laughter, or phrases, such as "right," "yeah," and "sure." Watch your listeners' nonverbal cues to get feedback.

Inconsistency between verbal and nonverbal feedback. Who hasn't experienced it? The drawn lips, the deep frown, the papers slammed on the table, accompanied by the words, "No, I'm not angry. Why on earth would you think that?" The verbal feedback contradicts the nonverbal feedback, and confusion results. Research reports that when the verbal and the nonverbal are inconsistent, people tend to believe the nonverbal. This grows out of a belief that it is easier to lie with words than with actions.

Communication does not really operate like the linear drawing shown earlier. To be completely accurate, the communication model should be a dynamic, moving image, changing as it turns and spirals. The sender and the receiver encode and decode almost simultaneously, taking in multiple nonverbal cues at once, assigning meaning to content and relational components of messages, filtering the context, watching for immediate nonverbal feedback, interpreting codes, heeding or ignoring noise in the channel within the span of seconds. A model slows it down to help you see elements you might not see as communication whirls around you.

The communication process underlies all the specific skills discussed in this book. Understanding the elements of the process and knowing how it works allows you to have a sense of where communication breaks down, what can improve communication, how to frame messages so your receivers are more likely to put together your puzzle pieces as you intend, and how you can successfully reassemble theirs.

Works Cited

Bickel, Harold. Personal interview. Oct. 1997.

Bickel, Harold, and Gregory Dieckmann. "Multifaceted POP Project Breathes New Life into Apartment Communities." *Problem-Solving Quarterly* 10 (Winter 1997): 1–7.

Community Policing Consortium. "Cultural Diversity." Community Policing Consortium Bulletin Series. www.communitypolicing.org/cultural/index.htm. 22 Oct. 1997.

Hall, Edward T. *The Hidden Dimension*. Garden City, N.Y.: Doubleday, 1966.

McLanus, Tina. "Creative Tactics: From Visual Disruption to Code Enforcement. New Ideas from Around the Country." http://www.ssc.msu.edu:80/~cj/newideas.html. 4 Aug. 1998.

Merabian, Albert. *Silent Messages*. 2nd ed. Belmont, Calif.: Wadsworth, 1981.

Peak, Kenneth J. and Ronald W. Glensor. *Community Policing and Problem Solving: Strategies and Practices*. Upper Saddle River, N.J.: Prentice Hall, 1996.

Postman, Neil. *Crazy Talk, Stupid Talk*. New York: Delacorte Press, 1976.

Trenholm, Sarah. *Thinking Through Communication*. Boston: Allyn and Bacon, 1995.

Watzlawick, Paul, Janet Helmick Beavin, and Don D. Jackson. *Pragmatics of Human Communication*. New York: W.W. Norton, 1967.

Activities

1 One- and Two-Way Communication

Supplies: Lego blocks and a lap board or desk

You need a partner for this activity. This activity also works well as a demonstration for a larger group sitting in a circle around you and observing how closely the emerging models match, or with several teams working at once.

One-Way Communication

Sit back to back with your partner. Decide who will be the source and who the receiver. Each person takes a matching set of about fifteen Lego blocks. Including a couple of wheels or some odd-shaped doors adds a challenge to the task.

The source uses the Lego pieces to build something, describing the steps to the receiver. As the source adds each piece, she uses one-way communication to describe her actions and tell the receiver how to duplicate the model. When both of you are out of pieces, compare the two models. The more alike they are, the more closely you and your partner encoded and decoded the messages. Often when the source thinks she's been clear about the car she's building, the receiver was building an airplane.

Recall that both you and your partner worked with the same Lego pieces. The similarity symbolizes common backgrounds, education, cultural values, and language. This is the ideal communication situation. Because you used one-way communication, there was no feedback and the receiver could not clarify errors in understanding.

Two-Way Communication

Switch roles and select a new batch of about fifteen matching blocks. This time use two-way communication: the receiver can ask questions and the source can request feedback. When you are out of pieces, again compare the two models. You and your partner should have much closer models, although the process took longer. Again, you have mimicked an ideal communication situation because you worked with the same pieces, which represent a common background.

Intercultural Communication

You have had it easy, communicating with people with common backgrounds. Now try a variation. You and your partner each select your own Lego pieces (in both number and shape). Don't show the other person all your blocks, but make sure you have a few pieces in common. Use two-way communication as the source instructs the receiver what to build.

How did you do? What strategies did you use to bridge the intercultural gap? Did you eliminate all pieces that did not match in size or color? Did you find that you could construct similar models by creatively letting two of one size equal one of another? Did you decide that color or size didn't matter? Were you able to use non-matching pieces in ways that made your final structures similar even though they didn't match exactly? Did you share any pieces?

In any intercultural exchange, some pieces go unused, and some information is not exchanged. Sometimes we can't say exactly what we want to, but we can get close. Consider how difficult this exchange would be with one-way communication.

2 One- and Two-Way Communication to Multiple Receivers

Supplies: Two pieces of cardboard for patterns of squares (described below), and enough paper and pencils for the audience

This activity makes the same point as the Lego activity, and is easier for a larger group. You need at least three other people, but you can also do this with a large audience.

Draw two different patterns of four or five squares in a variety of contiguous positions on the cardboard. Figure 1-4 shows one example.

Distribute paper and pencils to the listeners. Describe the first pattern of squares to the listeners to replicate. The listeners cannot ask questions or make comments, and can draw only what they hear described. After you complete your descriptions, compare images. See where messages do not coincide. This activity demonstrates visibly that messages get distorted.

Repeat this activity with the second pattern of squares. This time use two-way communication. Compare your results and how long the process takes.

3 Message Distortion Through Gatekeepers

This activity requires five people in addition to yourself, but it is more fun with a listening audience.

Ask for five volunteers. Send four out of the room. Describe details of a recent event to Volunteer 1. Your story should take no more than a couple of minutes to relate, but don't make it too simple. Call in Volunteer 2. Volunteer 1 tells Volunteer 2 the details of the event. Call in Volunteer 3. Volunteer 2 repeats the details to Volunteer 3. Continue until all five volunteers have heard the details. Have Volunteer 5 repeat the final story and see how the message changed in each retelling. Obviously, the more detailed and lengthy the initial story, the more likely speakers will distort it. Be aware that the activity may take too long if each volunteer has to relate a lengthy story.

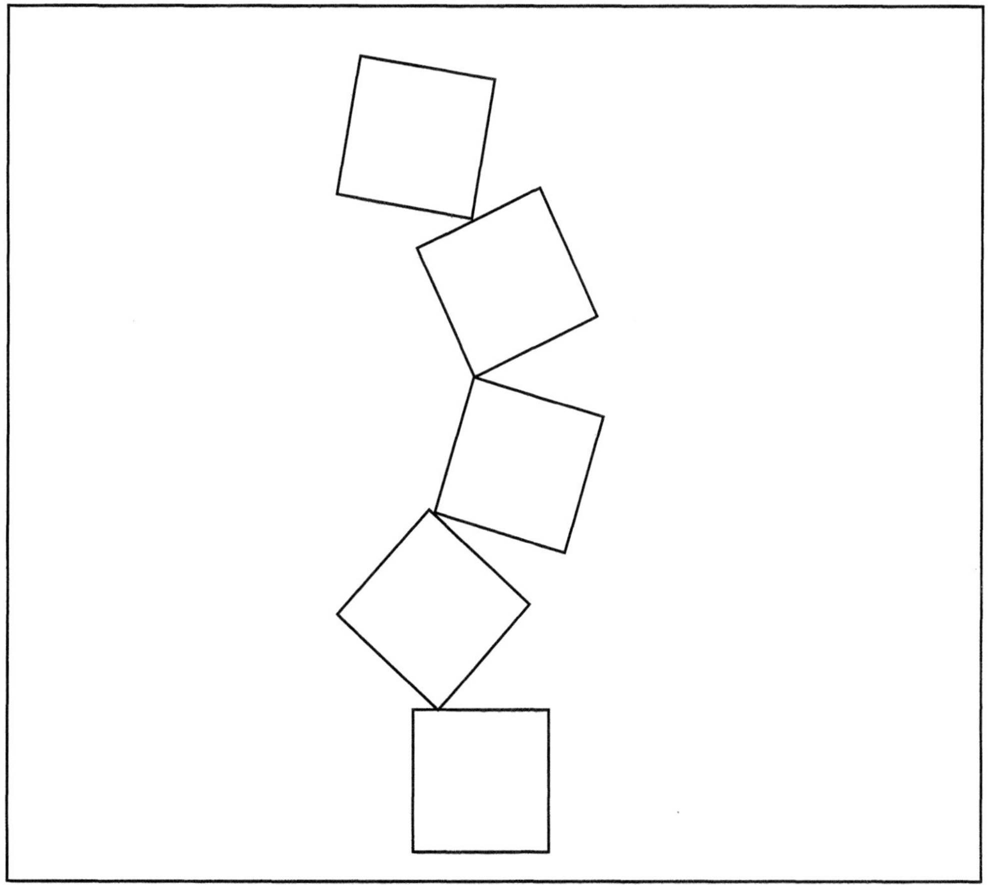

Figure 1-4: Sample pattern of squares

Discuss how messages sent through the chain of command in a police agency inherently go through this same process and suffer similar distortion and reduction. In addition, messages from officers to the community and back or messages between officers face the same limitations.

4 Messages, Channels, and Noise

Supplies: Paper and pen

This activity is designed to heighten your awareness of all the messages you receive and the channels through which they arrive.

1. Record all the messages you receive in one fifteen-minute walk. This becomes very difficult when you start adding in billboards, tee shirts, music, brief glances from people you pass, graffiti, and so on. Stop and jot down or draw each message as you encounter it so you won't forget.
2. For one day, make a note of all official messages you receive at your agency. Note through what channels they arrive. Include conversations with other officers; the grapevine is a channel, too.

3. For one ten-minute period when you are supposed to be listening at some public meeting or event, pay attention to the noise, both internal and external, that works against your hearing. If you can, record the noise as it occurs. If you cannot do that, think back later and make as complete a record as you can. This is especially useful at helping you understand how others might be distracted when you speak.

5 Context

How daring do you feel? One way to get a real sense of how the context influences a message is to violate the expectations of the context. In an elevator, ask strangers about their favorite movies. Talk about sports during a religious service, or talk about religion during a sports game. When out to dinner with people who are not officers, discuss rodent-infested public housing and some of the health problems you have seen. Check out the inside of the refrigerator at the home of an acquaintance. Take the seat next to someone when many empty seats are available.

You get the point. Unspoken rules exist that tell us what a behavior communicates in a *particular context*. Somewhere else, the behavior means something quite different.

6 The Communication Model

Part 1. Select a television show you enjoy watching. Watch one scene in which characters are talking. If you choose a sports show, watch the commentators or an interview. Answer the following questions:

1. Who is the source?
2. Who is the receiver?
3. What is the context?
4. How does the source encode the content components of the message?
5. How does the source encode the relational components of the message?
6. Does the receiver decode accurately? How do you know? Does the receiver give feedback?
7. What channel is used for their communication (within the scene, not with you)?
8. Is a gatekeeper involved? What does the gatekeeper do?

Part 2. Select a scene from a program you have not watched before. Try to find something that seems strange to your tastes, a religious show if you are not religious, a kids show if you have no kids, a PBS drama if you prefer action. Answer the same eight questions about this scene.

Part 3. Compare how familiarity affected your ability to decode the communication.

Chapter Two

Getting to Know You

Communicating Interpersonally

"Effective communication hinges on our ability to make emotional contact."

BERT DECKER (13)

"This looks great!" exclaims Officer Diedra Holland. She stands with community members Danny Lopez and Carl Ellison in front of a swatch of beige paint that was a multicolored confusion of graffiti just a half hour earlier. Both Lopez and Ellison hold paintbrushes, and Lopez carries a gallon paint can. The two men were moving systematically down Twelfth Avenue when Holland stopped to offer support and encouragement.

"Wanna take bets about how long it'll stay clean?" sighs Lopez. "I just hope we can paint over their garbage more often than they can write it."

"I agree," Holland nods. "Do you know the library bookdrop got tagged last night? Are you planning to paint that?"

"I'm really looking forward to the game tonight!" declares Ellison. "Marge and I have courtside tickets. It's gonna be a hot one!"

CONVERSATIONS ARE NEVER EASY. Some people like to talk a lot more than they like to listen. Some ramble on incoherently. Some state their opinions even when they lack basic or relevant information about the topic. Some, like Ellison, boom out responses completely unrelated to the sentences that precede them.

Unfortunately, as a community officer you can't just ignore a person whose style is unpleasant. One of the first things you do as a community officer is to get to know the active people in your area. The Community Policing Consortium advises officers to conduct door-to-door surveys, converse with neighborhood residents, chat with county or city employees, contact civic organizations, attend community meetings, team up with personnel from other agencies, and interact informally with community members ("Module Three"). This means you must communicate one-on-one with people, no matter what their conversational style, as you work together to solve community problems.

Your goal is to form partnerships. Nancy McPherson, director of the Community Policing Bureau in the Seattle Police Department, puts it this way:

> Partnerships, partnerships, partnerships. Everywhere we go we hear about partnerships. You know how difficult partnerships are. Give and take. Compromise. Win-win. Build consensus. Share information. Nurture relationships. Nurture relationships? Did I hear you right? This is a police agency, for Pete's sake! Our job is to enforce the law and solve crime problems, not nurture relationships!
>
> It is true. Partnerships are difficult. It takes time to build relationships, to learn to trust each other, to find mutual interests and concerns, and to learn a common language that results in problems being solved. But what we're learning from officers all over the country is that long-term solutions to problems require partnerships. (1)

And partnerships require interpersonal communication.

Communication is considered **interpersonal** when the message would change if the participants changed. In contrast to a public speech, for example, which would continue unaltered if one audience member slipped out the back door, an interpersonal message would change if spoken to someone else. How you talk to your family and how you talk to the cashier at the market are different. Likewise, how you talk to a cashier you know and one you don't know are different. The human element is central to interpersonal communication. People in interpersonal conversations matter to one another. It is the basis of relationships, friendship, and love. Often this kind of interaction is called relational communication or one-on-one communication (even when it involves two or three people) because the relationship between the participants is the prime factor. Interpersonal communication generally is conveyed in two-way conversation. This means interaction is constantly dynamic and changing because other people in the communication situation can alter the nature of the communication at many points.

Interpersonal communication, which focuses on how to talk to individuals, is also the foundation of many communication situations. This one-on-one communication occurs in all other types of communication. In meetings, for example, after a time you get to know the other group members and relate to them as human beings. In community work, after a time "the Glenview Neighborhood Association president" becomes "Eva Perlroth," a specific person you know and like. When you must generate solutions to problems, you come to know that Rita Lopez is a great person to work with and Carl Ellison is not. When you want something done right and on time, you learn to turn to Than Pham. In public speaking, you know your host, the person who introduces you, and perhaps a few audience members. Interpersonal communication principles tell you how to talk to another person, and consequently they play a role in all communication situations even when other elements overlay them.

Interpersonal exchanges are usually the first type of communication that new community officers have with community members. The natural beginning steps in a new district are meeting people, chatting with neighbors and patrol officers, interviewing shopkeepers, interacting with kids, talking and listening. In *Community Policing: How to Get Started,* Robert Trojanowicz and Bonnie Bucqueroux describe "What the officer should do first":

> Walk the entire area and begin to meet people at random, explaining that you are a full-service community policing officer who has been assigned to the area on a long-term basis and that you have an office in the neighborhood (giving them the location), hand out your business card. . . . After a couple of days, make contact with area clergy, business owners, local agencies, and school officials. . . . Make motor patrol officers in your area aware of your presence and keep them informed about what you are doing. (85)

All of these involve interpersonal communication.

No simple prescriptions can tell you exactly how to improve your interpersonal communication. However, some styles of interacting can help you convey more clearly what you intend to say and help you respond to others' messages in ways that show you care about them and their messages.

Randy Washington and Alan Richards met at the Teriyaki Bowl to grab a late lunch. As they finished the meal, the manager came out and stood by their table. Washington greeted him warmly; this was one of his frequent lunch stops.

"You guys hear about the robbery at the Pizza Oven last night?" The manager gestured across the street toward the red and green sign above the corner store. Both officers nodded. "My cook thinks he saw the guy that did it. The guy ran across the parking lot out there."

Richards looked up in surprise. "I talked to the patrol officers who answered the call. They talked to people all around here. This place was dark, closed up. They thought you were all gone."

The manager nodded. "We turn off the signs and turn out the lights so nobody comes in while we're still here cleaning up. When Leo went to his car, this guy ran right in front of him. He got a good look at his face."

"Did you tell the patrol officers about this?" Washington asked.

The manager shrugged. "No. But I know you guys, and I knew you'd take it seriously."

Later, Washington and Richards privately chalked up the arrest of the Pizza Oven robber to interpersonal communication, and celebrated their success with lunch at the Teriyaki Bowl.

Pay Attention to Your Relational Message

Recall that every time you talk with someone you send dual messages: the content component and the relational component. Because the relationship between speakers is central to interpersonal exchanges, the relational component is of vital concern in interpersonal communication. Your listeners give meaning to the words you say (the content component) at the same time that they reach conclusions about whether you like them or not, feel respect for their ideas, and accept them as equals, or whether you are a threat, and so on (the relational component). They read messages into your tone of voice, rate of speech, physical stance, eye contact, and other nonverbal expressions. As you get to know one another better, they will grow more accurate in their interpretations—but even when the message they interpret is not the message you intended to convey, it will be seen as what you meant to say unless further information changes their mind. In the same way, you will make inferences about their responses to you.

The most simple relational message is called **phatic communication**, the almost mindless communication that is designed to maintain human contact and has almost no content: "Hi," "How's it going?" "What's happening," "Have a nice day." Such exchanges indicate friendliness and courtesy.

For many community members, conversations with police inherently carry highly charged relational messages. Individual reactions run the gamut from fear to adulation but are rarely neutral so long as they see you solely as "police." For people to see beyond the uniform, you must become, for them, a specific individual with personal characteristics. Consider the situation in reverse for a moment. Imagine yourself interacting with a neurosurgeon. Dr. Alexa Canady voiced the challenge officers face when she spoke of her own role: "When you see me as a neurosurgeon, you're going to be nervous, you're going to forget what you came to tell me, your blood pressure is going to be elevated, you're not going to be able to communicate with me because you are intimidated." But in her work, as in yours, it is essential for people to give her information "even if they think it is going to be silly. . . . You have to see me not as a surgeon but as a person" (1).

> "If you're going to change kids' attitudes toward cops, you've got to do it early. I spent a year going to one elementary school. I'd go to different classes and read books, do math problems, basically I'd do anything whether it was police related or not. This let the kids see that I was a real person, just like them. So now when I drive down their streets, they wave at me with all five fingers, not just one. They talk to me when I'm in their neighborhood."
>
> —Deputy Lissah Norcross, Mesa County Sheriff's Department

To help community members feel comfortable with you, your messages *must make them feel understood and valued.* They need to believe that you hear and understand their words and that you appreciate their input. Think of a time when your words were heard, but you were ignored. Maybe your sergeant adopted your suggestion but took no notice of who offered it. Possibly you made a comment to someone who immediately turned away and began speaking to someone else as if you had not spoken. This kind of response makes you want to withdraw. You want to be acknowledged and appreciated and so do community members who work with you. The relational component of your message needs to convey that acceptance and appreciation.

Develop a Supportive Communication Climate

Your goal as you communicate interpersonally is to create a communication environment in which people feel safe to speak out openly. In a highly influential article, communication researcher Jack R. Gibb uses the metaphor of climate to illustrate how communication often is influenced by the environmental conditions in which it operates. Writing about defensive communication, he argues that specific kinds of comments create supportive and defensive climates. In a **supportive climate**, individuals feel comfortable speaking out, they tolerate differences, and are likely to engage in honest dialog. In a **defensive climate**, people feel threatened and under

POCKET GUIDE

Be Accessible

COP increases the interaction between you and the community. Combine this with increased accessibility through technology, and the demand for your time can become troublesome. A business card can help because you can control what goes on that card to limit access if you want.

- **Name**—In addition to your last name, list a first name that you want people to call you. Some people will want that level of familiarity.
- **Address**—List an address where you receive mail and one where you receive visitors. Be sure to designate which location is used for what purpose.
- **Phone Numbers**—Either list a number that someone answers twenty-four hours every day or a number with an answering machine or voice mail so that a message will get to you. If you use machines or voice mail, update your outgoing message to let people know when you are not going to return calls in a timely manner (such as when you are on vacation, in training, etc.).
- **Fax**—List a number where you receive material in a timely manner.
- **E-mail**—Only list if you are going to respond to e-mail messages.
- **Pager**—Only list if you will respond to *all* pages in a timely manner.
- **Cell Phones**—Only list if you want an unlimited number of calls.

Don't list numbers where you cannot be reached. For example, people expect to rely on your pager when you cannot be reached by phone. If you leave your pager off when you are away from the office, you can save yourself a tremendous amount of grief by not listing it on your business card. A delayed response can alienate volunteers. Also consider having two business cards, one with limited numbers for the general public and one for fellow officers, colleagues, or others who might need greater access to your time.

attack, and consequently they become cautious, unwilling to share, alienated, closed, and may withdraw. They feel attacked or perceive a potential for attack, and they protect themselves.

The last thing you want is for volunteers and neighborhood groups to grow defensive or hostile and stop working with you. What makes a person defensive? Feeling that their self-worth is attacked. Note that *feeling* attacked is not the same as *being* attacked. Because people interpret what you say based on their own perceptions, they may interpret some behaviors as an attack when that is not at all what you intend.

When people feel defensive, they tend to fall into the old patterns of flight or fight. Some people withdraw or take flight when they feel threatened. They stop participating either by growing silent or by leaving. Other people fight when they feel threatened. They may argue loudly, disagree with everyone or everything, dispute even insignificant points, sometimes insult officers and other community leaders. Also, their interpretation of the situation can become distorted. Gibb writes, "As a person becomes more and more defensive, he becomes less and less able to perceive accurately the motives, the values, the emotions of the sender" (141).

One cause of inaccurate perception that leads to misinterpretations of messages is that people automatically make assumptions about the motives behind others' communication. **Attribution** is the tendency people have to ascribe causes to another person's behavior. Often these causes come from past experiences of the person ascribing meaning, not from the source. Nonetheless, attributions influence the response. Consider, for example, a community member's interpretation of why police have not addressed a public safety concern in his or her neighborhood: *I'm a minority, I'm disabled, I'm on welfare, I'm a teenager, I'm poor, the cops don't care.* Once the person assumes such a cause, he or she may have trouble establishing a good relationship with police. Your communication must be proactive and supportive to help establish relationships that prevent inaccurate attribution.

In a supportive climate, ideas flourish, people take risks, and communication is more accurate. Gibb says, "The more 'supportive' the climate, the less the receiver reads into the communication distorted loadings. . . . As defenses are reduced, the receivers become better able to concentrate upon the structure, the content and the cognitive meanings of the message" (141).

Gibb identified six communication characteristics that tend to generate defensive responses. People grow defensive when we act as though we are *superior* to them; when our remarks make them feel *evaluated;* when we try to *control* them; when we are so *certain* of our position that we won't listen to alternatives; when we are *neutral* or indifferent about their feelings or ideas; or when we act in a *strategic* manner to manipulate them. And we, in turn, grow defensive when others act this way toward us. Gibb contrasted these characteristics with their opposites, which generate a supportive climate. People feel comfortable when we treat them as *equals;* make *descriptive* comments rather than evaluative ones; seek to *solve problems* rather than control the outcome; make *provisional* statements rather than speaking in absolutes; show *empathy;* and respond in a *spontaneous* style. Generally, defense-arousing behaviors center around controlling another person, while supportive behaviors are much more concerned with good listening and are more team oriented. Examining these in greater detail will help you develop a supportive approach.

Treat Others As Equals, Not Inferiors

People often become defensive when they interact with someone who is, or acts, superior to them in status, rank, education, knowledge, strength, or financial worth. They feel less defensive interacting with equals. This is easy to understand. How open and friendly do you feel in a courtroom talking to the judge? Even when you and the judge meet at a community function, a constraint exists because of your professional roles. You and the judge can breech that gap by being friendly, pushing aside any perceived superiority of positions, and finding a common ground to discuss. (It's not an accident that such conversations often turn to sports or weather).

POCKET GUIDE

Communication Behaviors

Supportive	Defensive
Equality	Superiority
Description	Evaluation
Problem orientation	Control
Provisional statements	Certainty
Empathy	Neutrality
Spontaneity	Strategy

Your interaction with many community members is similar. Community members may see you as someone in a higher position or may believe you think you are better. They may see themselves as superior to you because of their role in the community, age, status in their culture, financial position, or education. Signs of the type of superiority that generates defensiveness include ordering rather than requesting, talking rather than listening, making decisions without consulting, explaining when it is unnecessary as if to a child, or even always picking up the tab. You have to get beyond the image of superiority so community members see you as simply a responsible community member working with them to address a common concern.

Remember, too, that even your fellow officers can become defensive if you present yourself as representing the latest criminal justice philosophy in contrast to their old, out-of-date approach. Patrol officers may already see you as getting premium equipment while they make do with the old, receiving more recognition from the command staff and the community than they do, and having a more flexible schedule. It is just a short step to their assumption that you think you are better. Their next move is a defensive response.

Several techniques can help you convey a sense of equality to both community members and fellow officers. Go to the other people's environments. Be willing to travel to their office, meeting place, roll call room, or home, rather than demanding that they come to you. Break the ice by smiling and being friendly. Search out common interests. Ask their opinions. Don't always take the head of the table, and don't sit while they stand. Address people in ways that in their culture convey respect. Ask their opinions and listen to their responses. In a group, don't speak between every speaker. These and other responses you may think of convey a sense of equality.

Be Descriptive, Not Evaluative

"No, that'll never work. The city doesn't have the money" may be true in your opinion, but the remark itself will not encourage a speaker to continue participating in a conversation in a friendly manner. Change phrases from evaluative to descriptive.

"Mrs. Lopez, as I understand your idea, it is that the city buy the abandoned houses and refurbish them for the poor. Do we have any estimates on how much that would cost? The city has said it will spend no more than $200,000 on this whole project." When you are tempted to voice a judgment, think about its potential effect. "You're obsessed with this" brings a defensive response; "This seems very important to you" gets an honest explanation.

Focus on Problems and Solutions, Not Control

Attempting to control another person or group can provoke resistance. Efforts to control can be subtle. Gibb points out that methods of control are "many and varied," including "legalistic insistence on detail" and "conformity norms. . . . Gestures, facial expression, other forms of nonverbal communication, and even such simple acts as holding a door open in a particular manner are means of imposing one's will upon another" (143). Forcing a community member or group to accept your answers to a community's problems not only limits your solutions, it closes down the open flow of discussion. You may believe that before the group does anything else, they must clear up the abandoned houses in the neighborhood, but forcing them to focus on this when they are concerned about school safety does not build allies or encourage people to share their ideas with you. It simply generates defensiveness. Instead, focus on the problem. Ask for their interpretation of what the problem is, and search together for possible solutions.

Be Provisional, Not Certain

The provisional view is tentative, open to receiving data and listening to others' ideas. Certainty is akin to dogmatism. People who think they know all the answers and refuse to hear information to the contrary put others on guard. Being supportive does not mean caving in; voice your ideas honestly and directly. However, stay open to other options. Make clear that you will consider alternative perspectives to any you may hold. "Personally, I favor starting by clearing out the abandoned houses, but I'd like to hear your views. How do the rest of you feel we should start?" Sometimes being provisional can be indicated in words that tone down your stance, such as "It seems to me," "probably," "perhaps," "in many cases," "so far, I've noticed that," "very likely," "at the moment I'm inclined to think that. . . ." These suggest you are open to input.

Show Empathy, Not Neutrality

Empathy involves "experiencing another's perceptions—seeing and feeling things as the other does" (Tubbs and Moss 58). In contrast, neutrality communicates a lack of concern. Officer Holland probably will feel she has to defend her point of view if she voices a concern about abandoned houses to Carl Ellison, and he says, "Well, yes, there are a lot of abandoned houses. Of course there are a lot of other problems, too." He's expressing neutrality. Ellison doesn't have to agree with her to show empathy. He has to understand her perceptions. "I can see you are very concerned about what's happening in these houses. It's pretty bad, isn't it?" will get a more positive response from Holland.

Discounting another's problems also shows a lack of empathy. Gibb says, "Speech . . . that communicates little warmth or caring . . . sometimes communicates rejection" (145). For example, some people try to calm a distressed person by saying, "It'll be okay." The statement may be well intentioned, but the implication is that the person is unnecessarily upset. "Do whatever you want; I don't care" suggests a lack of concern. Instead, express your concern, listen to the other person and, if the situation calls for it, paraphrase (explained below) to be sure you understand clearly. If you desire, disclose similar experiences you have had. Avoid statements that tell another person how to feel, such as "Cheer up" and "Don't feel bad."

Practice Spontaneity, Not Strategy

Spontaneity is honest, candid communication. Strategy is manipulative, planning your behavior to produce a reaction. Gibb advises that you be sincere and "free of deception." People tend to see through strategic communication such as phony compliments, glib promises, artificial attention, and feigned appreciation. To illustrate the difference between spontaneous remarks and strategic ones, contrast your nephew's shout of delight at the new bike with your sister's strained smile when she unwraps the slippers with a genuine replica of Elvis on each toe. The value of spontaneous interaction is that honest behavior leads to trust between you and those with whom you interact.

Unfortunately, much traditional police work requires officers to engage in the very behaviors that make people defensive. On the street, you have to evaluate people constantly. You must be strategic, evaluate a situation, then move in and take control. You can legally control people to the point of arrest, even directing them when to talk and when to remain silent. Although these communication behaviors are effective when you need to restrain a crowd, make an arrest, or handle an emergency, they hinder communication in most community policing situations. Community policing requires you to broaden your communication repertoire to include supportive communication behaviors.

Listen Actively

A good listener pays close attention not only to the speaker's words, but also to the speaker's nonverbal signs, and through them to the speaker's feelings. Often we are not good listeners. Stephen Covey argues in *The Seven Habits of Highly Effective People*, "Most people do not listen with the intent to understand; they listen with the intent to reply" (239). The point is, if you are thinking about your own response, you may miss the speaker's real message.

Active listening means concentrating entirely on the speaker, making an effort to understand the speaker's meaning and feelings. The active listener takes in words, subtle tones, facial expressions, timing, and other nonverbal elements as well as the message context in order to understand what the speaker's message means *to the speaker*.

To be an active listener, it's not enough to *listen* to the speaker's message; you also must *show* that you are listening. Maintain eye contact, lean forward, nod, and vocalize agreement when appropriate by saying "I see" and "Um hmm." Even take notes if that is appropriate. Avoid actions that suggest you are not listening, such as glancing at your watch, focusing on outside events, wearing dark glasses, crossing your arms and leaning back, watching TV, or waving to other people.

After the speaker has finished, the active listener then feeds back to the speaker what he or she has heard.

Paraphrase to Express Your Understanding

You can verify your interpretation of a speaker's message and communicate your understanding by **paraphrasing**, or **reflective feedback**, restating in your own words the speaker's words and feelings. Paraphrasing takes into account the nonverbal signs you see and hear as well as the verbal. Paraphrasing also invites the speaker to elaborate and clarify. It also sends a strong relational message. Being able to express the speaker's position clearly says indirectly that you value him or her enough to listen carefully.

When paraphrasing, do not simply restate the speaker's words. That does not show you have received the whole message. Instead, restate the message in your own words, including your perception of how the speaker feels about the issue. Your paraphrasing must not sound artificial. Typically, your paraphrasing will consist of three parts: (1) acknowledging whose problem you are discussing, (2) reflecting the emotions of the speaker, and (3) summarizing the facts. This need not be complex. An example might be: "You feel (acknowledgment) very worried (emotion) about your son's safety coming through the park (fact).

> "You will learn more about a person and what they're thinking and feeling by reflective feedback than you will learn in almost any other way. Interrogations tend to turn people off because they are often perceived as threatening."
>
> —Gordon Shea (124)

Typical lead-in phrases for paraphrasing are:

"It sounds like. . . ."
"I can see that you. . . ."
"From your point of view it seems. . . ."
"The impression I get. . . ."

For example, as Danny Lopez examined the bookdrop defaced by graffiti, Officer Randy Washington came by. Lopez said, "It's a lot of work." Washington noted Lopez's tired face, flat tone of voice, the droop of his shoulders, and the downward twist of his lips, and replied, "You sound discouraged about the antigraffiti effort." Lopez opened up, describing his vision for the area and the emotional drain of the constant struggle against graffiti.

Paraphrasing is especially useful when information is complex, when you want to ensure the accuracy of vital information, and when people ask for your help and you want to be sure you understand the problem. Paraphrasing is also invaluable when you disagree with someone but must, nonetheless, offer some polite reply. For example, "So you believe a community advisory committee should decide when officers get promoted" summarizes someone's view with which you may thoroughly disagree. The summary simply allows you to show you heard the message.

Respond Sensitively

After listening, a person often responds to the speaker. The response offered is vital to the conversation. At the end of some conversations, do you feel as though you weren't really heard? At other times do you feel energized and understood? The difference is often in the kind of responses people give your remarks—whether their responses are disconfirming or confirming. **Disconfirming responses** are relational components in a message; they imply that the person responding does not value or confirm the original speaker. Carl Ellison's treatment of Diedra Holland illustrates this. She asks a question about graffiti, and he responds about game tickets. In essence, Ellison's conversation

POCKET GUIDE

Guidelines for Effective Listening

1. **Stop talking.**
2. **Paraphrase.** Because this is a descriptive, nondefensive response, it gives the other person an opportunity to clarify or elaborate without feeling attacked.
3. **Withhold evaluation.** Whether listening for factual understanding or for emotional content, it is important to withhold evaluation until after you understand. This is difficult and requires patience. Once ideas are understood, some degree of evaluation is appropriate. But you should evaluate ideas, not speakers.
4. **Take notes when appropriate.**
5. **Ask for specifics and/or clarification.**
6. **Watch for nonverbal cues.** Be sensitive to nonverbal messages, ask for clarification when needed, and paraphrase to ensure that your interpretation of the nonverbal cues is correct.
7. **Review and summarize.**

(cf. Phillips and Wallace 26–27)

would be the same if Holland had not spoken or were not there. **Confirming responses** show the respondent values the speaker as a person by acknowledging the speaker's views, attitudes, and feelings. Avoiding disconfirming responses and giving confirming responses are essential for building trust in the community.

Avoid Disconfirming Responses

Disconfirming responses are subtle. They can undermine the speaker without stopping conversation. People often use disconfirming responses to control the conversation or to appear superior—two communication behaviors that can cause defensiveness. Monitor your own communication to ensure that you avoid these disconfirming responses: interrupting, irrelevant response, incongruous response, ridicule, discounting the issue, and no response at all.

Interrupting. When people interrupt, they imply that they and their words are more important and relevant than the speaker and the speaker's message—so important, in fact, that the speaker doesn't even get to finish his or her words.

If you are the speaker being interrupted, you can finish your thoughts in two ways. First, you can confront the interrupter: "Do you mind if I finish what I was saying?" Second, if you want to avoid creating stress, you can simply wait until the interrupter has finished and then insert, "Anyway, as I was saying," and continue your remarks.

Be careful about your own interrupting. On the street, you probably learned to interrupt rambling responses. In interpersonal exchanges, however, those you interrupt will feel just as annoyed as you feel when you are interrupted.

On some occasions, however, interrupting can signal excitement, especially when you are talking interpersonally with several people who begin saying essentially the same thing, overlapping one another. This kind of interrupting usually elaborates rather than changes the subject. The speaker tends to feel rewarded, and the others feel energized.

> Charlie Brown: "I think that if I were happy, I could help others to be happy. Does that make sense to you?"
> Lucy: "We've had spaghetti at our house three times this month."
>
> —Charles Schulz, *Peanuts*

Irrelevant response. An irrelevant response is a reply that does not relate in any way to the last message. This change in subject implies that what the speaker is talking about does not matter. For example, neighborhood activist Eva Perlroth asks, "Do you think we should try to get a permit to block off the alley?" and Ellison answers, "We need to close that liquor store on the corner. How can we get started on that?" This irrelevant response symbolically dumps Perlroth's thoughts in the trash. A better response would be for Ellison to discuss Perlroth's issue or at least acknowledge her question before moving on: "That's one option. Let's make a note of it and consider other options too. What about closing the liquor store on the corner?" This response validates Perlroth's input before changing topics. Make sure your own responses relate to the speaker's remarks.

Incongruous response. A response is incongruous when a person says one thing and does another. We tend to doubt the verbal response and put more faith in the nonverbal behaviors. "Sure, it's a great idea" coupled with a deep sigh and an exaggerated eye roll comes across as a negative assessment of the idea. At best, incongruous responses are confusing. Your verbal and nonverbal messages must be congruent.

Ridicule. Ridicule discounts or makes fun of either a speaker's position or the speaker's level of concern about it. People tend to use this response when they feel threatened and want to minimize the issue at hand. Sometimes it is used by attention-seekers who are after a laugh and don't realize the impact on the speaker. Honest disagreement is fine; putting down ideas through ridicule is not.

> *After the flood receded, the emergency response team met to debrief the police department's actions during the height of the storm. After the usual issues were handled, Lt. Stefan Ivancic, who had been in charge of seeing that those facing long duty hours were fed, tried to alert the group to some of the problems his unit had faced. The deputy chief leading the meeting waved his input aside. "Hey, nobody's going to starve. Your guys'll get food. We never have to worry about cops eating." Nobody challenged the high-ranking leader as he said indirectly that Ivancic's concern was foolish. The topic changed and the food distribution issue was never addressed. Ridicule had effectively silenced communication.*

Discounting the issue. The **discounting** response is similar to ridicule, but it lacks the ironic twist. It directly denies the importance of the problem and attributes other causes to the speaker's remarks. Typical discounting responses include, "Sounds like you had a bad day" or "Oh, you're just in a bad mood." Sometimes the response is competitive: "That's nothing! Let me tell you about *my* problems." To avoid discounting, acknowledge a person's concern, even if to you the problem seems small or you disagree.

No response at all. Sometimes people ignore or just don't respond to a speaker's words or concern. At other times the emotional expression is so flat, people perceive the response as unconcerned. To avoid this appearance, show expression, make eye contact, and respond directly.

The most common versions of this disconfirmation are not returning phone calls, not answering letters or e-mail, and pushing people off on secretaries or volunteers rather than talking to them yourself. Unfortunately this disconfirming response is exactly the same as would occur through genuine oversight or when messages never got through. Depending on machines, mail, and other people to transfer messages is risky. Expecting people to remember all their obligations, especially ones made orally and not written in an appointment book, is unrealistic. Don't hesitate to send a message a second time by mailing a confirming letter that restates the details or by calling with reminders. If the people simply forgot, they will appreciate the reminder. If they intended to snub you, you will have called them on it politely. Make an effort to be a person who does respond. Develop a system to remember appointments, calls, and messages. This may mean carrying an appointment calendar or slipping index cards into your pocket to write notes on. As your life gets more complex, depending solely on memory is unreliable.

Provide Confirming Responses

Confirming responses cause people to feel that they are valued and their words heard. Such valuation is often energizing, which encourages people to contribute and communicate more. You can convey this relational message by acknowledging existence, acknowledging positions on issues, recognizing feelings, and acknowledging contributions.

Acknowledging existence. Let people know that you are aware of them. You do this by returning calls, responding to requests, and remembering people's names, views, goals, and even casual remarks.

Acknowledging positions on issues. Recognizing a speaker's position does not mean agreeing with it. You can convey acknowledgment by paraphrasing or by offering a thoughtful reply to the speaker's points. This is why, when you listen actively, your paraphrasing is important: it conveys that you respect the speaker enough to give him or her attention.

Recognizing feelings. Showing personal regard for people's experiences and acknowledging the weight they give an issue are ways to honor their feelings; you do not have to have the same feelings or values. Sometimes simply engaging in casual conversation at the beginning of meetings or chatting briefly about a person's family or hobbies is sufficient. This is why seemingly irrelevant conversation is in fact valuable interpersonal communication: it is confirming at the relational level.

Acknowledging contributions. Acknowledging contributions, commending good work, and offering to help with difficult tasks are all ways people tell one another they appreciate each other's efforts. Too often work is simply taken for granted. Appreciation is very important for volunteers whose only reward may be your acknowledgment of their contribution. When little note is taken of people's work, they often feel disappointment and might very well cut down on their efforts. In effect, this means gratitude is a commodity that you can trade for community effort, but hopefully, your appreciation is genuine.

Use Verbal Techniques to Enhance Communication

Four simple techniques for wording your messages can help you communicate more effectively: speak for yourself, make direct statements, ask "what" or "how" questions, and be specific. If you don't use these already, you may need to consciously practice them until they become natural. They are ways to enhance your day-to-day communication.

Speak for Yourself

One way to enhance interpersonal communication is to **personalize** your comments and take responsibility for your positions, opinions, and values, rather than generalizing, rendering judgments, or blaming others. This sometimes is called "**I-speaking**" because you use the word "I" quite a bit to directly acknowledge your own position. This approach reduces defenses by not placing general or even specific blame on others. Consider how the statements in each of the following examples differ:

"This project is going nowhere."
"I'm very concerned about how little we've accomplished so far."

The first statement can cause those involved to feel defensive. The second statement addresses the same issue, but is a comment about your own reactions, which invites discussion about the project's progress.

"You're late again!"
"I would like us to begin promptly at nine."

The first statement is guaranteed to evoke defensive reactions and provoke an argument. The second statement encourages a serious discussion of what the best start time is and allows you to voice your position.

I-statements can be useful in a conflict situation. In that instance, the statement has three parts. First, provide a neutral description of what the person is doing that bothers you. Second, describe the effect this has on you. Third, explain how this makes you feel. For example, "When you didn't show up at the meeting, I had to present our viewpoint without all the material. I was embarrassed."

Don't confuse taking responsibility for your position with focusing on only your own needs and feelings. A constant barrage of "I" rather than "we" can be off-putting. The key is to use I-statements rather than blaming, using vague statements, or not expressing yourself at all.

Make Direct Statements

Direct statements overtly express what you mean to say. Communication problems can arise when people bury their real positions in indirect statements and questions. Try to reword vague questions as clear statements about your own perceptions or preferences. Consider the difference between the following:

"Are you planning to wear that in public?"
"I would rather you would not wear that when we visit the neighborhood centers."

The first is really an attack, not a question. The second also conveys a negative comment, but it acknowledges that the statement is your opinion, not an absolute fashion judgment, and any ensuing discussion is more likely to be about appropriate attire on such occasions than about the degree to which your attitude resembles that of a Neanderthal. Again, compare the next two statements.

"It's very nice outside."
"I would like to hold the meeting outside. How do the rest of you feel?"

The first comment could get you general agreement, but you could still be sitting in a stuffy room an hour later. Saying what you mean in a clear, direct statement is simply more effective.

Ask "What" or "How" Questions Rather Than "Why"

Simple word choices can influence the response you get from another person. Consider the simple word "why." As a question, it calls for a justification, not information. Richards asks, "Why are you putting all that data on the computer?" Holland thinks, "Because I want to! What's wrong with it?" She feels she must justify her action.

Instead substitute "what" and "how" for the word "why." "What led you to decide to put that data on the computer?" focuses on the decision process. "How are you going to use that?" focuses on the result. A question such as "Why are you going to the coast?" can become "What will you do there?" or "How did you choose the coast?" or even "Are you going for work or a vacation?" Remember that how you ask a question can make a big difference in the response.

Be Specific Rather Than General

The minute you claim someone "always" does anything you get in trouble. Even a child can find one example of when he, in fact, "did, too, go to bed on time, so you're wrong." Specific information describes particular incidents, includes detail, and to a large extent, includes factual detail based on observation. General information is impressionistic, often includes inferences drawn from numerous occasions, and inevitably involves a level of abstraction. Although such generalizations are inevitable when preparing reports and assessing a community, during interpersonal exchanges, the more specific you are, the stronger your message is.

As a receiver, asking others to be specific rather than general is a useful technique for responding to general accusations. Respond to such charges as "The police department ignores our part of town," with "Can you give us a specific incident so we can see if we can get to the bottom of it?"

Be Sensitive to Intercultural Differences

Different cultures convey relational messages in different ways. Normal behavior in one culture can convey rudeness, incompetence, and even dishonesty in another. Learning what is normal behavior in other cultures and what that implies

POCKET GUIDE

Asking Someone to Change

On occasion you may want to ask someone to change a behavior. This is always a delicate situation. Built into such a request is an implication of criticism. Some techniques can help minimize the strain.

1. Choose an appropriate time and place to comfortably share personal data.
2. Remember that you are sharing your perceptions, not "facts" about the other person.
3. Focus your feedback on sharing information rather than on evaluating your listener. In particular this means describing:
   - specific incidents rather than general conditions
   - behavior that can be changed rather than personality traits
   - a given situation rather than advice on how to "fix" things.
4. Explain how the behavior you are describing makes you *feel.*
5. Avoid using phrases such as "you always" or "you never." Instead, be specific and descriptive.
6. Focus your feedback on the value to your listener, not on the release it may give you. Give the amount of information the person you are talking to can use rather than the amount you have. Don't overload your listener.
7. If you encounter rising defenses or emotional reactions, acknowledge these reactions rather than trying to convince, reason, or supply additional information.
8. Communicate your concern for the receiver, and your recognition of his or her right to be different from you.
9. Leave the responsibility for change with the receiver.

for communication is essential to establishing strong communication within those cultures. When you violate cultural norms, you inadvertently send a message. People of another culture may see you as just making a mistake or they may perceive you as intentionally rude. They may refuse to talk with you. Your mistake may be simply speaking to a younger person before an older one, but inadvertent error can close all lines of communication.

To overcome the potential of making serious cultural communication errors, you must learn the specific communication practices of each culture. Much of the research on **intercultural communication** has been conducted in foreign countries where traditions firmly entrenched are easily identified. The degree to which these traditional patterns prevail once people immigrate to the United States varies widely. Generally, the longer people have been in the United States, the more likely they are to understand Western communication practices even if these practices are not their usual way of interacting. Gradually researchers are finding out more about U.S. ethnic group practices and immigrant cultural norms. Such research also brings mainstream U.S. practices to our conscious awareness. As this knowledge expands, the potential for positive intercultural communication should open.

In the meantime, you need to learn the patterns of any specific culture with which you interact. Knowing typical patterns of Asian cultures will not be of much help in dealing with new Ukrainian immigrants or residents with historical ties to Nigeria. Develop a **confederate**, someone from the culture who will explain to you how the culture typically communicates. This can save you enormous time, possible embarrassment, and the potential of inadvertently offending the very people you seek as partners.

> "Oakland has a lot of immigrants who don't speak English very well. In contrast, the majority of our officers speak only English. It's easy to see why citizens and law enforcement aren't communicating very effectively."
>
> —MOLLY WEXYL, EXECUTIVE DIRECTOR, SAFE STREETS NOW!, OAKLAND, CALIFORNIA

What further complicates this issue is individual difference. Simply because Japanese interact in a particular way does not mean that Mary Tanaka will automatically follow suit. People are individuals with their own idiosyncrasies, life experiences, personalities, and interpretations of the world. These differences influence their communication. In addition, people belong to multiple cultures. A person can be influenced by ethnic heritage, education, gender, career, religion, and so forth.

Despite all these variations, many intercultural differences grow from five issues: the role of context in the communication process, the use of time, the use of space and touch, the weight of the social hierarchy, and whether the culture is oriented around the individual or the group.

High- and Low-Context Cultures

All communication operates in a context. Recall that context is the situation in which the communication takes place. It prescribes what is appropriate for one person to say to another given their roles in that situation. One communication difference in cultures is the degree to which information is transmitted in words and the degree to which it is implied by the context rather than spoken. These are known as low-context and high-context cultures.

Low-context cultures depend on spoken language to communicate. What a person says is what the person means (at least it is if the speaker is honest). The mainstream United States is a low-context culture (although this varies to some degree by region). Communication training in the United States, as demonstrated in this chapter, typically stresses the value of speaking directly and voicing a position clearly and openly. We search for the right word because the word implies the meaning. This is not a universal value, however. Low-context cultures include the German, Swedish, Euro-American, and English (Lustig and Koester 131).

In **high-context cultures** the context conveys much of an interaction's meaning. The particular situation and the roles of the people in it prescribe how a message should be conveyed and what meaning is given to verbal and nonverbal codes. Return to the analogy of context as a ball game. When you run onto the baseball diamond, you are expected to know the rules of the game without explanation. In high-context culture, when you step into the meeting or begin to talk interpersonally, you encounter the same expectation. People know the signs of courtesy, forms of address, timing of language, nonverbal codes, and so forth, appropriate for a given context, and they expect you to know, too. They filter all behavior and statements according to this understood standard. High-context cultures include Japanese, African-American, Mexican, and Latino cultures (Lustig and Koester 131).

> "What seems efficient and reasonable to one culture is seen as cold and, in fact, rude to others with a different cultural heritage."
>
> —COMMUNITY POLICING CONSORTIUM, "CULTURAL DIVERSITY"

As an illustration, consider a culture where offering food communicates hospitality. Rita Lopez offers Alan Richards a piece of cake. Because Richards already has to hold his breath to button his slacks, he refuses politely, operating on mainstream U.S. norms, in which you say what you mean directly. In the context of Lopez's culture, she is welcoming Richards to her home. His refusal could be a rejection, but she knows such a refusal can mean the person doesn't want to appear greedy. Therefore, she reassures him, "Oh, go ahead, have a piece. There's plenty." This is where communication gets tricky for Richards. He's already refused once. If he refuses again, will Lopez be offended?

Consider another situation. Many Japanese, from a high-context culture, tend to begin every interaction, even a group meeting, with polite inquiries about family and personal well-being. This communicates respect. Mainstream Americans, who tend to be task oriented and direct, often see this as "wasting time." They may view the polite inquiries as intrusive. Similarly, mainstream Americans state their opinions in a forthright manner with only minimal regard for the feelings of the listener. This is shocking to many traditional Japanese who value feelings, saving face, and preserving group harmony. Second- and third-generation Japanese-Americans, who have lived by Western norms all their lives, may still be influenced by their ancestral culture, beginning meetings with personal exchanges and showing polite concern for others without even realizing the source of the pattern.

Use of Time

How members of a culture use time shows up in how promptly they arrive for appointments, how tightly their calendar is scheduled, how rapidly meetings turn to the task, how fast the pace of conversation moves, and the amount of time devoted to elements other than business. Many Latin American, Pacific Island, and Native American cultures are notoriously less concerned about time than mainstream American business schedules prefer. People from these cultures have learned to live by U.S. standards in most cases, but some still have a much looser definition of "on time" than do the Americans, who run their lives by alarm clocks and time management literature. This difference can result in a situation where you wait for someone you think of as late who sees himself as on time. You expect an explanation, maybe an apology, and get nothing because he doesn't even realize that he is not "on time."

Use of Space and Touch

How near people can stand to one another comfortably, and when they can appropriately touch, varies by cultural background. The Community Policing Consortium describes this as "one of the most overlooked barriers to communication."

> Individuals within the dominant culture in the United States tend to stand four to twelve feet from individuals when speaking if they do not know the individuals well. To people of different cultures, this posture can appear to express aloofness, superiority, or an unwillingness to see others as "worthy" human beings. ("Cultural Diversity")

Those who stand close can be perceived as invasive or even as being too familiar by those from the Western culture. Communication professors Myron Lustig and Jolene Koester describe the European origins of these differences:

> The personal space bubbles for Europeans get smaller and smaller, as one travels south toward the Mediterranean. Indeed, the distance that is regarded as intimate in Germany, Scandinavia, and England overlaps with what is regarded as a normal conversational distance in France and the Mediterranean countries of Italy, Greece, and Spain. (196)

Not only do the northern Europeans think the southern Europeans are getting too close, but the southern Europeans see their northern European neighbors as "distant and aloof." What starts out as a space preference turns into a personality characteristic.

Touch is an extension of these standards about space. For example, Latinos often use touch to communicate friendliness, which can easily be misinterpreted by cultures that avoid touch. The Community Policing Consortium "Cultural Diversity" Internet page provides a vivid illustration of the power of touch as communication.

> Clashes between African Americans and Korean shopkeepers, particularly in the inner city, could be based partly on misunderstanding touch. Koreans raised in the traditional culture feel it is rude to touch someone they do not know well. So, they place change or goods on the counter rather than directly in someone's hand. African Americans and Hispanics, accustomed to conveying friendliness with touch, may feel this is a sign of someone feeling superior to them or rejecting them.

Social Hierarchy

Even though the United States is founded on the value that all people are created equal, in reality you are unlikely to speak to the mayor in the same way you do a homeless person on the street. The degree to which people's status and position determine how others communicate with them varies by culture. Vastly different standards operate about what is appropriate to say to those of "higher rank." That rank can be the result of family background, age, social position, financial standing, gender, education, occupation, or the authority of the badge. At one extreme are cultures that recognize few differences in position. People in this culture call the chief, the sergeant, and the community officer by their first names. The teenager feels equal to the experienced beat cop.

At the other extreme are cultures such as Asian that typically perceive social position and role as highly relevant. An officer at the front door may violate cultural norms if he speaks to the wife rather than the husband, or to the child rather than the parent. A group will make no decision without the endorsement of the patriarch. A person of high rank is offended to be spoken to as an equal by someone "below" him or her. In such a situation your casual friendliness can communicate rudeness, and the absence of your agency's high-ranking officers at a public ceremony of the culture becomes an insult.

Self-Orientation Versus Group Orientation

Cultures that value membership in a group, especially the family group, more than they value individual career advancement and personal achievements are called **collectivist cultures**. Members of collectivist cultures will repress their personal desires in order that the group may succeed or have unity. Members feel loyalty and responsibility for the group and take care of one another. That group attachment, however, does not extend to you—the community officer. Such cultures typically have a very strong sense of the in-group and the out-group, those to whom they feel loyal and those who are "others."

Individualistic cultures, on the other hand, focus on self-development. People pride themselves on their unique traits, their ability to get ahead, on thinking critically for themselves and not blindly conforming to tradition.

The differences in the two approaches affect communication in various ways. Consider conflict. Lustig and Koester write: " Individualist cultures train their members to speak out as a means of resolving difficulties. . . . Those with a collectivistic orientation are likely to use avoidance, third-party intermediaries, or other face-saving techniques" (147). Persuasion, too, is changed by this value. Programs to benefit families fare well in collectivist cultures, and as a community officer, you can use this to your benefit. In such cultures—Southeast Asian, Japanese, Chinese, Latino, to name a few—your strongest connection may be to set up family programs or programs to benefit children or the elderly.

No specific advice on interpersonal relations in different cultures will work in all cultures you encounter. Respect the cultures you enter and understand that communication may be interpreted differently in different cultures. Find out about the specific practices of each culture or ethnic group you work with regularly. The easiest way to do that is to get to know someone in each culture and frankly ask for help. Community leaders from such cultures will understand your problem. They have faced it, living in both their own and the mainstream culture. Focus particularly on the five areas discussed here and ask for advice. People who realize you are there to help them will assist you so that you communicate appropriately.

Trust: The Ultimate Goal

Communication works best in open environments where people feel comfortable enough to share information and trust one another enough to be honest. Beneath all the suggestions for good communication offered here and in other references lie the twin goals of individuals building trust and developing respect for one another. Your ultimate interpersonal goal, working one-on-one in the community, is to build such trust and respect. No techniques can replace the power of one human being's respect for another or the honorable behavior that results in trust, but communication techniques can help you communicate as you build such trust in relationships with people in the community.

Over time people have a chance to assess your trustworthiness, as you do theirs. What you do or say is compiled in memories until the community has a sense of who you are. Consistency is vitally important. Be honest in your interactions with others.

ACTION CLIP

Trust in a Housing Project

Officers Harold Bickel and Greg Dieckmann received the 1996 Herman Goldstein Excellence in Problem Solving Award for their work in two housing projects in Sacramento known for heavy juvenile crime and gang activity. They report getting information when they arrived in the complexes from "various sources, including property managers, resident councils, district officers, surveys, door-to-door conversations with adults, and conversations with children around the two complexes."

They looked for common ground to build on, and then "we communicated indirectly by performing. A message was sent by our behavior." Bickel and Dieckmann began to set limits about what was not acceptable. "We told it to those we arrested, said it at meetings, told the resident councils, let the managers know." Then they acted consistently with that message. Harold Bickel says, "My partner can run like a rabbit. I said to those we arrested, 'If you run, Dieckmann will catch you.' And he did. Word got around. We built a reputation."

Gradually others in the projects began to side with them as they acted to help the community in the ways consistent with their statements. "The resident council president at that time—she was a rock cocaine addict; even so, she worked with us. They put out a newsletter, and said in it, 'Who ya gonna call? The Crimebusters.' So then we got that reputation. We built trust."

(For a detailed report of the Bickel–Dieckmann project, see their articles in the *Problem-Solving Quarterly,* Winter and Spring/Summer 1997.)

Voice your wishes and dreams for the area carefully. Visions can guide a group, but don't let the group take them as promises. If you or the department cannot follow through on what was perceived as a commitment, they will feel disappointment and see you as making promises you can't keep. Chief Pat Parks of Petaluma, California, urges that when you forecast what community policing will accomplish for your community, you "under project; over achieve." This way, the community feels you have done more than you promised.

Your reputation goes on and on. Giving false information to a group can get you out of a bind today, but it puts you in one tomorrow. If you treat people badly, interact in ways that offend people, fail to do what you say you will do, community members will remember and the word will spread. If you treat them well, interact in a culturally sensitive manner, do what you say you will do, and show regard for other human beings, the word will spread about that, too. Interpersonal communication is complicated, but it is the foundation upon which neighborhood activation is built.

Works Cited

Bickel, Harold, and Gregory Dieckmann. Personal interview. 11 Nov. 1997.

———. "Multifaceted POP Project Breathes New Life into Apartment Communities." *Problem-Solving Quarterly* 10 (Winter 1997): 1–7.

———. "New Life in Sacramento Apartment Communities, Part Two." *Problem-Solving Quarterly* 10 (Spring/Summer 1997): 1–7.

Canady, Alexa. Quoted in Goleman, Daniel, Paul Kaufman, and Michael Ray. *The Creative Spirit*. New York: Dutton, 1992. 39–40.

Covey, Stephen. *The Seven Habits of Highly Effective People*. New York: Fireside, 1989.

Community Policing Consortium. "Cultural Diversity." http://www.communitypolicing.org/cultural/index.htm. 10 Nov. 1997.

———. "Module Three: Community Policing Problem-Solving—Taking a Problem-Solving Approach to Tackling Crime, Fear and Disorder." http://www.communitypolicing.org/mod3.html. 7 Nov. 1997.

Decker, Bert. *You've Got to Be Believed to Be Heard*. New York: St. Martin's Press, 1992.

Gibb, Jack. "Defensive Communication." *Journal of Communication* 11:3 (1961): 141–148.

Lustig, Myron W., and Jolene Koester. *Intercultural Competence: Interpersonal Communication Across Cultures*. New York: HarperCollins, 1993.

McPherson, Nancy. "Solution-Driven Partnerships: Just Six Steps Away." *Community Policing Exchange*. Sept./Oct. 1995: 1–2.

Norcross, Lissah. "Officers from Rural, Suburban and Urban Jurisdictions Share Views." *Community Policing Exchange* July/Aug. 1995. http://www.communitypolicing.org. 12 Nov. 1997.

Parks, Pat. "Community Oriented Policing and Problem Solving Training for Trainers." Folsom, Calif., 24–26 Feb. 1998.

Phillips, Dennis, and Les Wallace. *Influence in the Workplace: Maximizing Personal Empowerment*. Dubuque, Iowa: Kendall/Hunt, 1992.

Shea, Gordon. "The Power of Listening." *Managing a Difficult or Hostile Audience*. Englewood Cliffs, N.J.: Prentice Hall, 1984.

Trojanowicz, Robert, and Bonnie Bucqueroux. *Community Policing: How to Get Started.* Cincinnati: Anderson Publishing, 1994.

Tubbs, Steward L., and Sylvia Moss. *Human Communication*. 5th ed. New York: Random House, 1987.

Wexyl, Molly. *Community Policing Exchange* Sept./Oct. 1995: 5.

Activities

1 Listening Journal

Try this once a day for two weeks.

1. After a short conversation, try to write down what the person you talked with said. (Try this for conversations, not interviews where you are taking notes.) Observe whether anything seems vague to you or confusing or how much of the exchange you simply lost.
2. If you feel comfortable with the speaker, go back and ask about what you missed. Observe for yourself how much information is lost while listening.
3. Pay attention to the times when your mind wanders. When you suddenly come back to the conversation, make note of what was being said. Try to determine what caused the lapse of attention. Did you hear something that was said and think about it while the speaker continued speaking? Did some comment spark an idea? Or were you far from the subject, making no effort to pay attention?

2 Speaking for Yourself

Rephrase the following statements to speak directly, taking responsibility for opinions and expressing feelings, instead of blaming others or outside forces for what is happening. Also, be specific rather than general.

1. The club president didn't do her share of work in the group.
2. The sergeant doesn't let me express my ideas at all.
3. You're late again.
4. It's just not fair for you to shirk on your share of the team effort.

5. It's important that we meet before Wednesday.
6. Where were you this afternoon? We were all supposed to be there.
7. He won't ever let us have any fun. The minute we start telling any story, it's back to work.
8. This project is a mess.

3 Paraphrasing

Supplies: index cards or notepaper
This activity is designed to help you practice paraphrasing.

With a Partner

Practice paraphrasing with a partner.

1. On index cards, briefly describe an issue you feel strongly about. For example, you might believe that abortion should be every woman's option and that such issues should not be controlled by law.
2. Hand the card to your partner. Your partner makes one statement *in opposition* to your view.
3. You paraphrase your partner's statement as clearly as possible. *You may not argue the issue.*
4. Your partner must agree that you expressed his or her statement clearly before you can move on. If this has not happened, your partner explains what is missing. Then you restate your partner's position. Continue until your partner feels heard.
5. Your partner then makes another, longer statement *against* your view. Repeat Steps 3 and 4 until you have paraphrased three statements to your partner's satisfaction.
6. Switch roles and repeat the process.

On Your Own

Be aware of paraphrasing as a technique. For one week, consciously try to use paraphrasing, perhaps beginning with "Let me be sure I have this right. . . ." Watch the response of others. Note how often the speaker corrects your interpretation or elaborates with more information.

4 Putting It All Together

Consider a conversation you would like to have with a specific person. Select a situation with some complexity. It may be a problem in your agency or at home, the need to express emotion to a child, an occasion to give feedback to a romantic partner, or a need to ask a person to change a behavior you find unpleasant.

1. Write a description of the situation as you anticipate it. What do you want to say to whom?
2. Anticipate any problems you might encounter. Will your listener be receptive? Will your listener be surprised at your message? Will you appear to be outside your role? Will your listener likely say no or be embarrassed or reject your ideas? Will your listener be hurried, tired, hungry, preoccupied? Write a list of possible problems you might encounter.
3. Plan a strategy for avoiding or managing the problems you listed in Step 2. If your listener will be defensive, for instance, how will you minimize this defensiveness? What place will you choose to talk? What time? How will you frame the message? Write a description of your strategies.
4. Practice the beginning of your conversation (your part) out loud.
5. Visualize yourself being successful in this conversation. What do you see in your visualization that is not a part of your strategy? Add it if you can. Describe any additions. If several people do this activity, sharing strategies and getting feedback before Step 6 is useful.
6. Put your plan into effect. Talk to your friend, neighbor, spouse, partner, house mate, and so on. Assess your results. Consider what you would change for greater success in a future conversation.

5 Intercultural Opportunities

Increase your awareness of another culture.

1. Attend a cultural event to which the public is invited. Religious organizations, schools, and ethnic groups often host community events such as food festivals and community fairs to which they invite the public. Go. Mingle. Talk to as many people as you can. You can simply be a private community member enjoying the day, or you can speak to someone at a booth who is not too busy and tell him or her that you would like to learn more about the culture. You may develop some interesting conversations.
2. Buy your groceries for one week in a market that caters to a particular ethnic group. Go to a Chinese market, a Greek deli, or a Ukrainian shop. This is a very easy way to expose yourself to a small piece of another culture. Eat what you buy. If you have to ask advice, so much the better. It gets you talking. Explain that you have heard the food is good, but you don't know what to make—this is a natural way to begin.
3. Go to foreign films or film festivals, ideally, films shown in a theater in a part of town where people of that culture reside. You may not enjoy the film; that is not the point. Go for the experience of being in a different environment and seeing a different visual re-creation of culture. You may even enjoy it! Look for the less-seen films, such as those from Korea, the Philippines, or Hungary.

4. Watch cable TV in a language you want to learn or aimed at an audience whose culture you want to understand. TV is not reality, but the shows will expose you to some of the values of the culture.
5. Search the Internet. Find and talk with officers who live and work in the countries of origin of ethnic groups in your community. For example, if your community has a large Swedish group, find a police department in Sweden and chat with the Swedish officers online.

6 Supportive and Defensive Communication

Rewrite the following statements, likely to produce defensive reactions, into statements that will produce a supportive climate. Review Gibb's list of supportive and defensive communication behaviors, if necessary.

Evaluation

You didn't show much effort in this.
I think if you cared, you would have time to donate blood.
I'm glad you're finally doing something about that weight.

Control

Write the report and get it to me by Friday before noon.
That was just the most wonderful movie, wasn't it!
I know you're going to love the plan I have for you.

Neutrality

You're thinking of going to Hawaii? Well, whatever.
I heard you got promoted.
Everybody has to work on Christmas sometime.

Superiority

Let me show you; I've had years of experience.
Make an extra key for the office while you're out.
We'll take my car; there's so much more room.

Certainty

Nobody learns from pure lecture.
You have to get that lawn mowed.
You can't make a living as an artist.

Strategy

I think it would be inappropriate of me to comment on the Council's plans.
I'm sure that whatever the chief plans will be the right thing to do.
I think that whatever the union plans will be the right thing to do.

Chapter Three

Camels Are Useful on the Desert

The Work Group Meeting

"I think this co-operative scheme is an uncommonly good one. It's much easier to work on someone else's job than one's own—gives one that delightful feelin' of interferin' and bossin' about, combined with the glorious sensation that another fellow is takin' all one's own work off one's hands."

LORD PETER WIMSEY
(DOROTHY L. SAYERS)

Sgt. Emilio Fritz looks smug as Officer Alan Richards approaches. This is not a good sign, Richards thinks. He likes it better when Fritz barks out orders. His heart sinks as Fritz directs him to form a work group of interested business people and neighborhood leaders concerned about prostitution on Broadway. Richards' charge is to meet with them and set up a system to get their ongoing input. The work group should include representatives from the merchants association, the county public health department, the shopping center administration, the apartment complex known as Four Oaks, the Asian American League, and the Mexican American Citizens Alliance.

"Like a community forum?" Richards asks.

"Like a group meeting. Like a committee!" As he heads for the firing range Fritz smiles, "Better you than me."

THE PERSON WHO FIRST CAME UP WITH THE LINE "A camel is a horse put together by a committee" clearly was not enthralled with the group meeting process. Neither was the cynic who penned, "Meetings, the plausible alternative to work." But the fact is, in spite of the general frustration many people have with group meetings, they are one of the most effective and efficient ways to quickly exchange a lot of information, reach common agreement, generate ideas, and develop individual commitment to a goal. Whether your work group is called a committee, task force, board of directors, multi-agency team, crew, or a departmental staff meeting; whether it has three members or fifteen; whether it meets two times or twenty, the group process will influence your success.

In contrast to the public community meeting, called to allow the community to address an issue or share information, the **work group** tends to include a small number of people who meet for a specific purpose. Frequently, this purpose is to make a decision about an issue. Generally a work group meets several times; in ongoing groups and standing committees, they meet many times. Group members tend to develop relationships with one another and often evolve a sense of identity as a group. Researchers do not agree on when a "small" group becomes a "large" one. Although this book discusses community meetings separately in Chapter 5, these large and small meetings frequently overlap. At a community meeting, neighbors discuss an issue and then form a task force, which holds work group meetings. As you plan your meetings, use whichever techniques help you improve the community.

Groups can be very effective. *Business Week* says that group decision making can result in a 40 to 50 percent increase in productivity over individual decision making ("Payoff"). Groups usually make better quality decisions and do so faster than individuals working alone (Frey 7). And one thing you can be sure of is that as a community officer you *will* attend meetings! In the business world, managers spend 30 to 80 percent of their time in meetings (Mosvick and Nelson). The world of community policing is similar. Consider some examples:

- In Baltimore, a team looking at the connection between truancy and juvenile gang and drug problems held meetings with school officials to identify truancy violators and to target locations where illicit juvenile activities often occurred ("Youth" 1).
- The Austin Police Department decided to implement community policing. A task force oversaw such issues as changing the mission statement, training, developing an officer reward system, and revising the department manual (Peak and Glensor 319).
- In Milwaukee, the police Gang Crimes/Intelligence Division worked with the Medical College of Wisconsin to develop programs to prevent youth violence ("Youth" 1).
- In Reno, a Gang Alternative Program (GAP)—consisting of representatives from law enforcement, the district attorney's office, juvenile probation, the school district, private agencies and citizens—shared resources and information concerning gang violence, seeking to balance enforcement with diversion and intervention (Glensor).

The starting point for each of these projects was a work group meeting. This trend is likely to continue as federal grant programs increasingly mandate **collaboratives**, efforts in which a variety of social agencies work together to solve problems, as a condition of receiving funds. As organizational consultant Len Silvey explains:

> The reality today is that educators are pulling together probation officers, police officers, school teachers, social service professionals, mental health professionals and recreation specialists to address the truancy problem. The reality today is that probation officers are pulling together community based organizations, police professionals, employers, labor groups, social service professionals, mental health professionals, and educators to address issues . . . in the juvenile justice system.

Communicating well in groups is, and will continue to be, essential.

Elements of Group Meetings

Much of what happens in one work group meeting happens in all meetings. Some elements of group interaction are completely predictable, no matter who is meeting or what the group wants to accomplish, whether it is a formal business meeting or an informal working session. Simply handing out an agenda and proceeding to talk about items on it does not really explain the communication of people who meet together for some time. Knowing what to expect, and understanding why these elements occur, will help you feel more comfortable and work in your group more effectively.

Primary Tension

Whenever a group of people first get together, they experience **primary tension**, a state of mild anxiety that comes from not knowing what to expect socially. They wonder whether they will appear overly authoritative, unprepared, poorly dressed, or ignorant—whether others will view them with hostility, friendliness, or prejudice. People are wary about talking until they figure out the unwritten rules. Is this meeting to be formal or informal? Do you address people by first names or last? Can anyone speak or just those in authority positions? Is it okay to joke and tease others or should you be businesslike? Do lines of rank operate when community members are present? If you make a joke, will you seem frivolous? If you plunge in with a suggested policy, will you seem to be pushing a cause? This uncertainty results in awkward silences intermixed with inane remarks and excessive politeness. It is the main reason ice breakers were invented.

> "Refreshments are a hospitable touch that have put many a potentially contentious meeting on a civilized track."
>
> —Elaine Cogan (51)

Especially for the first meeting, try to plan activities that help release this primary tension. Many ideas are simple and inexpensive:

- Have refreshments available when people arrive to encourage them to mingle.
- Ask participants to wear name tags, which can include, in addition to their names, their special interests, hobbies, affiliations, and so on to serve as conversation starters. Generally, people will take their cue from your name tag, so make sure your name tag includes all the information you want others to provide. Also write your name as you want people there to call you. This is the difference between "Andy Taylor," "Sheriff Taylor," and "Andy."
- Arrive early to greet the participants; shake hands and introduce them to one another. If you feel awkward in such situations, urge an extrovert or two in the group, who can do this naturally, to arrive early to greet people.
- Start with an **ice breaker** to relax people if you have time and it seems appropriate. (Sample ice breakers appear at the end of the chapter.) At the very least, as you start the meeting, have people in the group introduce themselves, and, if time allows, comment on the project or purpose (or do a full-scale powwow). These activities not only help break the ice, they also signal that participation is appropriate and each person's contribution is important.

Group Size

The number of people attending a group meeting affects the communication patterns in it. A group can have as few as three members, but the ideal size for a work group is five to seven people (Bormann *Small Group* 2). In a meeting this size, everyone can

Powwow

Walt Disney is credited with advocating the powwow as a way for people working on a project to get to know one another. Based on the Native American notion of sitting together around the fire and sharing ideas, the powwow is a great way to begin a project that includes strangers from differing agencies or community groups. The group sits in a circle and does the following:

1. Each person introduces himself or herself and then describes personal skills and experiences related to the issue the group faces. This identifies resources the group can call on.
2. The group goes around the circle again. This time, each person describes activities, related or unrelated to the project, that he or she likes to do. This builds ties between people with common interests. If you know people might make up part of your golf foursome, you are more willing to listen to their ideas.
3. The group goes around the circle a third time. This final time, each person offers thoughts about the project while the others listen. Note that this is not a discussion, but rather a chance for each person to listen, without interruption, to others' views.

At the end of the powwow, the group has a much better overview of its members' strengths and attitudes—a common foundation to build on. Be careful not to dive into business. In *Think Out of the Box*, Mike Vance and Diane Deacon warn, "It's important to resist the urge to come to solutions at a powwow. Powwows are not designed to produce closure" (161).

POCKET GUIDE

express a point of view and speak freely and the group has enough people to get the work done. You can push the size a little, but by the time thirteen or more people attend a meeting, research indicates that five to seven of them will do most of the talking. The larger the group becomes, the more some people sit quietly rather than actively participate, and the more cliques and subgroups develop.

The size of your group changes the strategies used to run the meeting. For example, if you want to make decisions, smaller groups can discuss issues and reach a consensus; larger groups generally must resort to a vote. When you have a choice, try to keep your group meetings small (five to seven people). A larger group (more than seven or eight people) is useful only when you want representation from many areas or when you are trying to generate enthusiasm for a project.

Task and Social Dimensions

The cry to "keep the group on the subject" is common from people who want to get their business done and get away. But focusing entirely on the task will not eliminate human relations. Group work involves more than the obvious business agenda and goals of the meeting. Because human beings are involved, group meetings also entail human emotions and reactions. These dual components are called the task and social dimensions. The **task dimension** is the actual content or business of the meeting, the task to be accomplished. The **social dimension** is how people relate to one another. (Sometimes this is referred to as the socio-emotional component or the climate.) Figure 3-1 lists examples of the task and social dimensions. People are concerned about being acknowledged as individuals. No matter how important the task is to people, they also have a need to belong, be respected, and have their contributions recognized. These needs can be more important to some people than whatever task brought the group together. Sometimes they seek status and power. Some seek to play politics, and possibly to achieve hidden goals.

Task Dimension	Social Dimension
Discussing factual information about the issue	Shyness
Clarifying the goal	Feeling included
Enthusiasm about the possibilities of the project	Irritation because one person monopolizes the discussion
Developing steps to achieve the goal	Longing for recognition
Long-range planning	Pleasure being in another person's company
Dividing up work	Feeling left out or unneeded
Conflict caused by differences in positions on issues	Anger and conflict caused by disregard for others' feelings

Figure 3-1: Examples of task and social dimensions

Dr. Ernest Bormann uses an example of a purely task-oriented "group" to illustrate the two dimensions:

> Five carefully programmed computers, their memory storages filled with information, can be connected with one another so that information is fed back and forth among them. . . . The computers in this small group can be programmed so they are completely task oriented. Such a group has no social dimension. One of the computers will not short circuit communication because he feels a loss of status within the group, nor will one computer resist instructions transferred from another because it dislikes the attitude of that computer. (*Discussion* 138)

Human beings, however, will resist. As much as you might want to focus on a task, how people are treated affects how willingly they communicate and how diligently they participate in the project, which, in turn, affects the quality of the group's decisions and actions.

The social dimension does not license people at meetings to talk about themselves at length or to show you their latest vacation photos. A good group meeting focuses primarily on the task, but group members still take the time to treat one another with respect, show concern for each other's emotions, and appreciate one another's contributions. Before and after meetings group members engage in casual chitchat, and during meetings they enjoy occasional quips or stories that release tension. They pay attention to the particular nuances of how ideas are voiced. Sometimes fostering the social dimension is as simple as listening to everyone and making sure all points of view are heard.

A good group achieves a balance between the task and social dimensions. Too much focus on the task leaves some people unmotivated and disinterested. Too much focus on the social prevents work from being done. The social dimension should be the interaction that smoothes the way to get the task done pleasantly.

Tension relief. The social dimension also serves as tension relief when groups begin to feel conflict. Joking, telling stories, asking with concern about a problem someone expressed previously, or getting off the subject into a brief discussion of the latest Bulls–Jazz game gives the group time to cool down or to relax at the end of a line of discussion before the group takes up a new topic. Few contributions are as valuable to a working group as good tension relief. It is the oil that lubricates the machinery of group meetings.

Group Norms

What happens early in a group sets the standard for later meetings. Initial behavior establishes group **norms**, or what is normal behavior for that combination of people. Setting the tone you want from the beginning is important. Do you want everyone to speak out freely? Then get them to talk within the first ten minutes. Do you want a casual tone? Then take off your jacket and hang it over your chair. Is it okay to have coffee at the table? Then bring it. Do you want a formal meeting focused on a task? Then have all necessary material ready to go and establish the work tone from the onset. Remember that group members don't know what's expected of them at the first meeting. They watch what others do and copy whatever seems successful. By doing this, groups gradually develop their own norms of what is appropriate behavior.

Officer Randy Washington wanted his first meeting with the executive committee of the Lakeshore Asian American Association to go well. He knew that sometimes speaking in public can be stressful for traditional Asian Americans, and he wanted group members to feel comfortable. For the meeting he arranged for refreshments and even brought fresh flowers. He set the chairs in a circle so everyone could make eye contact. He decided to start the meeting by having people introduce themselves and say a little about their backgrounds. His goal was not just to help them get to know one another; it was also to set a norm of participating.

He knew what the first person said was very important. Participants tend to watch their neighbors and then copy what seems successful. If the first person said only, "Hi, I'm Than Pham from First Avenue," others would do likewise. In advance he asked his friend Mary Tanaka to go first and model what to do. They arranged that Tanaka would not only give her name and the area where she lived but also briefly voice her concerns about vandalism around the lake. At the meeting Washington smiled as others followed suit.

Phases Groups Go Through

Groups go through predictable phases. Ongoing groups cycle through four predictable phases: orientation, conflict, emergence, and reinforcement (Ellis and Fisher 158–160). Even groups meeting only once or twice have touches of these phases.

Orientation. Groups begin with an orientation phase, which grows out of primary tension. At this point, participants are getting to know one another and exploring the range of their task. They are still hoping to impress one another, so they make tentative comments and use ambiguous wording. The group easily agrees on small issues. Everyone is nice and careful.

> "Debate and verbal conflict are not necessarily signals of members' dissatisfaction with their group; as long as they occur in the spirit of producing the best group decision rather than as a personal attack on a particular group member, they signify involvement and a high level of participation in the group's deliberations."
>
> —Ronald W. Toseland, Robert F. Rivas, and Dennis Chapman (345)

After a while, however, the honeymoon is over.

Conflict. At this point, the group is getting down to work. The participants have come to understand the task, the issues involved in the task, and the group norms. More confident of themselves and fed up with the "over-niceness" of orientation, participants take positions on issues and are willing to argue for these positions, make firm comments, and voice unambiguous statements. Disagreement follows. It is at this point that group members begin to wonder what kind of mutated genes spawned the other group members. The conflict phase is one of the reasons people dislike working in groups.

The good news is that conflict and disagreement are normal. Nothing is wrong with the group. Conflict can even have some positive outcomes. Disagreement on issues leads to well-thought-out conclusions and stronger decisions. It prevents the blind conformity known as **groupthink**. Conflict on issues shows participants' commitment to the goal and the group's concern about making correct choices. It is the group version of clear, critical thinking. It helps group members get to know one another better. People who experience conflict over issues are showing that they care about the project. Only people who don't care will ignore issues.

Unfortunately, people can feel personally hurt when their ideas are rejected, even when these are rejected for good reasons. People often equate the fate of their ideas with their social status, and feel less valued by the group when their ideas are rejected. Your best strategy is to assure them nonverbally of their value to the group. Give them attention; it is a reward in a group. Listen to them intently the next time they speak, and agree with them on issues whenever you honestly can. Be sure you show your appreciation of their contributions.

> "Groups making effective decisions and proposing high-quality alternatives are willing to engage in open conflict over the ideas, evidence, and reasoning presented in the group. They vigilantly test all information and ideas for soundness."
>
> —John K. Brilhart and Gloria J. Galanes (269)

Conflict can arise over issues and over personalities. When conflict is clearly over issues, the best resolution procedure is to reason clearly and to seek factual information that explains the issues. In discussion, group members do not have to abandon their positions, but they should try to be as flexible as conscience will allow. The group should look for solutions that will satisfy all parties of an issue conflict whenever possible.

Conflict is troublesome when it is about personalities. When people start to evaluate one another, show concern only for themselves, and display very rigid attitudes, the conflict does not help the group reason to a better conclusion. Group members sometimes forget the relational component of their messages. They speak tactlessly, do not help in giving one another ways to save face, and ignore one another's feelings. At this point, less committed group members will stop attending meetings.

One myth people often have about group work is that the best way to deal with conflict is to avoid it. They engage in what is known as **flight taking**, ignoring issue conflict in the name of harmony, pretending nothing is wrong and suppressing their ideas and opinions to retain a superficial group unity. *This is a very unproductive response. Without open discussion of ideas and problems, a group can make very poor decisions.* Their "unity" is false, growing out of a fear of giving their honest opinions. A far more functional response is to openly discuss the group's problems. Agree to listen politely, consider one another's positions, and speak honestly about your subject.

Individuals cope with conflict in one of five main styles: **avoiding**, repressing their own views or withdrawing; **forcing**, attempting to force others to accept their ideas or opinions by arguing, providing evidence, even shouting, power plays, manipulation, or threats; **smoothing**, trying to minimize the impact of conflict by smoothing over it, pretending it is less severe than it is, giving in for the sake of interpersonal relationships; **compromising**, seeking ways each side can give up something; and **collaborating**, seeking solutions that will satisfy all sides in a conflict. Although compromise is often touted as a useful strategy, it always leaves both sides disappointed because they each must give up something. When the group uses collaborative efforts to find a solution that satisfies all concerned, the group members feel more commitment to the decision. Collaborative solutions require a statement of the goal and issues. Participants must keep the goal in mind, but be flexible about how to reach it. If the group reaches a stalemate, people should concede on low-priority issues.

Sometimes conflict is worked out by individuals talking in twos and threes outside the group meeting, negotiating solutions in more private circumstances, feeling each other out, searching for new ideas.

Emergence. In the third phase, the miracle occurs: the group agrees on a solution. Dissent lessens and ambiguity reappears in language, which enables people in conflict to unite. Within the social dimension, harmony blossoms again. Frequently members feel closer than ever before, and display the strength of a team that has survived conflict. They begin to develop real cohesion, to think of themselves as a group, and to feel loyalty to their team.

Reinforcement. During the fourth and final phase, decisions that emerged somewhat vaguely are stated clearly. People begin to provide reasons to accept the decisions. Unity develops as members become committed to the decision. At the social level, members become comfortable with the contributions they are making.

Groups may cycle through these phases a number of times as they consider new issues. Such movement is natural.

Cohesiveness

Groups that work well together begin to develop **cohesiveness**, an esprit de corps or group loyalty. Cohesiveness is described by communication professor J. Dan Rothwell as "the degree of liking members have for each other and the group and the commitment to the group that this liking engenders" (62). The more cohesive the group, the more efficient the communication and the more enjoyable the meetings. Rothwell adds, "Common sense indicates a close relationship between productivity and cohesiveness" (62).

Cohesiveness grows from attention to social relationships in an environment of compatible membership, open communication, shared goals, a history of success at the task, and a positive history of cooperation.

Sometimes cohesiveness can be carried to extremes. Groups develop an "us versus them" orientation that is unhealthy. They see themselves as pitted against outside forces and picture their task as a war. This can prevent cooperative solutions and lead to groupthink. Such groups would be better off maintaining an open communication system.

Understanding principles that influence interaction among group members helps you as you work in your group. Much of that work is done in group meetings. Learning how to make meetings more effective can improve the whole group process.

Groupthink

The term "groupthink" refers to a condition that occurs when group members strive for excessive unanimity at the expense of clear thinking. Recognizing groupthink is very important in policing. Officers often feel a pressure to present a united front to those outside law enforcement. Such pressure can make you reluctant to oppose fellow officers. While unity is a worthy goal, groupthink is very dangerous. Research by sociologist Irving Janis illuminated a number of significant historical decisions now recognized as blunders that came as a result of groupthink, such as the Bay of Pigs, Watergate, and the escalation of the Vietnam War. When groupthink takes hold, group members sacrifice critical thinking and effective decision making in the interests of avoiding conflict, reaching agreement, and preserving friendly relations.

Three symptoms characterize the groupthink phenomenon. First, the group overestimates its potential for success and the inherent morality of its own position. Second, because the group believes it is right and will succeed, it becomes closed to any evidence to the contrary. Group members ignore evidence that contradicts their position. They develop stereotyped views of those with different perspectives outside the group, describing them as wrong, stupid, weak, or evil, thus justifying their decision to ignore these people's evidence. Third, group members feel pressure to conform. This happens in several ways. Group members begin to censor themselves. They hold back doubts they feel. This leads to an "illusion of unanimity," even though a number of people may privately have doubts. If group members do openly express doubts, they often encounter direct pressure to change, either from the whole group, the leader, or more vocal members. Other times the group simply ignores the dissenter's input. Sometimes groups have "mindguards," people who keep contradictory information from the group by omitting conflicting data when they give reports, preventing outsiders from presenting evidence, and so on.

Several techniques can help prevent groupthink:

- **Recognize the symptoms.** Just being aware of groupthink is one guard against it.
- **Appoint a devil's advocate.** One person or even a subgroup can serve as critical evaluator and intentionally ask questions or bring up opposing viewpoints.
- **Take steps to prevent insulation.** Communication researchers John K. Brilhart and Gloria J. Galanes urge group members to get feedback on tentative proposals from trusted associates outside the group, and then report back to the group. They also suggest that outside experts be invited to discuss their views with the group.
- **Minimize status difference.** Too often groupthink occurs because people accede to the views of a person in authority, even when the person is wrong. One experiment of groupthink among airplane personnel illustrates this in a frightening way. In the study, captains feigned serious errors that would lead to certain disaster. Twenty-five percent of the time, crew members did not take corrective action to override the flight captain even though they realized the error.

Avoid groupthink. Don't just go along with the crowd because that is the easiest way. Think clearly and urge your group to fully analyze issues.

Step-by-Step to a Productive Work Group Meeting

> "The Rule of Temporal Integrity: Do not jerk those members around who have prepared to accommodate the schedule of those who have not prepared."
>
> —John Tropman (43)

Almost universally, people hate poorly run work group meetings. Advance planning can make a meeting a pleasant experience of getting together with effective group members who get the work done. People who know what to expect from a meeting, who come prepared, meet in an environment that supports their needs, and move through a well-thought-out agenda, accomplish more and feel better about group meetings. Whether you are the group leader, a participant, or advising a community member who leads the meeting, understanding how to lead a meeting enables you to help your group achieve its goals.

Determine the Meeting's Purpose

One reason people so often leave a meeting muttering "What a waste of time," even though the group accomplished a lot, is that the meeting was not what they expected. Being clear about purpose and structuring the meeting to achieve that purpose are the keys to a satisfying meeting. The most common meeting purposes are for making decisions, exchanging information, establishing rapport, generating ideas, or creating enthusiasm.

Making decisions. The decision-making meeting brings together people, typically with different viewpoints, to reason together and make decisions about issues. This is the most common work group meeting. Business books abound on how to lead such meetings, and the bulk of group-communication research has centered on them. A decision-making group might hammer out policy, set strategy, decide about specific details, or coordinate actions.

Exchanging information. People who work together on a project or in an agency must meet regularly to keep one another posted about ongoing activities. Exchanging information keeps participants informed about what the others are doing, helps them notice overlooked details in project plans, prevents much duplication of effort, and keeps people from feeling left out and resentful. (The latter, for example, is a common response patrol officers feel when community officers plan special events in the patrol officers' district without informing them.) Just make sure that group members understand that the meeting is not for decision making; otherwise they might complain that "nothing was done."

Establishing rapport. Sometimes a meeting is called just so people who will work together can get to know one another. Rapport-building meetings are especially common and helpful when new officers come into a neighborhood or when new projects begin. Often such meetings include presenting the goals of a program.

The key to a successful meeting when the goal is essentially social is simply to remember the goal. Too often task-driven officers or community volunteers turn social meetings into business meetings by cutting off comments, shortening the social time, and addressing issues. The "business" of these rapport-building meetings is to help people feel comfortable with one another, to share information about interests, needs, what strengths they bring to the project, and so forth. Group members must remember the purpose.

Generating ideas. Certain projects require that a work group meet to come up with ideas. This type of creative meeting requires positive responses from those at the meeting. Research consistently confirms that ideas flourish in a nonjudgmental environment and shrivel under criticism. For a work group to successfully generate ideas, group members should not comment on or evaluate ideas until the group has compiled a long list of possible solutions. (See Chapter 7 for more information on generating ideas.)

"One tactic I would encourage other city leaders to consider is to hold extended meetings between officers and the city employees they'll be working with."

—Darryl Herring,
Asst. City Manager, Springfield, Ohio

Creating enthusiasm. People need to have some emotional investment in a project to feel a part of it. They must develop a sense of ownership. Sometimes meetings accomplish this. You invite people to meetings as a way of persuading them to your point of view, asking for their support, or seeking their input. The important task of such meetings is to make those who attend feel like part of the team so that they volunteer themselves and their group to sell tickets, volunteer at neighborhood centers, hand out fliers, or do whatever you need.

Knowing what kind of meeting you are attending or hosting makes a difference in your preparation and how you define success. A meeting can provide those who attend with a great deal of information, but if they expected to make decisions about an issue, they will view the meeting negatively. Be sure all participants are clear about what kind of meeting you hold.

Plan Your Meeting Carefully

A good meeting begins long before the participants pull up their chairs to a table. Careful advance planning can make your meeting proceed much more smoothly than it would if group members simply show up with no sense of what will be discussed. Keep these steps in mind as you plan.

Consider the purpose and participants. When planning a meeting, start with the purpose and participants rather than the agenda. Consider carefully who will come or who should be included in your meeting. After you have a sense of who will participate, arrange the meeting agenda to engage their interest, facilitate their contributions, and build their trust. Important questions to consider include: What do the participants expect to get out of the meeting? What do you want from the participants—an orderly discussion? ideas? involvement in a project? sharing strategies for attacking a common problem? How much do they know about the issues? How do they feel about the issues? Should any of them help plan the meeting? What alliances, rivalries, or animosities exist in the group?

Plan for the social dimension. Consider how you want the participants to relate and interact at the meeting. If it seems at all appropriate, serve coffee, tea, juice, and water and perhaps cookies and fruit to set a friendly tone for the meeting. If people don't know one another, have name tags or name tents for the table. If you anticipate certain problems, take steps to avoid them. For example, remember traffic patterns and schedule the meeting to avoid catching people in rush hour. If two people are running for the same council seat, make sure each knows the other will be at the meeting.

Plan the task dimension. Put together a meeting agenda. An **agenda** is a schedule of items to be discussed in the order they will be discussed. Also include the meeting location, starting and ending times, and a contact number to reach you. Gather any documents or data the group must read in advance so the group meeting can focus on discussing issues.

In *Making Meetings Work*, John Tropman recommends dividing the agenda items into three unequal parts. The first short part includes easier items, such as announcements, minutes, or a recap of the last meeting, and an overview of what the meeting will address or why the meeting was called. This establishes a sense of accomplishment and rapport. The second longer part arranges all the hard items—controversial and arguable—for participants to address before they get tired. The last short part is one item for discussion only (not involving decision making) to allow the meeting to end on an agreeable note.

ACTION CLIP

Interagency Communication

Illinois State Police report that participants in an Illinois multi-agency program discovered a lack of communication between police departments and local public and private agencies, and even between police departments. Some police departments, especially smaller ones, felt isolated. Corporate resources went unused. Many officers lacked knowledge or resources to refer problems to other agencies such as mental health facilities. Agency participants found that the lack of communication "resulted in a disjointed and inefficient approach to problem solving." They assessed that "the lack of communication was prolonged and had the effect of duplicating itself."

The response to this problem was to develop a six-person work group, including a trained problem-solving officer, a community policing officer, and agency representatives. They held monthly meetings. The group developed objectives and manuals for a Community Service Resource Network, including a page on the state police Web site for referral information (Illinois State Police).

One of the most common agenda errors is to try to deal with too much. With an overloaded agenda, the group either rushes through items without discussion or puts some off until another meeting. A better plan is to put fewer items on the agenda and potentially even to finish early—a rare treat in group meetings. No guideline exists on exactly how many items is too many. This depends on the group, the issue, and the process for addressing issues. With an ongoing group, you will get a feel for this after a few meetings.

Send the agenda to all group members in advance, along with the information they need to study before the meeting. (Bring extra agendas to the meeting for those who forget theirs.) Tropman suggests if you have regular, ongoing meetings, you send out this material three-fourths of the way between meetings. Giving people a chance to think almost any topic improves discussion. Often when group members see material for the first time at the actual meeting, they will either thumb hopelessly through it or sit silently and read during the meeting.

Arrange for someone to keep notes of the meeting. Ideally the notekeeper is someone who does not participate. If a group member must keep notes, however, select someone in advance or use a fun or unusual selection criteria such as: the notekeeper is the person who traveled the longest distance, has the next birthday, has been in police work the shortest time, and so on.

Plan your meeting strategy. Sometimes careful thought about your meeting can help the group avoid problems that might otherwise erupt. Planning can help you achieve your goal smoothly. Thinking about how you want the meeting to turn out can help you make it happen. If you want the group to accept a certain position or take a particular action, think about what information they would need to respond favorably. If you can predict that one person will respond negatively, consider inviting his or her input on a draft of the idea. If you want some members to develop a supportive relationship, think about what would help them develop trust.

Before the meeting, you may want to talk to a few influential people you expect to attend to get their opinions on issues and their perspectives on what new items might be added to the agenda or how others in the group are likely to respond to issues. Don't let big disagreements come as a surprise. Anticipating problems can help you prevent them. If you discover potential crises brewing, think of how you will handle these. If you know one person will have a strong reaction to another's idea, let the first person know about the possible reaction. Before the meeting discuss privately any issue that may make a person uncomfortable, so he or she is not surprised or embarrassed.

Determine your room arrangement and resources. Think about how you want to set up tables and chairs and what resources you need. How the room is set up affects the kind of meeting you will have. Room arrangement is vital in determining communication flow. For example, it is very difficult to have a good, open discussion when chairs are lined up in rows facing the front like a lecture hall. If you stand in front of a group seated that way, people will expect you to talk while they listen. On some occasions you may hold meetings in a home rather than a meeting room. There, too, you need to arrange the space as much as the host will allow.

Whenever possible, plan the seating so that each participant can make eye contact with everyone else in the group. Figure 3-2 shows a variety of seating arrangements for work group meetings. Chairs in circles or horseshoe shapes allow each person to see and hear all the other group members. If that's not possible, be sure the person leading the meeting sits where he or she can make eye contact with everyone. In a horseshoe arrangement, the leader usually sits at the head of the table or in the opening.

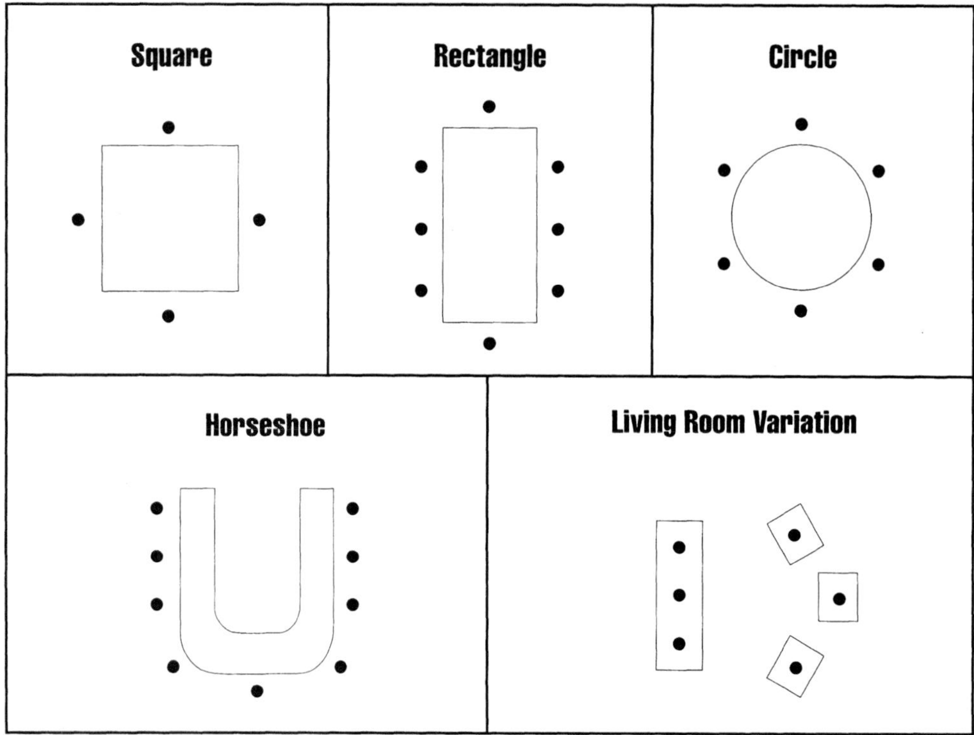

Figure 3-2: Seating arrangements for work group meetings

If you want everyone to sit around a table, make sure the table is big enough to fit everyone. People sitting away from the table are excluded from participation in many ways. They are visually in the position of audience rather than participant, have a hard time getting the leader's attention, and if they sit behind someone else they miss that person's facial reactions.

If you want subgroups, you can set up smaller tables so the subgroups are set up from the beginning. However, this arrangement impedes the whole group operating together.

Also determine what supplies and equipment you need for the meeting and reserve these from your agency or the meeting site. Think about an overhead or slide projector, easel charts, and writing pads. Bring along spare bulbs, extra markers, and so forth.

A few days before, remind participants about the meeting. Don't assume that people will remember an upcoming meeting, especially if it is not at the usual time or if the agenda was mailed much earlier. Give all participants a courtesy reminder. E-mail, if available, is an easy and convenient way to remind participants. If members don't have e-mail or if you have time, call each participant. A personal call enables you to check in with the participants, get a sense of what's important to them, maybe even catch something you overlooked. *Ensure a good turnout by reminding people a few days before your meeting.*

Start the Meeting Effectively

Some simple steps as people first arrive can start the meeting off on the right foot. You are central to that effort because you can help set the first norms with your welcome.

Arrive at least a half hour early. Use the extra time to get things set up (room, supplies, equipment, refreshments, extra agendas, and so forth). As people arrive, greet them and chat informally before the meeting starts to help break the ice.

Begin the meeting on time. People have schedules, babysitters, commuter drives, other appointments. Those who show up on time deserve the courtesy of the group keeping to the schedule. If you start late in an ongoing group, members may begin arriving late. Remember, too, that you operate in an environment in which many people see meetings as a waste of time. Starting on time and proceeding in a business-like manner will help dispel that notion.

Welcome the group. Take a few moments to say hello and ask people how they have been. If you are leading a new group, and you want people to participate at the meeting, have them introduce themselves to the group to set a norm of participation. If you have a new member, which often happens in community meetings, have everyone introduce themselves. This is where you might want to use an ice breaker to help the group members get to know one another.

Explain the "rules." Let everyone know what is acceptable at this meeting. For example, if it is suitable to leave the table to get more coffee, say so. If you are having a long meeting, explain when the breaks will be and mention where the bathrooms are.

Briefly outline what the meeting is to accomplish. In essence, give the group a table of contents. Don't dwell on the items; they already have their agendas (hand out extras to those who need them). The verbal restatement simply reminds the group and unifies their attention about a common purpose.

Ask for additional agenda items. Your conversations with influential group members before the meeting should alert you to any new agenda items. But ask for the group's input. Add new items to the agenda or make note of them for future meetings.

During the Meeting

Whatever a leader may be on the street, in the meeting room a leader's role is not that of an action hero. A leader in a work group meeting controls the flow of information and recognizes speakers.

POCKET GUIDE

Planning Chart for Work Group Meetings

Purpose of the Meeting

Participants

Space Arrangement

Room?
Seating?

Resources Needed

Visual aid equipment?
Handouts?

Preparation for Social Dimension

Refreshments?
Name tags or name tents?
Talk to significant participants in advance?

Preparation for Task Dimension

Agenda input solicited?
Agenda prepared?
Agenda and supporting documents sent?
Reminder messages left?

Encourage various points of view. The group leader is not an advocate. If you are the leader, the group must perceive you as fair if you want to maintain all group members' respect and not be drawn into one side against the other on divisive issues. One technique is to keep a "speakers list," a register of those who signal they wish to address an issue. You call on participants by moving down the list, thus assuring that everyone who wants to speak has a chance to do so. If time limits prohibit everyone from speaking, be sure those who do speak represent various viewpoints.

Don't talk too much yourself. Your job is to encourage participation from the other members and keep the meeting on track, not to voice your opinions.

Encourage equal participation. Draw out the quiet members by asking open-ended questions, ones that can't be answered with just a yes or no. Ask about something you know they can answer; a safe choice is to ask for their opinions on an issue. Don't assume that because people are quiet, they are not actively involved in the group.

Even as you encourage the quiet ones, you need to rein in those who would dominate the meeting. This is, of course, a particularly demanding task if they are of higher rank than you. Appeal to the group's sense of fair play. "Thank you for your input. We do want to make sure everyone has a chance to share ideas. We have a tough problem here and we need all viewpoints." (Figure 3-3 provides additional suggestions for dealing with possible problems.)

Watch the time. Move the meeting along so you can get to all the agenda items before the stated end time. Generally, the group is in favor of moving along if an issue has been discussed to their satisfaction. You can say something like, "Well, I think we have discussed this fully. We seem to be saying that. . . ." Or, "I'm hearing agreement in our remarks. Are we decided that. . . ." Summarize the discussion or decision on an issue, then move to the next agenda item. You can even bring a large clock and set it rather ostentatiously in front of the group as a reminder that time is ticking away.

End the Meeting on Time

The meeting should end when the group has dealt with agenda items or reached the stated end time, whichever comes first. At that point, you're ready to close the meeting.

Summarize the activity of the group. Restate what decisions or discussions occurred during the meeting. Recap what participants will accomplish by the next meeting. Thank everyone for coming. Make positive comments about people's honesty or participation if any topics were difficult, hurtful, or touchy. Let them know that you know the discussion wasn't easy.

Don't rush away. Linger for ten or fifteen minutes after the meeting to chat with people. Sometimes quiet people will share an opinion or idea that they were apprehensive about voicing in the group. Their input can be very valuable.

Check in with group members a week before due dates. Be sure you have an accurate record of who is to do what. If actions have due dates, write these on your calendar with the name of the people responsible. Make a note to call them about a week before the due date to see "how things are going." This call is an indirect way of reminding them to "get this done."

Challenges of Working in Groups

One of the major sources of meeting frustration is *Other People*, those individuals in positions of prominence who talk too much, disagree, look out for their own interests, seek attention constantly, nit-pick about petty issues, and, in general, thwart your plans for a friendly, efficient meeting. Certain behaviors seem to recur in group after group. You can anticipate dealing with some of these at some point in meetings you lead and attend.

Power Struggles

A major source of problems in groups is **power struggles**, where people vie for unspoken positions of influence or status. These are considered "leadership" struggles,

If a group member	Try to
Is silent, doesn't participate	Ask for an opinion on an issue. Ask open-ended questions (not ones that can be answered with a simple yes or no) that you are sure the person can answer. For example, "Luis, what do you feel is the most important crime issue in your neighborhood?" Or talk to the person outside the meeting.
Talks too much	Sit beside the person so you never make eye contact. When the person does speak, do not let the long speeches go on if they are detrimental. Interrupt politely and move the discussion on, perhaps by remarking on the need to take up a new subject or to hear from other group members. For example, "Michela, your concern about kids playing basketball is a good point. Another issue is the problem of truancy and how we can help the schools. Lupe, what are your thoughts on this?"
Is a joker, the life of the meeting	Encourage this when the group needs tension relief. Ignore it when the jesting is inappropriate. If necessary, remark that time is short, and the group must get to work. For example, "I love how open our discussion is, but all kidding aside, we need to stay focused if we're going to complete this project."
Is argumentative	Paraphrase the person's ideas to be sure you understand and to give yourself time to relax. Sometimes good ideas are expressed in offensive way. Remember that a good critic is helpful to the group. If the arguing disrupts the group, move on to another agenda item. For example, "I think everyone is getting a little upset here. Manuel, let's focus on finding ways to keep the kids out of your garden and get them back on the playground." You may need to talk to the member privately during break, urging the person to help maintain group effectiveness by softening the presentation.
Challenges your leadership	Be very prepared and have facts at your fingertips. Treat everyone fairly. Between meetings attempt to win allies by helping people and chatting with them. In time, people trust those who are competent and fair, and they recognize inappropriate behavior. For example, "Maribel, you make a good point. Let me pass out the latest crime information for the neighborhood and as a group we can discuss how to move forward. If anyone thinks of a problem we need to discuss next time, please let me know and I'll provide as much information as possible."

Based on ideas from Bormann, Ernest G., and Nancy C. Bormann. *Effective Small Group Communication.* 6th ed. Edina, Minn.: Burgess, 1996.

Figure 3-3: Problem members in groups

even though someone may officially, on paper, already be designated the group leader. A member contending for that position of power will disagree with the designated leader, voice personal opinions, and push for his or her own way of doing things. Arguments over procedure are one sure sign that a leadership struggle is under way, rather than a genuine difference of opinion over an issue. When Raul and Gina disagree on whether to seek consensus or take a vote, the real issue is whether the group will listen to Raul or Gina. Often the rest of the group, the "audience" for the battle, decides such issues by ultimately siding with one or the other. The person who "loses" the battle may drop out of the group or may become a troublemaker. Generally a leader contender is a person of power, who has much to contribute to a group. If you want to keep that person's energy, you must court him or her back to the group, often by assigning the person tasks of some importance.

Personal Interests

Another challenge is when a person puts his or her own concerns ahead of the group's. **Personal interest** occurs when a person with a cause to support loses focus on the group's overall goal. For example, people regularly show concern for their own neighborhood or agency over others. The group leader must either raise the level of effort beyond personal goals or come up with a way to show that person that the group goal will further his or her personal goal.

Hidden Agendas

Sometimes people have **hidden agendas**, or unstated purposes, for being in a group. If you are lucky, these hidden agendas are simply to make friends or to raise the property value of their homes or to advance their careers. If you are unlucky, the agenda is to see the neighborhood association president fail or to see a current city council member ousted. Issues totally unrelated to the topics on the table can be secretly directing the way the vote goes. Knowing what hidden agendas people have can help you understand how these agendas influence your group. However, finding out what hidden forces are operating is not always easy. Sometimes community members have insight into what's really going on. Sometimes background information on the people or neighborhood can help you.

Long-Winded Monopolizers

Another challenge for a group is **long-winded monopolizers**, individuals who talk at length. These people can be among the most difficult to deal with simply because they don't mean any harm, may have something useful to say, and often don't even realize how long they are taking. They think their comments are helping the group, unaware that whenever they begin to speak others suddenly develop an inordinate interest in the growth of foliage outside the window. A variation of the monopolizer is the **recognition seeker**, the person with entertaining, but irrelevant, accounts of personal adventures that divert attention away from the task. A brief anecdote can relieve tension and warm up the group, but long drawn-out descriptions, or frequent ones, pose a problem. Group leaders can try such phrases as "Let's get comments from others in the group" and "Interesting, Ramon, but I think we'd better get going on the agenda now" to end the monologues and diversions. While the monopolizers often miss the point, generally others in the group get it and will take the floor.

Empty Promisers

The world is full of people who respond to ideas with excitement and energy, who make you think the group will succeed in everything, who throw out promises of contributions like confetti at a parade, and who then do nothing about them. At first, it is easy to be misled by the high energy of these **empty promisers**. But by the second or third meeting, when they still haven't talked to the contacts they said they would call, written the report they said they would write, or brought the supplies they promised to bring, you know to simply take their ideas as input but ignore their promises to help. You can try a few steps to encourage their work: set a deadline for what they said they would do, and then call to check on their progress as the deadline approaches; put commitments in writing, at least in the form of public minutes where their obligations are recorded; put them on teams with others who will work alongside them. If the issue is time management or priorities, sometimes these techniques help.

Deserters

Deserters gradually abandon your work group. They may stop coming to meetings entirely, come only intermittently, or attend meetings but pay no attention and contribute nothing to the discussion. The best possibility for dealing with deserters is to persuade them to take a more active role. If deserters do not feel needed by the group and neither the social dimension nor the task gives them status or satisfaction, sometimes giving them attention and a task the group values can gradually draw them back into the group. At other times, however, deserters are simply uncommitted and will contribute little to the group. In that case, allow them to drift away and replace them with more promising group members.

Fortunately, the majority of people work well in groups. If you are lucky, your group develops a kind of **synergy**, where the combined efforts of all the group members are greater than the sum total of individual efforts. The work group process allows you to make stronger decisions, generate more creative ideas, draw on more resources for your work, and function together as a team. When that happens, you will be glad to be part of a group.

Ice Breakers for Work Groups

Know Your Neighbor

Supplies: None

Purpose: Starts conversation and lets people get to know one another. This activity is easy and immediately lets one person get to know at least one other person.

Procedure: Ask people to pair off with someone they don't know. Have them talk for ten minutes. Each is to learn at least five things about the other person he or she can share with the group to introduce that person. If you want to use this with an established group, change the rules slightly. Each person is learning something about the other that is not yet known by the group.

What Do You Bring to the Table?

Supplies: Sheets of paper with the letters of the alphabet down the side, pens or pencils

Purpose: Demonstrates that the combined resources of a group of people are stronger than the resources of each individual. This activity is easy and nonthreatening, and gives a group of strangers something to talk about.

Procedure: Put attendees in groups of five to seven people. Give each group a sheet of paper with the letters of the alphabet down the left side. Their task is to find an object whose name starts with each letter of the alphabet in the items they happen to have with them. They "bring these to the table" by placing them on the table between them. They might, for example, find a key for K and a wallet for W. The challenge comes as they reach Q and X and other letters with no immediate object. (One enterprising group member sat on the table, rolled down his waistband, and claimed he represented the U for underwear.) After about ten or fifteen minutes (judge by how the groups are doing or how much time you have), time is called. Either have the group with the most items show what they have or, if time permits, have each group share their items.

Autograph Hunt

Supplies: A page with a list to be signed for each participant, pens or pencils

Purpose: Helps a mid-sized group of unacquainted individuals mingle and find out information about one another.

Procedure: Prepare a list of ten or fifteen items that could apply to a number of people, but not to everyone. Samples are included below, but the exercise works best when you include items specific to your group. If you know, for example, that you have several avid golfers in the group, make that an item so they will find something in common. Or if you have a neighborhood group, include streets so they can find their neighbors. Or include an item to help you find out about the group, such as "Volunteers in the community," then when the people are identified you can ask where they volunteer. Or if you know you will need some design work done on a poster, slip in "Can design posters," and pay attention to who signs. Vary the number of items depending on the amount of time you have.

At the meeting, hand out a list and pens to everyone. All people must stand and mingle to find individuals who fill the roles listed. People must sign their own names next to the item. This is important, because the real purpose is to get people to meet one another. Without that step, people will just copy from a third person, sit down, and declare "I'm done." It helps to tell people at the outset that the real purpose here is for them to get to know one another. The task-oriented folks in your group will then have an understanding of the task dimension and will be less impatient.

After most people have a majority of the list filled in, ask people to sit down. Go down the list and find out not just who can speak a foreign language, but which language it is; not just who plays a sport, but what sport. This is an ice breaker, after all. You have time for a little conversation that gets people to know one another and feel comfortable together.

Your form should have instructions at the top as shown below.

Autograph Hunt

Get the autographs of people in the group who match these descriptions. Each person must sign her or his own name and can sign for only one description. Find someone who:

Commutes from your part of town ______________________________

Can speak a foreign language ______________________________

Has a hobby much like one of your (your hobby ____________________)

____

Is a firstborn ______________________________

Does community service work of some sort ______________________________

Plays a musical instrument ______________________________

Saw a movie over the weekend ______________________________

Can name all seven dwarfs ______________________________

Plays a sport on a team ______________________________

Lived in a country other than the United States ______________________________

Went on a cruise recently ______________________________

Likes to cook ______________________________

Has been to a NASCAR race ______________________________

Was a Boy or Girl Scout________________________________

Plays golf ____

Is a Libra (pick the sign coming up next)__________________

Is from New York (or Tucson or Chico or wherever) __________

Just bought a new car _______________________________

Loves deep-sea fishing _______________________________

Getting to Know You

Supplies: Paper and pens or pencils

Purpose: Reacquaints members of ongoing groups that haven't met for a while.

Procedure: Group members each write three things they think others in the group don't know about them. These could be personal, social, or professional (for example, I once had a job as a turkey impregnator, I won second in a pie-eating contest by eating six lemon meringue pies, and so forth). Collect the lists. Read them one by one and let the group guess who goes with each list. This generates a lot of laughter and surprise.

Works Cited

Bormann, Ernest G. *Discussion and Group Methods*. New York: Harper and Row, 1969.

———. *Small Group Communication: Theory and Practice*. New York: Harper and Row, 1990.

Bormann, Ernest G., and Nancy C. Bormann. *Effective Small Group Communication*. 6th ed. Edina, Minn.: Burgess, 1996.

Brilhart, John K., and Gloria J. Galanes. *Group Discussion*. 9th ed. Boston: McGraw-Hill, 1988.

Cogan, Elaine. *Successful Public Meetings*. San Francisco: Jossey-Bass, 1992.

Ellis, Donald G., and B. Aubrey Fisher. *Small Group Decision Making*. 4th ed. New York: McGraw-Hill, 1994.

Frey, Lawrence R. "Introduction." *Innovations in Group Facilitation*. Lawrence R. Frey, ed. Cresskill, N.J.: Hampton Press, 1995.

Glensor, Ronald W. "Engaging the Community in Problem Solving: A New Synergism." *Community Policing Exchange*. July/Aug. 1995.

Herring, Darryl. "Interview: Police Chief, Assistant City Manager and Budget Director Focus on What Works." *Community Policing Exchange*. Nov./Dec. 1995. http://www.communitypolicing.org/exchange/e5interv.htm. 20 June 1998.

Illinois State Police. http://www.policeforum.org/popnet/. 9 June 1998.

Janis, Irving. *Victims of Groupthink: A Psychological Study of Foreign Decisions and Fiascos.* Boston: Houghton Mifflin, 1982.

Mosvick, R. K., and R. B. Nelson. *We've Got to Start Meeting Like This.* Glenview, Ill. Scott-Foresman, 1987.

"Payoff from Teams." *Business Week.* 10 July 1989: 57.

Peak, Kenneth J., and Ronald W. Glensor. *Community Policing & Problem Solving: Strategies and Practices.* Upper Saddle River, N.J.: Prentice Hall, 1996.

Rothwell, J. Dan. *In Mixed Company: Small Group Communication.* 3rd ed. Fort Worth: Harcourt Brace, 1998.

Sayers, Dorothy L. *Whose Body?* 1923. New York: Perennial, 1987: 36.

Silvey, Len. Personal communication. May 1998.

Toseland, Ronald W., Robert F. Rivas, and Dennis Chapman. "An Evaluation of Decision-Making Methods in Task Groups." *Social Work.* July/Aug. 1984: 339–346.

Tropman, John. *Making Meetings Work.* Thousand Oaks, Calif.: Sage, 1996.

Vance, Mike, and Diane Deacon. *Think Out of the Box.* Franklin Lakes, N.J.: Career Press, 1995.

"Youth Firearms Violence Initiative Fact Sheet." http://www.uadoj.gov/cops/wyouth.htm. 4 Aug. 97.

Activities

1 Prevalence of Groups

For one month, keep a list of all the group meetings you attend. Note the meetings you found most effective. What did the group do that made the meeting work well? Consider the ones that were least effective. What went wrong? What did the best leaders do? What did the worst leaders do? What problem people appeared in the groups? How were they handled? Try to be as specific as you can in assessing these meetings.

2 Groups Make Better Decisions Than Individuals

This activity has you first solve a problem alone, and then try to solve the same problem with a group. Contrast people's success when working alone with their success working with others.

Jelly Beans

Supplies: A jar of jelly beans and one person who knows how many jelly beans are in the jar

1. Each individual guesses how many beans are in the jar. Record the guesses on the board or on a flip chart.
2. Put participants in groups. Direct the groups to figure the average guess of each group. Record those guesses on the board or a flip chart.

Usually the average guess of the group is closer to the real number than are the individual guesses.

State Capitals

Direct individuals and then groups to name the fifty states and their capitals. (By the way, bring the right answers so you can say which are correct.) If time is limited, ask them to name a limited set—the West Coast, states beginning with A to G, all the states whose borders touch a seacoast, and so forth.

Classic TV Shows

Direct individuals and then groups to name at least ten characters from each of these classic television shows: *Andy Griffith Show, Bewitched, I Love Lucy, Perry Mason, Dick Van Dyke Show,* and *Leave It to Beaver*.

3 The Social Dimension

Make a list of ten different ways you could improve the social dimension of a group. Now consider a group meeting you will attend in the next two weeks. Select one item from your list and try it out. This can be a small action, but carry it through. Actually improve your group's social dimension in some way.

4 Planning an Agenda

Take an agenda from a meeting you have attended or make up a hypothetical agenda for some group meeting you will be attending. Now arrange the items as Tropman suggests, beginning with easy ones, taking up controversial issues, ending with a discussion-only item. Speculate on what difference such a pattern would make.

If you are in a position to actually plan an agenda for a coming meeting, plan it according to Tropman's formula. Follow the agenda in your meeting. Again, attempt to assess what difference the pattern makes.

Chapter Four

Americans' Greatest Fear

Public Speaking

"Have some 15–20 minute
'canned' speeches prepared.
Suggested topics:
The 911 priority system,
why citizens should report crimes,
why citizens are needed to help,
how to avoid crime in
certain circumstances, etc."

HELEN CREEK
FOR THE PORTLAND, OREGON,
POLICE DEPARTMENT

Officer Alan Richards exhales a sigh of relief as his speech ends and he begins to answer audience questions. His confidence builds; he even begins to think of public speaking as "no big deal, a piece of cake." Then, like a lightning bolt, a voice from the back booms out, "I've lived in this community twenty-five years and all I've seen from the police is abuse! You're just like those cops who beat that poor man on the news last week. You just sit around donut shops and drink coffee for free. . . ." Richards retreats farther behind the podium, wishing he could escape out the back door.

What could he have done to prevent this? Or how could he have lessened the blow? Experts say preparation is the key to success, but what is preparation in this case? Is it preparing a speech, making notes, providing handouts, or, as an alternative, doing what you can to dump the assignment on someone else?

RICHARDS IS NOT ALONE IN HIS DISLIKE OF GIVING A SPEECH. Americans' number one fear is public speaking. In one survey it ranked even ahead of death (*Spectra*). Yet those who are skilled at speaking in public—or even willing to stand up and speak, skilled or not—have an opportunity to convey their ideas to a large number of people at once, to be influential, to make contacts, and to become recognized in their communities.

At its base, giving a speech is nothing more than talking with a group of people instead of just one or two, but for many people the phrase "public speaking" invokes an ominous image of a cavernous room filled with row after row of sneering judges all waiting for the speaker to look like an idiot so they can snicker and then go tell their friends.

Because "giving a speech" has a negative connotation for so many people, just think of it as "talking." How hard is it to talk to people? You do it on every call every day. You drive up to an incident, talk to strangers, give them information, and answer questions. Often, a crowd gathers. You go on talking. Talking to an audience is pretty much the same, except you get to plan in advance.

The key to making a talk easy and successful is to *say something that your audience wants to know.* Yes, it's that simple. Of course it's nice if your material is organized and you feel comfortable speaking. Even if you don't, if you and your audience care about what you have to say, you will succeed. Imagine yourself in these situations:

- You sit listening as your lieutenant says, "The, uh, City Council just voted that if we, uh, do these, uh, three things, we will, uh, receive a pay raise." Do you sit in bored judgment wishing he would speak more clearly, stand straighter, and stop saying "uh"? Or do you listen attentively to hear what he has to say about your pay raise?

- The Police Athletic League is raffling off free tickets to a sold-out NFL playoff game. You are about to call out the winning numbers. Will those holding raffle tickets criticize your speaking style?
- You are asked to address Sisters in Crime, a group of mystery authors. You have step-by-step procedural information on how homicide detectives caught the last murderer to hit the headlines, including some clever fingerprinting techniques just developed by the FBI. Will they be interested?

If you and your audience care about what you have to say, you will find talking in public a fairly natural process. It's even better if you also are clearly organized and speak fluently. This comes about with some advanced planning.

Understanding Your Speaking Situation

The success of a talk is determined long before you stand before an audience. Devote some time to preparing your presentation, and you will feel much more comfortable in front of a crowd.

Investigate the Occasion and Expectations

You were invited to speak for some particular reason. The audience may be eager to know about community policing or about crime in their neighborhood, or they may simply be a civic club that needs a speaker talking on anything. Talk to the person who invited you to find out as much as you can about your speaking situation. You want your presentation to successfully meet the expectations of the group that invited you. Find out the answers to these questions:

- What generated the need for a talk? What is the occasion? Is this a regular meeting that needs a speaker or is it a special event? Were you asked to address a particular issue? Did the person who invited (or assigned) you to talk want to know about something in particular? What will be done with your information?
- How long does the host want you to talk? How much of that time should you devote to questions and answers?
- What will precede and follow your talk: a business meeting? a meal? a hot political item on the agenda? Does the program include other events? Are you the only speaker or are you part of a panel?
- How many people will attend? This affects how you plan the presentation of your material. A large audience demands a more formal structure, less interaction. A small room of people can involve much more back-and-forth exchange if you want it. Is the group accustomed to listening quietly or to interacting with speakers? Do they expect a formal address or casual chatting?

- What is the physical space like where you will talk? Is it indoors or outside, a small room or a large auditorium? Will you have a microphone? At the very least ask about the space; if possible, look at it. Picture yourself there, talking successfully. Anticipate potential problems with sound or line of sight or room arrangement, and prevent these or prepare for them.

All of these elements are part of the speaking situation you are given. Beyond that, you have choices to make about your talk.

Decide What You Want to Accomplish

Being clear about the purpose of your talk can help you frame a talk that will achieve your goal. Traditionally, speeches have four purposes:

- **To inform.** Is this strictly a talk to give people information? to introduce yourself to a neighborhood watch program? to explain a new procedure to fellow officers? The focus of a speech to inform is good information, very clearly organized.
- **To persuade.** Is your goal to build support for the department? Sway voters? Get kids to fear drugs? In the speech to persuade, you seek to get your audience to change their beliefs or their behavior. Sometimes your persuasive goal is to move the audience from one point of view to another; more commonly it is to move them from apathetic to concerned to active. Convincing requires strong evidence, and in addition, such talks frequently include an emotional dimension.

  Sometimes you want to do more than simply convince an audience; you want them to actively join your community effort to fight crime. You seek to activate them. To do this you need strong evidence and emotionally moving material that makes them feel their support will make a difference. You also should designate clearly a specific action you want them to take. Urging an audience to "get involved" seldom motivates instant response.

ACTION CLIP

DARE Speeches

The experience of Garden City, Kansas, is typical of Drug Abuse Resistance Education (DARE) and the experience involves a lot of speaking. The Garden City DARE program started in 1990. Officers visit fifth-grade classrooms every week for seventeen weeks to tell students how to refuse drugs and alcohol. Later, they do follow-up in middle schools. By 1996, the program had served 3,085 fifth-grade students. Of these, only 1 percent have had police contact for drug-related incidents. These results indicate that the officers used effective persuasive speaking to accomplish their goal.

- **To inspire.** Perhaps your goal is a simpler one: you want the audience to know their efforts make a difference. You want them to keep working. People get tired of trying against almost insurmountable odds. Volunteers grow tired, and so do city employees, teachers, parents, and police officers. Sometimes the audience needs to hear that they matter, that each action they take will help create a more beautiful environment. In this case, you fill your speech with moving success stories and stress to them what they are accomplishing.
- **To entertain.** Your goal may be to roast a retiring officer or to recount true-life adventures to a group of police cadets. Humor and dramatic storytelling help accomplish these.

Talking to people seldom involves only one of these purposes. Perhaps you want to inform, but you would like to be at least mildly entertaining as well. Or you want to activate, but to do it you have to inform them about problems in the neighborhood. The value of recognizing the main types of purposes is that it helps you consider your options and clarify for yourself what you really want to do.

Analyze Your Audience

Understanding your audience is one of the most important, but often overlooked, aspects of a successful talk. If you know about them, you can build on what you have in common and anticipate potential negative responses. Assessing an audience requires work well in advance of your talk. You want to find out as much as you can about the people who will be listening to you. Ask your host. If you know people who may be in the audience, give them a call or get their input over coffee. In some cases, you may be able to estimate potential audience reaction. For example, a civic group will likely support any actions that lead to civic betterment; a high school student group will undoubtedly have some members who have had negative experiences with police. The more you can go beyond general stereotypes to information about your specific audience, the greater the likelihood your speech will provide what the audience wants and you will experience a sense of success. Try to find out the following information:

- **Determine what unites your audience.** If you are talking to an organization, what is its purpose? If it's a club, what links the members? For example, if you talk to the Rotary Club, you are speaking to a group dedicated to community service. They will be interested in what you are doing for the community. If you are in a class, what are they studying? A class in creative problem solving will have different interests than one in criminal justice.
- **Consider demographics.** What are the audience members' ages, genders, ethnic backgrounds, occupations, religions, economic levels, and education? Such demographic details give a hint of some of the common experiences and expectations of the audience, even an implication of their values.

Demographics suggest appropriate use of language, what kind of examples might reach them, what will be out of bounds, what will attract their interest, and so on.

- **Assess the audience's attitudes about your subject.** How much do they already know about it and how much does it interest them? What do they want to know? What are their attitudes about law enforcement in general? What are their perceptions of the level of service they should be getting—and *are* getting—from police, government, and schools? Do they have any attitude toward you personally?
- **Try to find out about the audience's popular tastes.** What movies have they seen? What TV shows do they watch? What sports do they follow? Mentioning something you all have in common is a great way to create a bond. Media and sports are usually easy links. You may have a hard time finding out their preferences, but demographics will give you a hint, and you can ask the person who invited you. If all else fails, you can refer to the number one movie of the last month or the most popular TV show or the next game of any local team.

In many ways, you assess your audience for a public talk as you would for any call. Think about the preparation you do before you handle a disturbance call. While responding to the call, you research any history of violence, arrests, the absence or presence of a restraining order or arrest warrants. You prepare yourself by gathering as much information as possible to help you resolve the situation. The same is true for a public presentation.

Assess Co-Presenters

If you are on a panel or part of a group presentation, you need to have a sense of what others will say. Knowing what others are going to discuss not only helps you anticipate audience response but also leads to a more compatible and comprehensive presentation.

> *Officer Diedra Holland was asked to be a guest speaker at the local university. The topic for the Contemporary Issues in Criminal Justice class was her effort at community mobilization. Holland learned that she was to be joined by a community leader who was supportive of the police efforts. Holland did her preparation by talking to the professor and learning about the audience—how many students were majors, how many were upper division, their experience in theory and practice, and what they hoped to hear.*
>
> *The day before the lecture, Holland was told that her co-presenter had been changed. The new speaker would be a community leader who was unhappy with local policing. He distrusted government in general and the*

police in particular. Holland's plans had to change. She mentally prepared by expecting to hear negative remarks about law enforcement, and her topic expanded to include issues regarding tolerance of diverse views and opinions encountered during the mobilization process.

The change in speakers greatly affected how Holland approached the presentation. Planning for the other speaker allowed her to adjust her presentation to take this into account.

Preparing Your Talk

After you assess your situation, it's time to get down to business. Gather the information and examples you will want to talk about, and plan your speech.

Organize What You Will Say

Organizing what you will say is central to an effective talk. If you have a clear framework for your presentation, your audience will understand your talk more easily and remember it better. Trying to just wing your talk is the path to disaster. Plan your introduction, body, and conclusion and think of relevant examples to illustrate your points.

But don't write it all out. This is a *talk*, remember, not a public reading. The more you write out, the more you'll read. An outline helps you talk conversationally. Write an outline of major points you can see at a glance. Use keywords to remind you of what you want to say. Under each major point, write in a word or two that reminds you of examples, statistics, quotations, or other ways to develop your talk. By the way, lighting at public events is often awful. "Dim the house lights" translates to "Make it hard for the speaker to read notes." Use black felt-tip pen and write larger than you normally would, so you can see a reminder word with a glance.

The best idea is to use note cards. Index cards (3"x5" or 4"x6") are an excellent aid to remembering both the content and the structure of your talk while providing you the freedom to adapt to your audience on the spur of the moment. Here are some tips for using note cards:

- Use only keywords on your note cards, never sentences.
- Limit the number of cards you use. The fewer you have, the freer you are to interact with your audience. One good rule of thumb is to use one card for your introduction, one card for each main point, and one card for your conclusion.
- Use index cards, not slips of paper. Paper is sloppy and unpredictable, whereas cards are easier to handle and uniform.
- Always number your cards. This can save you a great deal of embarrassment if you drop them (Thomas 34).

Plan the Introduction

Prepare your talk's **introduction**. At the beginning of your talk, your goal is to develop rapport with your audience, establish your own credibility, and arouse audience interest in your topic. The first few minutes proceed in a fairly standard pattern.

Thank the group for inviting you. Acknowledge the group's work or the occasion or event that brings you all together. This affirms something you all have in common. "It's a special pleasure for me to have a chance to meet with the Rotary Club as you begin your discussion of the role of business in crime prevention and to tell you how much local officers appreciate the support of groups like yours." If you've met with some of their members ahead of time, mention it. It will boost their spirit, and show that you cared enough to find out about their problems.

Tell them a little bit about yourself. Sometimes the person who introduces your talk tells the audience about you; sometimes, however, you may choose to do this yourself or to expand what was said. In essence, you're saying, "Here's who I am. Here's why I'm here." Describe your work in law enforcement. Generally, the public is fascinated with police work. A great mystique surrounds the profession, and audiences hang on what a cop's day-to-day job is like. Describe what you do or have done. (But don't overdo it. Don't brag.) Tell them one or two of your favorite policing stories. Such stories break down barriers at the same time they build your credibility, and if you are speaking to fellow officers who do not know you, the stories will help convey your qualifications.

If it suits your personality, use humor. Humor does wonders to break barriers and relieve your own tension. Generally, the public doesn't expect humor from officers, so it is doubly appreciated. It raises your credibility in their eyes because you are comfortable enough to laugh with them. Be careful, however, that your humor is in good taste and doesn't offend anyone.

Introduce your subject. Begin your talk with something that will grab the audience's attention and focus it on your subject. A good beginning makes them eager to hear what else you have to say. Standard introductory techniques include:

- **A story**—"I was recently called out to a gang-related shooting. Where did I go? Not to the ghetto, but to Edison High. The boy who was shot was 15. When he was young he loved baseball and was a Little League star. He said he wanted to be a firefighter. But somewhere along the way, he became a skinhead. His sister is a cheerleader, his mother a librarian; his dad is an engineer. It's a normal family, probably a lot like yours and mine. How did this happen? Could it happen to your kids or mine?"
- **Startling facts or statistics**—"Each year gang members contribute to more than 100 homicides in our county. Over 70 identified street gangs operate here. We can no longer pretend that gang activity won't affect us."
- **References to historical or recent events**—"Last year's devastating floods hit everybody. Who can forget the tragic pictures of farmers in the valley losing their crops, the desperate efforts of the people near the river to save their

homes? What you may not know is that prisoners from the minimum security prison were on the lines trying to save—of all things—the county jail."

- **A quotation**—"In 1764, about the time this nation was being born, an Italian economist wrote: 'It is better to prevent crimes than to punish them.' It's not an accident those words come from an economist. Preventing crime is good for the economy, and cleaning up the community is good for business." (Cesare Bonesana, the Marchese di Beccaria 37)
- **Humor**—"You know the mind is a wonderful thing. It starts the minute you are born and only stops when you get up to make a speech."
- **Suspense**—"We have a plague hitting our county. It's not drugs. It's not gangs. It's not prostitution or car theft or mugging. It's not even higher taxes. It's apathy."
- **References to any preceding speeches**—"It was good to hear Principal Devereau talk about the importance of a good education today. In the Sheriff's Department, we're concerned that your kids not only have a good education, but a safe one as well."
- **If you think you will be really nervous, let the audience talk first**—Some speakers find they are more comfortable if they begin with questions that ask for responses. "How many of you have been a victim of crime? How many of you know someone who was a victim of crime?" Ask for a show of hands, call on a few people if you want. The audience looks around at those who are responding, and the attention is off you for a moment. In addition, this sets up a conversational tone from the start.

Sometimes you may be addressing a small audience, such as a Neighborhood Watch group. In that case, it is wise to take the time to go around the room asking those attending to introduce themselves to you. This breaks the ice, lets you learn about the audience and their motives, and helps you connect with them.

Give a preview statement. Finish the introduction to your talk with a **preview statement**, which is essentially an overview of the talk: "I want to explain our new community policing program to you today." In *How to Make Presentations That Teach and Transform,* educators Robert Garmston and Bruce Wellman offer this advice:

> Research has clearly shown that listeners remember better and remember more if they have a sense of the shape of the talk. Because a grasp of the pattern is important to participant understanding of your material, the best technique is to make each individual section, as well as the overall organization, simple, logical, and clear. The best presenters make the organization of their talk boldly obvious to their listeners. (8)

Organize the Body of Your Talk

The introduction is followed by the body of your talk. This is the substance of your talk, what you really have to say. A very clear organizational structure helps the

POCKET GUIDE

When Your Audience Disagrees

An **opposed audience** may disagree with the position you are taking. You may know in advance that they hold a different view or favor a different solution. (An opposed audience is different from a hostile audience, which is emotional, angry, and potentially out of control. Techniques for handling hostile audiences are discussed in Chapter 5.) If you know from the outset that your audience opposes your position and is unlikely to be receptive to your point of view, try to establish a common ground with them during your introduction. This usually means that your introduction is much longer than it might otherwise be. Show a friendly attitude. Use humor; a group that laughs together has that moment in common, which begins to break down the resistance. Invest time in finding and describing common ground. This is where your audience analysis really comes in handy. Refer to attitudes, beliefs, and experiences you and audience members share. Help them to understand that you all have similar goals, though you may disagree on particulars. When you can, quote people who are respected by the audience. Even better, quote someone in the crowd. Without being hypocritical, offer tactful compliments of the audience's abilities and accomplishments.

audience understand your message and remember it. The material you present should be organized into no more than three or four major points. You can organize the main points in different ways. Usually your subject matter implies which of these you choose.

- **Topically**—Divide the main topic into smaller subject areas and discuss each one. For example, a talk to introduce new COP programs in River Heights could be divided into four topics: (1) preventative patrolling; (2) neighborhood programs; (3) youth camp; and (4) anti-drug strike force.
- **Chronologically**—Order the main topic by dates or time. For example, a talk describing new service centers in the sheriff's office might proceed this way: First, we select volunteers; next we train them; then they staff the service centers to take crime reports.
- **Problem–solution**—Describe a problem, then present a solution to it. A speech on public inebriation would have two sections: The problem—drunks on the streets; the solution—expanding detox center facilities.
- **Cause–effect**—Mention or explain a condition, and then expand to describe its consequences. A talk starts with cause—the drug problem in your county—and then describes the effect—an increased crime rate. You may describe other effects, such as violence in the schools and school dropout rates. Also, this organizational scheme can be reversed: describe an effect and then ponder its cause. A talk describes the alarming increase in school dropouts, asks why this is happening, and then traces the answer back to drugs.

- **Spatially**—Discuss your subject by geographic divisions. A talk on crime in River Heights could describe a crime in the downtown area, surrounding districts, suburbs, and countryside.
- **Monroe's Motivated Sequence**—This five-step standard sales approach leads the audience toward a specific action you want them to take.

  1. **Attention.** Use your introduction to grab the audience's attention and focus it on your topic, as discussed earlier. Your introduction also sets up the problem you will discuss. For example, you tell the story of a young student who was expected to win the state high-jump competition, but succumbed to drug use in high school.
  2. **Need.** Stress the need aroused by your introduction. Here is where you show the extent of drug use in high school today and its terrible toll. Try to connect directly to individuals in the audience by showing immediate effects of drug use in the local high school or on families like theirs and potential future effects on groups of which they are members. Arouse them to the point where they begin to wonder what they can do to stop the drug use.
  3. **Satisfaction.** Tell the audience what you want them to do. Here is where you show how the new Police Action Team (PAT) fights drug use in high school, and how audience members can help by volunteering at the after-school recreation center PAT wants to establish.
  4. **Visualization.** To sell your idea, paint a verbal picture of how the future will be if your project becomes a reality. Alternately, you can describe the future without your project. Depict the safe, happy future for kids who have the center versus the growing power of drugs if the center is not built. Visualizing is a vital step in this persuasive process; it is the real selling of the proposal. If possible, reinforce the verbal picture with an actual picture or architect's rendering of what the drug center will look like. By the end of this step, the audience should be ready to act.
  5. **Call to action.** This is a short finale. Quickly urge the audience to take part in your project, and tell them how. "Sign up with the volunteers here tonight" or "fill out the card you were given and drop it in the box."

Whatever organizational technique you use, develop each major point with detail—facts, stories, statistics, quotations, explanations. Whenever possible, give specific examples to illustrate your point. Sometimes an example can clarify in ways a direct statement cannot. Examples are frequently stories, which audiences love, so you hold their attention.

Plan Your Conclusion

No, you can't just stop and say, "Okay, you can applaud now because I'm done." But even that's better than, "Uh—any questions?" Your final remarks to your audience should be the climax of your speech. The conclusion is the last thing they will hear, and consequently is something they are likely to remember. It is your chance to emphasize your major points or restate your message in one last moving appeal. With careful planning you can end with a strong impact.

Choose your closing words. To signal you are concluding, you can use signpost words such as "finally," or "in conclusion," or "let me leave you with this thought." Then rely on one of the standard techniques:

- **A summary.** Summarize your talk in general or emphasize the major ideas.
- **Return to your introduction.** Refer back to something from the beginning of the speech.
- **A moving story.** A story that illustrates your point can bring the elements of your speech together in a memorable way.
- **A quotation.** Sometimes a relevant quotation or memorable phrase will stick with the audience.
- **An appeal to action.** Clearly lay out for the audience what you want them to do: "Come out Saturday and help paint over graffiti" or "Join your Neighborhood Watch and help the community stay safe." This is the common ending of a speech using Monroe's motivated sequence and is also a frequent choice for any speech that aims to persuade.

Practice a well-worded final phrase. Don't let your audience's final view of you be of a speaker fumbling for words. Don't rely on inspiration at the last minute. Practice the last words of your talk out loud, and end smoothly.

Dressing Up Your Talk

An audience sees a speech as well as hears it. What you have to say is the backbone of your address, but you can enhance that basic presentation in a number of ways that add visual interest to the message or help strengthen the positive reaction to you.

Add Visual Aids

Visual aids help your audience understand your points. Many people are "visual learners"; they grasp information better if they see it as well as hear it. Visual aids also add interest to a talk. Prepare overhead transparencies, slides, video, handouts, or whatever you might need to supplement your talk, especially if you want to inform people. An audience trying to understand new information is more likely to succeed when they receive it through multiple channels, such as both eyes and ears. These few tips help to ensure that your visuals remain aids and don't become hindrances:

- **Never use visual aids without trying them out.** Not knowing how to focus overhead projectors or rewind videotapes can undermine your credibility.

- **Always have someone else proofread your overheads or handouts.** Handing out written material with errors or projecting your misspelled words onto a screen is embarrassing. Proof your work carefully and use computer spell-check functions, but then have someone else proofread your final copies. Computer spell-check functions will not catch misused words such as *their* and *there,* or the fact that *it's* means it is and *its* is possessive (parallel to his, hers, ours). Spell-check functions will not catch that you misspelled someone's name or that you are urging people to come to an event on Saturday, March 14, when March 14 is actually Sunday.
- **Do not hand out written material at the beginning of a talk unless you want the audience to follow along.** Otherwise, wait till the end. If you give people a handout or flier while you are talking, they will read it, which means they won't be listening to you. They will also read ahead on transparencies. Place a blank piece of paper over any material you are not discussing and don't show that information until you get to it.
- **Be sure your visual aids are easily visible from the back row.** Two common problems are too much text and too small print. Avoid both of these. *Never simply take something that works in print—such as a page from a handbook—and expect it to work as an overhead transparency.* Print should never be smaller than 18-point font and ideally should be larger. Write in upper- and lowercase; ALL UPPERCASE LETTERS ARE HARD TO READ. Use a sans serif type (plain, with no curls or feet) such as Arial or Helvetica.

Practice Your Talk

Once you have planned what you want to say and what visual aids you will use, practice out loud. As consultant Marjorie Brody explains: "Practicing in your head is not practicing. We are all quite eloquent in our minds. However, when we speak out loud, something entirely different comes out. The only way to practice correctly is to practice out loud" (167). Also, practice your talk while looking into mirrors set in various spots around the room. If you have the time and equipment, videotape yourself. You can draw faces on cardboard and hang them around the room to practice making eye contact (maybe you can cajole your family or friends into listening several times). This also gives you a chance to rehearse with your visual aids, so you know how to gesture without blocking the audience view of your visuals, when to turn on the overhead projector, and how far the slide projector control cord reaches. (This is also good advice for preparing for the oral portions of promotional exams.)

Decide Whether You Will Wear Your Uniform

Your talk begins before you step to the front of the room or the podium. The audience sees you before they hear you. You need to decide whether you want that view to be of an officer in uniform. How do you want to come across? Recall that a uniform gives you instant credibility, but it also sets you apart.

POCKET GUIDE

Visual Aids

Many people understand information better when they can see and hear it. Well-used models, maps, slides, video, handouts, overhead transparencies, and demonstrations can add interest to your talk.

Slides

Ideal for audiences of 35 or more.
Require a dark room, which separates you from the audience.

Overhead Transparencies

Powerful for audiences of 50 or less.
Let you keep the lights on and use eye contact.
Lose their power when the audience is too large.

Video

Hard to see if the audience is larger than about 40.
Can be reshown to individuals later.
Remember that you can make a video of photographs or other illustrations that are too small to show.

Presentation Graphics Programs

Need specialized projecting equipment if the audience is larger than about 40.
Very impressive if the equipment is available.
Never use for the first time in front of an audience.

Handouts

Give people something to take home and refer to.
Let people add their own notes.
Can distract the audience; they will read them instead of listening to you.
Unless you want the audience to write on the handouts, don't distribute them until after you finish your talk.

If you don't wear your uniform, you still must make a choice about what to wear. Your clothing is really part of the first nonverbal message your audience gets. As Garmston and Wellman put it, "With one quick scan, the audience judges whether you are conservative or brash, sloppy or neat, one of them or an outsider. The basic rule of thumb is to dress one notch up from your audience. Audiences see this as a sign of respect" (62). (See Chapter 1 for more information about wearing your uniform.)

Gather Department Public Relations Material

You also may want to bring some departmental items to hand out as a public relations gesture. People love free things. Take department crime prevention tips, home

Overhead Transparencies

- No more than 6 to 8 lines per page
- No more than 50 words per page.
- No more than 5 points per page.
- No more than 6 to 8 words per line.
- Use only the top 2/3 of the page. The back rows can't see the bottom.
- Use large fonts (18 point or more). *Never just turn a printed page into an overhead.* One useful idea is to enlarge material on a copier before making a transparency.
- Use upper- and lowercase letters. Words printed in all uppercase are hard to read.
- If you can't read the overhead comfortably in less than 30 seconds, simplify it.

Avoid humiliation:
Know how to operate equipment before you get in front of people.

POCKET GUIDE

security booklets, Neighborhood/Business Watch fliers, junior badges, list of commonly used telephone numbers, business cards, stickers, and so on. Always take more than you think you need. You don't want anyone to leave disappointed, and you can save those you don't need for next time.

You can hand out these materials yourself or just leave them on a table. However, don't hand them out just before you talk or at the beginning of your speech. The audience will focus on the reading material you give them instead of listening to you.

Delivering Your Talk

Writing your speech is only the beginning, and for many people it is the easy part. Now you have to stand in front of a room of eyes staring at you and talk to them; you have to *deliver* your message. This is the point at which those who fear speaking more than death begin to sweat. They believe the phrase "a good speaker" refers not to the talk's wise words and exciting ideas, but to the single element of **delivery**—*how* the speaker talks, stands, and gestures. In reality your delivery is not as important as what you have to say. Nonetheless, strong delivery can add to your talk's effectiveness. Several suggestions can help you.

Set Up Your Space

Arrive at your speaking location before your audience. If you have not met this audience before, arrive about half an hour early; if this is a group you speak to with some regularity, arrive with everyone else or about five minutes early. If possible,

ACTION CLIP

Speaking of Homicide

Detectives Mauro V. Corvasce and Joseph R. Paglino of the Monmouth County Prosecutor's Office in New Jersey began presenting information about homicide investigation procedures together when they taught at the police academy. Today they are a popular presentational duo, recruited by serious mystery writers to talk about criminal procedures.

A typical presentation lasts four hours. The detectives stand on opposite sides at the front of the room. They begin their talk with a definite attention-getter: house lights dim, a red light circles as if from an emergency vehicle in the back of the room, a slide introduces the title of the presentation, and an audio tape plays the *Dragnet* theme song. The audience is instantly hooked. The tape then turns serious, playing a sample 911 call reporting a murder. The detectives talk about what the scene would show as they respond to that call, moving through the slides as they talk.

To adapt to their audiences, they change their material for each presentation. When they talk to mystery authors, for example, they point out common errors about police procedures in detective fiction. They also involve the audience by asking them periodically to list what clues they see and to speculate what these clues mean. Then the detectives explain the actual case.

Their presentations have been highly successful, leading to invitations to speak at the international mystery writers conference and the publication of two books: *Murder One: A Writer's Guide to Homicide* and *Modus Operandi: A Writer's Guide to How Criminals Work.*

arrange the room to suit your purpose. If you want a lot of audience participation, arrange the chairs in a semicircle with yourself in the opening. If you want a formal talk, arrange the chairs in rows. If a white board or chalkboard is available, print your name on it clearly. People often miss hearing the name of the speaker in the flurry of getting settled as a talk begins. If you want people to contact you, also put a phone number or e-mail address on the board. Your sense of time can get distorted when you are speaking. If you are concerned that you might go overtime, either bring someone with you to keep time or ask someone who will be sitting in the front row to signal you when you have about five minutes left.

If you cannot arrange the space, still arrive ten to fifteen minutes early. As the audience arrives, chat with people informally. This will warm you up and may give you a little extra information about your audience.

Whether other business precedes you or your talk is the only business of the day, the audience will get an impression of you before you open your mouth based on your nonverbal behavior—how you act and look. Let them see you paying attention to what is happening in their group. If the group has other business, show an interest in what is said. Overcome any urge you might have to check your notes.

Someone will have to stand up and say, "And now here's Officer Alan Richards to talk with us about community policing in River Heights." This person has a speaking obligation, too. Help him or her out by being prepared to share a little about yourself. Give the person who will introduce you information about yourself that will help the audience relate to you, or send or bring a brief bio for the person to use to prepare their introduction.

> "Will your audience be so bored that your speech is constantly disrupted by the sound of bodies falling asleep and sliding out of chairs? . . . Well, no."
>
> —L. Todd Thomas (20)

By the way, one of your most common speaking assignments will put you on the other side: you'll be the one introducing a speaker. In those cases, seek information in advance so you can pull out the most important points in a speaker's history. You want to say enough to help the speaker establish credibility without talking more than two or three minutes and without discussing the speaker's topic.

Move Beyond Barriers

After you are introduced, you step to the podium. Or do you? Where you stand depends on your goal. As an officer, you have learned that placing barriers between yourself and other people can improve safety. You know that standing in the "V" of the car door provides protection, remaining concealed allows you to check out an area safely, and cover increases the odds of survival.

But standing behind the podium will get you nowhere. Podiums separate the speaker from the audience and can increase negative perceptions that some may have of police as aloof and distant. One of the best ways to become part of your community is to move out from behind the barrier and get closer to people. In some situations, of course, you must stand on a stage or at a podium because the occasion is formal, the audience is large, or your microphone is stationary, or so people in the

Introducing Speakers

Time: 2 to 3 minutes.

Purpose: To make the audience eager to hear the speech.

Your goal in introducing a speaker (or speakers on a panel) is to help the audience look forward to hearing the speech. Imagine the audience sitting and staring at the speaker, thinking, "Who are you, what are you talking about, and what gives you the right to take my time?" Very briefly, answer that.

Help the speaker build credibility. Explain who he or she is, state the topic of the speech (but don't talk about that subject; that's the speaker's job), and explain the speaker's expertise in that area.

End with the speaker's name—pronounced correctly.

Be careful not to praise the speaker at a level he or she cannot live up to.

back of the room can see you. However, when the situation gives you options and you still stand far away, you suggest a disinterest in your audience. Closing the distance not only moves you physically closer to the audience but also symbolizes empathy for them and a desire for closeness.

Look at your audience and *smile*. This is not crowd control—it's fun! Begin your planned introduction.

Use Anxiety as a Stimulus

Almost everyone feels some sort of anxiety or **stage fright** the first time he or she talks to an audience, even a small gathering of neighbors. Palms sweat, hearts pounds, knees seem on the verge of giving way. Such fear can be debilitating or it can be a source of energy. Joseph O'Connor, who works with athletes at the Sports Performance Institute, reports:

> The feeling we might label as "nerves" in a performance situation is often the same as the feeling we would label "excitement" in another context. We need that extra energy in testing circumstances, and my experience . . . suggests that without it, performances suffer. So the question becomes, . . . if there are butterflies in your stomach, how can we persuade them to fly in formation?" (30)

One source of anxiety about giving a talk is what researchers call "performance orientation." This means you focus on your potential success or failure as a person giving a talk rather than on the message you have to convey and the audiences who want to hear it. In *Public Speaking Anxiety*, L. Todd Thomas reports:

> When we adopt a performance orientation to public speaking, we tend to think of the speech only in terms of how well we will do as an actor. . . . The fact of the matter is, if we were to ask the audience members after the speech whether or not the speech was successful, most of them would base their answer on one thing and one thing only. Did they understand what the speaker was trying to accomplish? (17)

Remember that the real focus of a talk is communication. Your audience has come to hear what you have to say, not how you say it. Thomas stresses, "If you allow yourself to think of public speaking as a conversation, rather than as a performance, you will find that you have relieved a great deal of pressure that goes along with being an actor" (18).

Your audience is on your side. They will identify with what you are going through. Fear of public speaking is one universal that cuts across ethnic groups, economic levels, educational backgrounds, even bigoted attitudes. If small signs of your nerves show, the audience will be sympathetic. If you feel comfortable admitting your discomfort, you can even make a joke of it: "I think it's easier to chase a bank robber down a dark alley than give a talk."

One way to enhance your success in giving a talk and to overcome stage fright is to visualize your success. Athletes use visualization to enhance their performance in upcoming games or races. You can use the same technique, much like a dress rehearsal in your mind. Imagine yourself in the room where you will talk, see your audience, visualize yourself interacting naturally and pleasantly with them before the talk, then picture yourself walking with ease and confidence to the front of the room. Picture yourself as you deliver your talk, confident, in control, and sharing useful information with the audience.

"For dry mouth: Take no milk products, soda, alcoholic beverages, or ice cream. Lightly coat your teeth with petroleum jelly; it will stop your lip from sticking to your teeth. Bite the tip of your tongue (this helps you to salivate)."

—Marjorie Brody (147)

Develop a Lively Speaking Style

Perfectly charming human beings, who can tell a joke that will crack you up, can suddenly turn into wood in front of a group. A ventriloquist could stand behind them and speak, and they could just move their jaw up and down and achieve the same effect. Don't do that! Easily said, right? Learning to be lively in front of a group is a bit like learning to shoot: you may not hit the bull's eye the first time, but you get better with practice.

Aim for a relaxed delivery. The model for a public talk is the same as it is for conversation. *Look at your audience, maintain eye contact, speak naturally and conversationally, be concerned for your audience rather than yourself, and speak loudly enough to be heard.* Speaking in an organized and lively way demonstrates concern for your

Overcoming Stage Fright

- Know your audience.
- Be prepared.
- Re-create the speech environment when you rehearse.
- Visualize your success.
- Know your introduction and your conclusion.
- Be organized.
- Use deep-breathing techniques.
- Act calm to feel calm.
- Focus on your message rather than your fear.
- Seek speaking opportunities.

(Beebe and Beebe 34–36)

audience. Looking at them for ongoing feedback indicates you care that they understand. Don't just scan the audience. Practice looking individual audience members in the eye for at least two to three seconds. Being well prepared helps you relax during the talk, which often leads to that dynamic delivery. Speaking dynamically enhances your credibility. Studies of credibility all rank "dynamism" as one of the key elements that lead an audience to trust someone.

> "A good speaker may occasionally stutter, or perhaps have a voice that is a little softer than might be desired. But if that speaker has information that the audience needs to have, or has an opinion that the audience recognizes as compelling enough to consider, then the stuttering, soft-voiced speaker is a more effective public speaker than the slick, smooth, fluent speaker who really has nothing to say."
>
> —L. Todd Thomas (18)

You have undoubtedly heard speakers who drone on in a monotonous voice, insert "uh" between every third word, have an accent that makes their words hard to understand, or pace back and forth from one side of the room to the other. Often, fear of giving a talk stems from a fear of seeming to be like those speakers. As a reaction to hearing such speeches, you may be overly concerned with aspects of delivery. In reality, saying "uh" a few times, having a slight accent, or letting a nervous tremble slide into your voice from time to time will not hurt your talk.

You can prevent some potential problems. Slow, hesitant delivery often stems from lack of preparation. If you have to think of what you are going to say during your speech, your examples will not come quickly (if at all). Monotone delivery most often comes from reading a speech, which changes the inflection in your voice, or from not really looking at and talking to the audience. Pacing stems from not concentrating on the listener. If you stop and look at your audience, you stop pacing. If you want to expand your ability, think about taking a speech class or joining a local Toastmasters Club.

Adapt As You Go

What do you do if you get to your talk and:

The topic is not what you were told?
The public address system doesn't work?
Twenty families have brought their kids?
The chief and the mayor are there?

Adapt to the situation, just as you would when you answer a call. If you're called out on a spousal abuse and it turns out to be a loud party, you'll change your game plan. The same applies here. You have to handle the calls and the talks as they come. For example, Capt. Braziel was set to provide supporting testimony to a legislative committee about allowing public housing authority to have access to applicants' criminal history. He recognized that he followed long lines of testimony

ACTION CLIP

Human Bar Graph

Bill Moyers used a wonderful technique in a speech on political power to an audience that numbered in the hundreds. He called it a "human bar graph." During a talk on political power and responsibility, he asked the entire audience to stand. This came in the middle of the speech when minds might be wandering and bodies were growing tired of sitting. He told the standing audience they represented the American populace.

He then drew two imaginary lines up the auditorium with his hand, dividing the audience into thirds. He asked the left third to sit. These, he said, represented people who did not register to vote. They were irrelevant to the conversation of political power.

He then turned to the right third and asked them to sit. They represented the third of the American populace who registered to vote, but did not do so.

One third of the audience remained erect, a visual representation that less than a majority make decisions about American government.

He then pointed to a lone figure in the front row, asked him to continue standing, and had the rest sit. This gentleman, Moyers said, had the money to gain direct access to political leaders.

Not only had Moyers made his point visually, he had also stimulated audience involvement in his speech. (In addition, he had not embarrassed people by asking those who *really* didn't vote to admit it and sit down.)

and the committee was more than ready to leave. He simply stood and voiced departmental support and sat down. The next speaker missed the cue. He began speaking at length and was cut off sharply in the middle of his words by a cranky committee chair demanding to know only if he supported the bill or not. The point is, every speaking situation demands flexibility. The more experience you have, the better you'll handle it.

And what if (oh no!) your audience is falling asleep? One of a speaker's worst nightmares is to look out and see the audience nodding off. What do you do if your audience is falling asleep? Change awakens a group. Because of the fast pace of television and movies, audience attention spans are growing increasingly shorter. The audience expects frequent changes of pace. If you stand in one spot and talk at a predictable rate, they may grow bored. Add movement to your speech. This can be verbal or visual. Tell a story, use humor, offer concrete examples, pick up the pace of your delivery. If you have several points to make, move from "point two" to "point three" in your talk. Switch to a visual aid. Make a direct reference to someone in the audience by name. Even walking to another side of the room will attract their attention again. Involve the audience directly. Ask for a show of hands or tell a hypothetical story that places them directly in the speech. If all else fails, end your talk sooner than planned.

End on Time

Remember how much you love it when a speaker drones on overtime? Your audience feels the same way. Stay within the time allotted for your talk.

Leave time for questions and answers. Find out how much time the host has allotted for questions and answers (Q&A), and stay within it. Most speakers relax during the Q&A part of the talk. Watch for this when you are in the audience. This is true in part because when people talk back and forth in two-way communication, they have a greater chance to understand one another than when one person explains and one listens.

POCKET GUIDE

When Your Audience Is Small

Community policing often demands that you talk with small audiences. Often this is a group of neighbors gathered in a living room or church meeting room. Don't underestimate the need to prepare for such a talk. Do the same background research into occasion, setting, audience, and purpose you would do for a large audience. Prepare your introduction, body, and conclusion. When delivering the speech, however, you often encounter differences.

A talk to a small audience generally is more informal and interactive. For example, the group may want to ask questions as you go rather than waiting till the end. If you want a more formal tone, dress formally and stand as you speak. If you want to encourage informality, sit with them and invite them to offer comments or ask questions as you go.

Plan ways to be flexible. A question may draw out information you had planned to present at the end, but once interest is expressed, you may decide to answer immediately. If you anticipate this, you can organize your notes accordingly.

- Write each topic or point on a different note card. That way you can discuss point four before point two, and easily locate the keywords of each point.
- Print essential information in one color of ink, optional information in another color. Before the end of the presentation, quickly scan your cards to be sure you covered everything essential.
- Or if you prefer, you can ask the questioner to hold the question until after you present another point.

Watch the audience's nonverbal feedback. You can easily see how a small audience is responding. Are they dozing off, glancing at their watches, drawing interesting variations of freeway graffiti on their notepads? Get them involved. Move from the general to the specific, provide an example, or ask for a show of hands on something. "How many of you own a Toyota truck? Be sure you lock it. That's the most commonly stolen car in the county this month." Are they frowning in confusion? It's okay to remark on that: "You seem puzzled. Let me explain another way." Are they listening intently and nodding? You're in good shape.

Keep your purpose in mind. A side issue that comes up in discussion may be more useful to your purpose than what you had planned. Go with it.

Admit when you don't know the answer. If someone asks a question that you cannot answer, it is okay to say, "I don't know." Answer as well as you can, but don't make up information. If you are willing to get back to someone on an issue, say so. If you know a source from which they can get their information, tell them. But remember, it's okay not to know everything.

If questions are irrelevant, ask that the questioner hold the question until after the official meeting. (For information on hostile audiences or questions, see Chapter 5.)

To end the session, ask for "one more question." Don't just stop the Q&A session abruptly. Give some warning by saying, or having the moderator say, "Last question" or "One more question." If you want to interact with people, tell them at the end of Q&A, "I'll be here for a while" and point to a designated spot where they can find you. This ends the questioning session on a positive note. Don't feel you must answer all questions in front of the group. Some members of your audience may be eager to leave.

After Your Talk

Wait! You're not done yet! What you do after your talk depends in part on your purpose. As a general rule, be prepared to stay after your talk for about half an hour to talk with anyone who didn't feel comfortable asking a question in front of the larger group or who might want to give you information. Community policing is about building relationships, and this is a chance to do that. Have business cards if you want to encourage future contact.

POCKET GUIDE

Preparing for a Talk

1. **Find out everything you can about the audience.** Who are they? What do they expect? Why are they gathered? What is the background of the situation?
2. **Research the subject.** Find out all you can about your topic, keeping the audience in mind. What will work on these people? Vivid examples? Statistics? Comparisons to other cities? Quotes?
3. **If possible, use visual aids or handouts.** Some people understand more by seeing than by hearing.
4. **Organize what you have to say.** Plan an introduction and conclusion; for the body, try to have 3 or 4 points.
5. **Plan ways to build your credibility.** Part of your credibility comes from expertise and part from friendliness and humanizing yourself.
6. **Practice your talk.** *Never read your talk!* Converse with your audience. If you need notes, keep them on a card.

Never go over your allotted time!

Assess Your Success

After you leave, think about both the good and bad moments of your talk. What do you wish you'd said that you didn't? What went over really well? What would have been great to have remembered to bring? Make notes right away. No matter how sure you are you'll remember, you will forget something. Write it down now.

Steal from Yourself

Save your speaking notes, visual aids, list of materials, and self-critique. Next time you're asked to speak, you won't have to start over at ground zero.

As you become a more practiced speaker, you will begin to enjoy the speaking experience. Seek opportunities to speak. In time you will become comfortable with talking in public, and you will develop your skills and provide a vital service for your community.

POCKET GUIDE

Giving a Talk

Smile. Look at the audience. Make sure everyone can hear you. (It helps to stand up.) *Converse* with your audience.

Introduction: Introduce yourself if you have not been introduced. Say something about the occasion or what immediately preceded you. Then move into your talk in a way that arouses interest in the topic—a story, startling fact, quotation, humor, suspense.

Preview statement: Give an overview of what you will talk about.

Body: Organize your ideas into 3 or 4 major points. Use examples, facts, statistics, quotations to enrich your points, especially ones that are relevant to your audience.

Conclusion: This is what audiences will walk away with. Conclude with a firm statement or a summary or a plea for action. If appropriate, leave time for questions and answers.

Be lively! Look at your audience!

Works Cited

Beebe, Steven A., and Susan J. Beebe. *Public Speaking: An Audience-Centered Approach.* 2nd ed. Englewood Cliffs, N.J.: Prentice Hall, 1994.

Brody, Marjorie. *Speaking Your Way to the Top*. Boston: Allyn and Bacon, 1998.

Bonesana, Cesare, the Marchese di Beccaria. *The Great Thoughts*. Ed. George Seldes. New York: Ballantine, 1985.

Corvasce, Mauro V., and Joseph R. Paglino. *Murder One: A Writer's Guide to Homicide.* Cincinnati, Ohio: Writer's Digest Books, 1997.

———. *Modus Operandi: A Writer's Guide to How Criminals Work*. Cincinnati, Ohio: Writer's Digest Books, 1995.

Creek, Helen. "Some Tips on How to Better Prepare for and Make Community Meeting Presentations." Booklet entitled "A Community Policing Seminar on Community Policing: The Process." Portland, Ore., Police Dept., 1994.

Garmston, Robert J., and Bruce M. Wellman. *How to Make Presentations That Teach and Transform*. Alexandria, Va.: Association for Supervision and Curriculum Development, 1992.

O'Connor, Joseph. "Dealing with Performance Anxiety." *Anchor Point* 6 (May 1992): 30–34.

Spectra 9 (Dec. 1973): 4.

Thomas, L. Todd. *Public Speaking Anxiety: How to Face the Fear*. Fort Worth: Harcourt Brace, 1997.

Activities

1 Video Practice

Pick a topic that interests you. Prepare a seven- to ten-minute talk using the guidelines in this chapter. Give your talk in front of a video camera. Review the recording to identify:

- Your five best qualities.
- Your five worst qualities.

Repeat the talk focusing on accenting the positive qualities and improving the worst qualities. Review the second recording. How did you do compared with the first recording? You can also ask others to evaluate your talk.

2 Audience Adaptation

Assume you have been asked to speak on "The Daily Life of Today's Police Officer." You can make only three points to your audience. What three points would you make to:

- A college criminal justice class.
- A group of senior citizens concerned about their safety.
- A neighborhood home association.
- A third-grade class.

Consider what you would include or exclude, how you might change the order of presentation, how much you would involve the audience, how much detail you would include, how long you would speak, what elements of your job you would highlight in each case, and how you would begin.

3 Eye Contact

Give a short talk on any topic in front of an audience. Have at least five people act as your audience, more if you can get them. Instruct each audience member to raise a hand and keep it raised as you talk until you make continuous eye contact with him or her for at least three seconds. The activity is complete when all hands are lowered. This activity trains you to look at people in your audience, not just scan a sea of faces.

4 Elements of a Good Talk

Interview three people about the last good talk they heard. Ask them what made it memorable. Your goal is to find out what an audience wants in a talk.

5 Practice Makes Perfect

The more you speak, the easier it gets. If you are a novice, volunteer to give a talk to begin your practice. If you feel apprehensive about speaking, start with an audience who will be eager to hear you—a local elementary school. Talk with the teacher about how long to talk (young kids won't listen for long) and how much to involve them. Then plan your talk carefully and give it.

If you have experience speaking, try adding a new element. Plan your talk carefully, using one technique discussed in this chapter that you have not used previously.

Chapter Five

The Only Certainty Besides Death and Taxes

Community Meetings

"Community policing in Chicago means meetings, as often as once a month in each of 279 beats. In church basements and police meeting rooms, some turn into gripe sessions, putting even the most-patient police officers on the defensive. But often strategies are hammered out to address specific problems: a building housing drug dealers, gang activity, graffiti and property damage."

COMMUNITY NEWS PROJECT

Randy Washington and Diedra Holland have a bet. He's just returned from a meeting with the Glenview Neighborhood Association, where members presented him with a litany of complaints about the alley behind Kennedy High. Holland bet Washington a cafe mocha she can guess eighty percent of them. She's systematically calling out items from the list about M Street Park she compiled last week at a Neighborhood Watch meeting. So far she's correctly guessed syringes, razor blades, condoms, and broken glass littering the ground; meetings that appear to be drug exchanges; loud music late at night and the crash of breaking bottles. He gives her only partial credit for graffiti on signs because graffiti hits garage doors and fences in the alley, too. She misses petty theft from nearby backyards.

"It's the same problem," she says, restlessly pacing the small apartment that houses their neighborhood office. "Even over by the movie theater, it's the same problem."

"We need to get these people together," responds Washington, "and the school officials, too. Have one big community meeting to identify the common issues. Then you can lead them through some problem-solution activity and put together a process to work together as a team."

Holland stops pacing abruptly. "Why should I lead them? How about you lead them?"

They stare at each other for only a second before both grin. "Alan can lead them."

THE COMMUNITY MEETING IS A CENTRAL WEAPON in the arsenal of community policing. Alternately known as a forum, town-hall meeting, public hearing, public meeting, or advisory meeting, the **community meeting** brings together involved community members for open public discussions. Attendees may live or work in the area or represent schools, businesses, religious groups, government agencies, medical facilities, or community-based organizations that operate there. Typically the purpose of a community meeting is for information exchange or problem solving rather than decision making.

Community meetings vary widely in form and size. You may have fifteen people at a neighborhood watch gathering or two hundred at a public meeting after a major incident. Sometimes you have one large general meeting of everyone, which you follow with **breakout groups**, smaller meetings designed for discussion. A well-run meeting can be an efficient way to integrate yourself into the community, build trust, and advance your fight against neighborhood crime. As Elaine Cogan points out in *Successful Public Meetings*, "Enlisting the public as a partner . . . can help you defuse potential opposition, acquire allies in unlikely places, and unite a community and its leaders around a common purpose" (2).

The community meeting differs from the work group meeting, discussed in Chapter 3, primarily in that community meetings are open to the public and revolve around discussion of public issues. In contrast, work group meetings involve a limited number of people who frequently are members of an ongoing group with an agenda. The work group members may think of themselves as a team, committee, task force, board of directors, support group, or planning staff, but their meetings are not open to the public and more often result in decision making and action.

Consider some ways police have used community meetings:

- Delta Township, Michigan: Police and managers of apartment communities meet monthly. Police give managers crime statistics for their areas, as well as gang awareness information and security tips, and managers help police gain insight into neighborhood problems.
- Benton County, Oregon: County officials sought public perspectives on plans for a new jail in a community meeting of residents, police, and corrections officials.
- El Paso, Texas: A community meeting brought together a state senator, the county attorney, a member of the city's antigraffiti committee, representatives of the corrections department, and the public to talk about what to do about graffiti after it is on the wall.
- Wynne, Arkansas: Sheriff's deputies in Cross County, Arkansas, faced problems typical of rural agencies with a large geographic region and few officers. One of their priorities was finding a way to establish communication with the county's farmers. *Sheriff Times* reports: "The department resolved this dilemma by arranging regular meetings on location at the farmers' shops—hubs of activity where workers maintain equipment, organize daily activities, and meet to discuss issues and upcoming events. The shop gatherings turned out to be the perfect place for the department's community-oriented deputy to meet with farm owners and their employees. On these occasions, the deputy shares local legal updates, reviews the regional game and fish laws, . . . and suggests strategies to prevent theft of farm equipment and agricultural products" (Brinkworth 8).
- Chicago, Illinois: Beat meetings are a staple of the 279 Chicago police beats. The department hosts meetings led by an officer from the beat, sometimes with a coleader from the neighborhood. Meetings are held monthly, bimonthly, or quarterly. Their goal is for officers and neighbors to determine the priority crime problems on the beat and develop strategies to address them, as well as for officers to let neighbors know what progress police are making. The Chicago Police Department says: "It is at these meetings that police and residents identify, analyze and begin to solve neighborhood crime problems."

Probably the best known of all such meetings is **Neighborhood Watch**, a gathering of ten to twenty neighbors from a one- or two-block area who are devoted to stopping crime in their area. Typically an officer talks about crime prevention and neighborhood problem-solving strategies for thirty to forty-five minutes, then the group takes another forty-five minutes or so to organize their program or exchange information. A neighborhood meeting operates essentially the same way as the larger community meeting, except that the neighborhood meeting is less formal, needs less planning and advertising, is often held in a home or a backyard, and consequently is easier to manage.

Despite their frequent use, community meetings are not easy. Cogan offers this description: "Public meetings are unpredictable. They are messy. They often become arenas where people confront each other on issues that they would rather avoid. They can be time consuming to organize and boring and tedious to attend" (1). In addition, because public meetings of all kinds are held regularly, your audience could well have expectations about your meeting based on their prior experience with a hearing on the city's sewage treatment plant. You need to separate your meeting from being just another "public meeting."

Careful planning can help you do this. First, put together a planning committee. Your planning committee then selects the community meeting **format**—the arrangement of information and presenters—best suited to your purpose. Formats tend to fall into three basic categories: informational, advisory, and problem solving. For clarity this text presents each format as an isolated method. In action, however, formats can be mixed creatively in any fashion your planning committee thinks will accomplish your mission. The formal presentation is often followed by breakout groups or an open forum where audience members ask questions.

Whatever format you choose, remember that your underlying purpose in a community meeting is to create a partnership with the community, and your relational message is vital in that effort. *Sometimes a smile matters more than a logical argument.* Whenever you get a chance during the meeting, and especially as people arrive, be sure that you and other officers interact with those who attend. Some community members are hesitant to approach officers, either from a polite reluctance to take up your time or because they are uncomfortable with police. Take the first step. Don't stand against the wall, arms crossed, carefully surveying the room. Instead, come forward, smile, be friendly, learn their names and their neighborhoods, talk about sports, the weather, traffic, or any of the mundane topics that say little in content but at the relational level establish a common ground.

This chapter details how to plan a large, formal meeting in order to explain all the steps for any meeting. Smaller community meetings, such as Neighborhood Watch, require far less preparation. Any of the formats that work in a large group will work in a small one; however, more informal conversation occurs in the smaller meeting, and procedural rules are more casual. It is much easier to allow community members to give input in the smaller meetings. Your interpersonal skills come to the fore. These are very likely the people you will work with over and over, the core of your support, and you want to build strong relationships with them.

Formats for Informational Meetings

Informational meetings are designed to relate facts and figures to the community. Formats for informative presentations, such as a symposium, panel discussion, and interview, rely primarily on one-way communication, with one or more informed speakers presenting material to an audience. Open forums often follow to allow the two-way communication of audience questions and comments. Configure the room for presentations with rows of chairs facing a podium or tables at the front and easily visible screens for projections. Figure 5-1 illustrates possible room configuration.

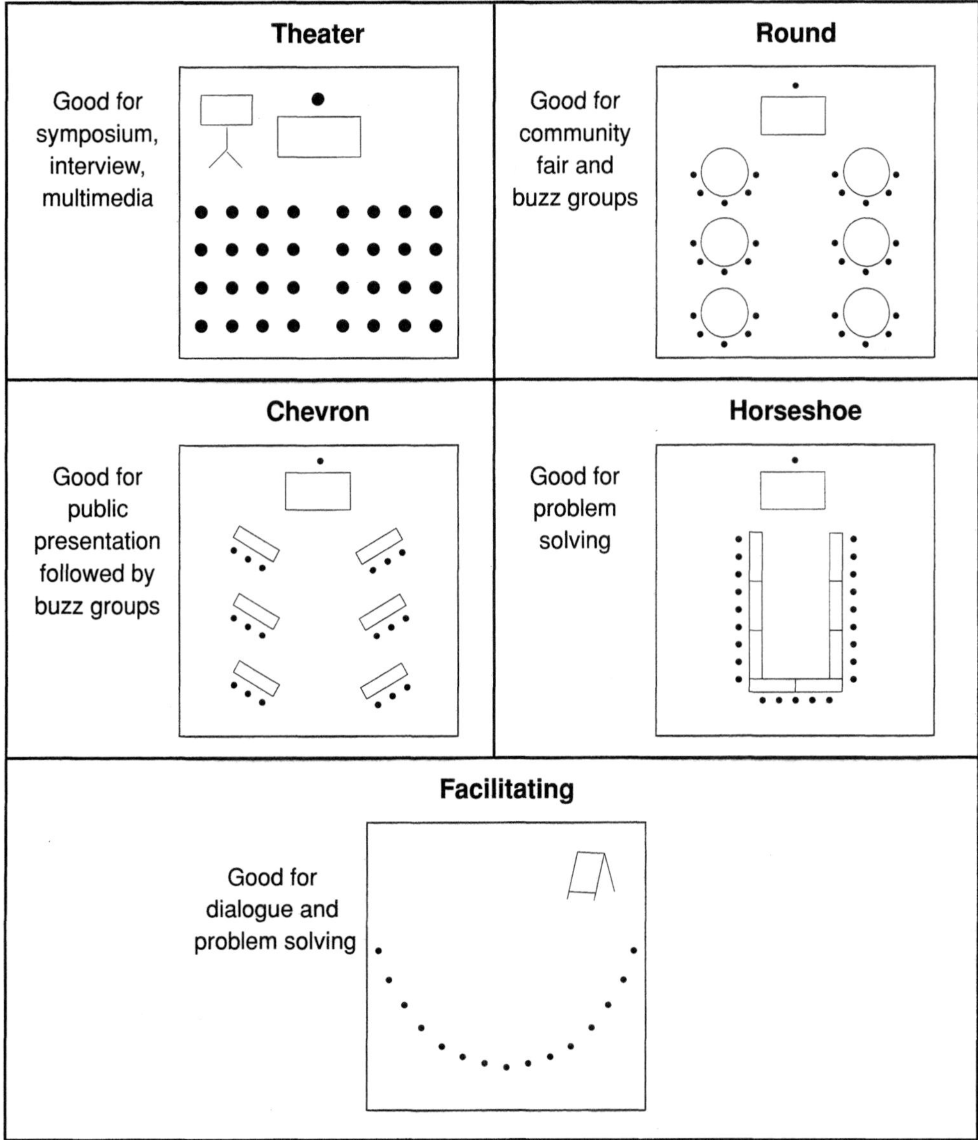

Figure 5-1: Community meeting room configurations

Symposium

A **symposium** is a series of speeches around one topic from a number of speakers. The format allows an audience to hear from experts in a variety of areas or from multiple agencies. A symposium on problems in the Glenview neighborhood, for example, might feature speakers from the school district, park and street maintenance, the community officer or sergeant, the president of the neighborhood association, and possibly the high school student body president. Each speaker discusses his or her group's perspective on the problem and possible ways to deal with it.

The advantage of the symposium is that good speakers can present a lot of information in a short time. The disadvantage is that a symposium is only as good as the speakers. The process of hearing from one speaker after another at a predictable pace lacks the dynamism of a discussion with interaction and differences of opinion. For a symposium to be interesting, very good speakers must present vital information.

Panel Discussion

More free-form and lively than a symposium, a **panel discussion** features three to five speakers who discuss a common issue with the guidance of a moderator. Any panel member can make a comment, respond to another panel member, or add a new viewpoint. More stimulating panels include speakers with differing points of view. The moderator should be articulate and informed, but neutral on the issue, such as a reporter or news anchor, a judge, or a university professor. The moderator might ask the Glenview panel about causes of the problem in the alley. This could generate a difference of opinion, with the community representative blaming students, the student arguing that out-of-school forces are responsible, the officer asking how students are monitored between classes, and the school district representative decrying the lack of after-school activities. Such genuine disagreement can be thought-provoking and exciting for listeners.

The panel discussion enables informed speakers to present useful information in a lively and engaging manner. Like the symposium, the panel discussion is better when the speakers are interesting, but even with weak speakers the panel is livelier than the symposium. The panel's disadvantage is that time is more difficult to control in a panel discussion and a moderator must be careful that one speaker does not speak much more than another and that all important issues are addressed.

Public Interview

Face the Nation and *Meet the Press* provide the model for the **public interview**, in which an interviewer asks questions that one or more speakers answer. The interview format has several variations: multiple interviewers can question one expert, much like a press conference; multiple interviewers can question multiple respondents; or one interviewer can pose questions to either a single or multiple respondents. For example, in the Glenview community meeting, the interviewer might be a representative of the community-based organization Safe Streets. Or the presidents of the Glenview Neighborhood Association and the apartment council can pose questions, and the rest of the panel responds.

If several persons answer questions, the interview can proceed much like a modified symposium: each speaker responds to the same question before the interviewer asks a second question or poses another situation. The advantages of the interview over the pure symposium are that each speaker responds to the same issue and the discussion moves faster. As an alternative, the interviewer can ask a question and the response can jump from speaker to speaker in any sequence, and not all speakers address every issue.

A very common variation of the public interview is to let the audience do a portion of the questioning. Ask audience members to submit questions before the presentation, and then have the interviewer or a community representative sift through submissions and select the most commonly asked questions. This process helps overcome the common problem of speakers responding to the loudest audience members instead of the most significant questions. This process works best when it follows a short presentation—a symposium, a panel, or even a speech. To better prepare your speakers to provide strong information, ask your informal community contacts in advance what questions or issues are likely to arise.

The advantage of the public interview is that an astute interviewer can force certain issues into discussion. An informed interviewer can probe, demanding answers from each person about subjects that would never come up in a symposium and that might be ducked in a panel discussion. This gives an audience a sense that nothing is being hidden, especially if they trust the interviewers. The disadvantage is that important material can be overlooked if the interviewer does not ask about it.

Multimedia Presentation

Sometimes **multimedia presentations**—such as film, video, slide shows, and audio—supplement traditional discussion formats. A symposium, panel discussion, or interview can precede a multimedia program, or the multimedia presentation can be a springboard for discussion. If you decide to show videos or slides, be sure to project them onto a screen large enough for everyone to see.

Multimedia can enthuse an audience, and some information is conveyed much more efficiently and vividly with images. For example, in Green Bay, Wisconsin, even though a business district was plagued with bars serving intoxicated people, city council members had a hard time believing that the problem was serious enough to declare a moratorium. Officers videotaped the intoxicated people and showed the tape at the next council meeting. The reaction was immediate: a bar moratorium was declared unanimously (Bongle).

Community Fair or Open House

At a **community fair**, people visit tables or booths scattered about a room seeking the information they want and sharing their opinions. Each table is staffed by a representative of a particular agency who presents information to community members or listens to their comments. Tables also can feature informational displays, resources, demonstrations, continuously running videos, and so on. People move from table to table. The advantage of the community fair is that people can attend at a time that is convenient for them, and they are more involved than when they simply sit and listen. The disadvantage is that they may not get all available information because they choose which tables to visit.

The keys to making this approach work are having the appropriate agencies exhibit and making sure every table is clearly marked with signs visible at a distance, written in all the languages of those attending. A good fair stretches several hours (for example, from 2:00 P.M. to 8:00 P.M.) to accommodate people's diverse schedules. The community fair is time-consuming and requires effort to set up, but as Cogan points out, "The very openness of this format—sending the message that the agency cares enough to meet the citizens on their own terms—creates a wellspring of positive community reaction" (29).

Formats for Advisory Meetings

Advisory meetings are set up to allow participants to share their concerns with those in authority. Your goals are twofold: to receive possibly useful information and to give participants a sense of significance by listening to the concerns they voice. *The audience must understand that their input is merely advisory.* They need to feel that they are heard, but they also must realize they are not there to make decisions. Be very clear in how you promote the meeting. Advertise something like: "We want your input to help with our decision making." A meeting can be fully advisory, or an advisory session can follow some other format, such as a panel discussion.

Configure the room to enhance audience participation. Ideally, be sure everyone can see and hear each other, not just those answering questions. In a smaller group, put people in a circle. For a large group consider setting up a microphone for questioners to use so the person who answers doesn't have to repeat the question or comment for the rest of the audience. For an especially large audience, set up a microphone on each side of the room, alternating questions from side to side.

Record all issues the audience brings up. Keeping a record signifies that community remarks are taken seriously. This confirms that you are listening and that the ideas will not be forgotten. Ideally, record ideas so all can see—on large easel-pad paper taped around the room, on a projected overhead transparency, or on a computer projected onto a screen. Also give participants comment sheets to take with them and mail back if they want to provide other input.

Advisory meetings can take several forms, including open forums, the mini open house, buzz groups, Phillips 66, and nominal group technique (discussed later).

Mini Open House

The **mini open house** asks your panel or symposium experts to move to selected spots around the room after the presentations. For example, one speaker could move to each corner. Audience members then circulate, asking questions or offering comments to the speakers one on one. This allows the whole audience to get an overview of an issue, after which individuals can address their personal concerns to the appropriate presenter.

Open Forum

An **open forum** is a format that allows anyone to speak on an issue. Audience members can offer comments or ask questions. Many public meetings are set up for this purpose alone, and most community meetings culminate in an open forum. Announce a time limit at the outset so people who don't get to ask questions or make comments don't feel cut off arbitrarily. You can also set up a large clock with a timer, so everyone realizes time limitations.

The advantage of a forum is that anyone can participate. The disadvantage is that planners have little control over what will emerge. Participants can present incorrect information, hostile comments can erupt, long-winded speakers can dominate, and tired people may begin to drift away. To prevent such responses, you must carefully moderate your forum. Use some techniques for additional structure: limit comments to one per person, limit the time for each speaker, put a cap on the time for each subject, or turn to a special technique, such as the buzz group.

Buzz Groups

A **buzz group** divides an audience into smaller groups of about six that discuss a specific issue for a limited time. This encourages input rather than leads to specific decisions. Often a buzz group follows another format, such as a panel discussion. After the main presentation, divide the audience into small groups. Give the groups a limited, specific task, such as, "In the next fifteen minutes identify the occasions when these teen gangs gather," or "Suggest four actions we might take," or "Determine one activity your group is willing to engage in to help fight this problem." Each group selects a spokesperson to report their conclusions to the larger group at the end of the allotted time. During these final group reports, write the responses where all can see. Washington and Holland, for example, might set up buzz groups after their public presentation, asking each group to suggest actions to take on the acknowledged problem.

Buzz groups allow wide participation even when a group is large. The activity also breaks up a long meeting. The buzz group does not work well when you need a detailed analysis of issues or thoughtful weighing of ideas.

Phillips 66

A variation of buzz groups is Phillips 66, where six-person groups discuss a topic for six minutes. Named for the idea's originator, Donald Phillips, and as a pun on the Phillips 66 Petroleum Company, this technique provides quick audience involvement. An easy version when you don't want to physically move people around is to have every other row turn to people behind them. Then have them divide into groups of six.

POCKET GUIDE

Buzz Groups

A way to involve the audience in discussion and encourage their input.

1. Divide the audience into small groups of six or so.
2. Charge them with a specific task.
3. Give them a limited time for discussion.
4. Have each group select a spokesperson.
5. Ask each spokesperson to share his or her group's conclusions with the larger group.

Revolving Speakers

Rather than having one speaker address a large group, you can break the group into smaller groups, and have speakers move from group to group presenting and receiving information. This process of **revolving speakers** is particularly useful if you want to stimulate discussion because most people feel more comfortable talking in a smaller setting. If the group needs some sense of action coming from the meetings, ask each group to come to some conclusion or generate solutions.

Open Dialogues

Sometimes you stage a meeting between two groups to address the specific problem of lack of trust between them in the hope of bridging the groups. Such residual problems are common between police and teens, residents of areas where police activity is common, and new immigrants who bring fears of police from another country. In such meetings, the primary goal is overcoming mistrust, although problem solving may follow a period of trust building. This meeting is different from other community meetings because the emotional level is so high. You need **open dialogue**, where issues of the past can be put to rest.

When dialogue is your goal, seek a **facilitator** who is used to working with groups in conflict. This person should be skilled in interpersonal relations and conflict resolution. A facilitator can moderate a meeting between two historically hostile groups because of his or her neutrality, noninvolvement, and skill.

Two examples illustrate this type of meeting. The Dispute Resolution Center at John Jay College of Criminal Justice, with the New York Police Department's 24th Precinct, developed Resolution Is the Solution. The program is designed to address problems between teens and police in Manhattan Valley. The Westside Crime Prevention Program realized that "seldom, if ever, do the police and young people have a chance to interact in a nonthreatening setting" (Cohen 8). Their attempt to change that involves two-hour facilitated meetings between police and teens where questions and answers are exchanged. The program "trains young people in basic conflict resolution skills and gives them the rare opportunity to spend two hours with police officers in a no-holds-barred question and answer session" (Cohen 1).

Hampton, Virginia, started the Youth Community Oriented Policing Effort (Y-COPE), a "prevention program that targets youth violence through nonconfrontational involvement with police officers. It brings young people and officers together to discuss the behaviors that each exhibits and encourages working together to improve neighborhoods" (Stephan 4). Reporting on the program, Jacqueline Stephan states that two components make the program successful—having a trained facilitator and ample space for activities. "The facilitator . . . begins each meeting with an exercise to strengthen communication and encourage tolerance of others' opinions . . . . After the ice-breaker, the facilitator opens a topic for discussion. Working in small groups, the members analyze the issue and come up with suggested solutions" (Stephan 4).

Formats for Problem-Solving Meetings

Sometimes simply presenting or exchanging information is not enough. The community needs to come to grips with a problem and solve it. In those cases, you need a problem-solving format. Typically, this is why neighborhood meetings are formed. People want to feel they can have an impact, and problem-solving meetings provide that feeling. Also, people who have a hand in shaping a solution are more likely to buy into its implementation.

Every problem-solving meeting should begin with a summary of the problem or the information participants need to know. This prevents rehashing old material during the problem-solving time and assures that everyone has current information. Two main techniques for problem solving, reflective thinking and the nominal group technique (NGT), are discussed here. Ways to generate new solutions are discussed in Chapter 6.

> "To stimulate small-group discussion, the facilitator must eventually ask the group to make choices or come to a conclusion. This step should be a natural outcome of the process of discussion. . . . List choices the group has discussed and ask participants to talk about the advantages and disadvantages of each. If discussion is framed in these terms rather than in absolutes of yes or no, even the most stubborn members of the group may see other points of view."
>
> —Elaine Cogan (37)

Reflective Thinking

Still recognized as one of the best agenda formats for problem-solving discussion or logical decision making, reflective thinking was first advanced by John Dewey in 1910. **Reflective thinking** provides a very logical, systematic, five-step procedure to ensure open, fair, and logical decision making.

1. **Define and analyze the problem.** Discuss the problem in order to clearly define it and understand what the problem entails. This discussion clarifies any unknown terms, specifies the problem's symptoms, and assesses its size, scope, and urgency.

POCKET GUIDE

Beat Meeting Agenda

The Chicago Police Department provides this model agenda for meetings where beat officers and their community engage in joint problem solving.

1. Welcome and introduce participants.
2. Give feedback on progress since the last meeting.
3. Discuss current crime conditions and new problems. This includes reports from beat officers as well as input from neighbors. Decide if new problems warrant the group's attention, given what they are already doing.
4. Develop strategies to deal with these problems and coordinate responsibilities. Identify a community contact person to coordinate efforts on any new problem.
5. Set the next meeting date. Schedule working groups to carry on between meetings.

(http://www.ci.chi.il.us/CommunityPolicing/BeatMeetings/Tips/Agenda.html. 7 June 1998.)

2. **List possible solutions.** Generate as many possible solutions to the problem as possible but withhold judgment about these solutions.
3. **Weigh alternative solutions.** Discard unrealistic solutions and consider the strengths and weaknesses of the remaining proposed solutions.
4. **Select the best solution.** Determine which solution is best from the list of proposed solutions.
5. **Implement the solution.** Determine the steps to put the solution into action and make any necessary follow-up plans.

This format is essentially a logical agenda for discussing an issue. Reflective thinking requires little more than sticking to the agenda and proceeding systematically. That, however, is easier said than done. Human discussion does not always flow in ordered patterns. Creative thinking, especially, proceeds erratically. People tend to discover ideas out of sequence, and groups reach accord through sudden insights rather than systematic procedure. If this occurs, record ideas as they emerge, put them on hold, and continue to proceed logically through the reflective thinking agenda to ensure that nothing has been overlooked.

Nominal Group Technique

So what do you do about those people who turn up at every community meeting and talk and talk and talk and . . . talk? Is there any way to have a fair, open forum and still shut them up? The answer is **nominal group technique** (NGT). Developed in 1968 by Andre L. Delbecq and Andrew H. Van de Ven, NGT blends the benefits of brainstorming with the advantages of quick decision making. In NGT, participants are put into small groups where a facilitator leads them through a tightly structured process that produces a ranked list of ideas. Research shows that NGT

Reflective Thinking

A logical procedure for problem solving.

1. Analyze the problem, including definition of terms and establishing group goals.
2. List possible solutions.
3. Weigh alternative solutions.
4. Select the best solution.
5. Take steps to implement the solution.

POCKET GUIDE

generates more and better ideas than other techniques (Van Gundy 345). It is used widely in business and public service agencies.

The advantage of NGT is that this format "provides equality of participation among group members. In a less structured group, personality or status differences often sway the direction of group discussion" (Van Gundy 345). The disadvantage is that it restricts genuine discussion of ideas. It also does not encourage the creation of new solutions from the blending of divergent positions.

Preparation. NGT is not a spur-of-the-moment technique. You need to prepare carefully to make maximum use of your time.

1. **Generate a triggering question about the problem or issue to be discussed.** Address only one question at a time. The triggering question asks something about your issue, worded so that each person can create a list of responses, such as "What are the major law enforcement problems this area faces?"

   The type of question you ask determines whether the responses are advisory, problem solving, or both. If your triggering question asks groups to identify problems, you have an advisory meeting. If you already know the problem and want solutions, your triggering question asks for solutions to the problem. You might ask, for example, "What suggestions do you have for dealing with the problem in the alley behind Kennedy High?" Or you can do both, first identifying the problem, and then searching for a solution.

2. **Train facilitators and recorders.** Facilitators lead the small group sessions, and recorders keep notes. The facilitators are vital to the NGT process. They need careful training. Recording is a less-demanding process, but recorders also benefit from training. The best way to train facilitators and recorders is to bring them together, explain the process, and then lead them through an NGT session.

3. **Gather supplies.** Each NGT group needs an easel, easel pad, marking pens, and tape to post the easel pages in clear view. If you want to use written ballots (discussed below), prepare them.

4. **Determine your NGT group setup.** At the community meeting, after the official welcome by your master of ceremonies (see below), divide the audience into groups of five to ten members for the NGT portion of the evening. Delbecq

and Van de Ven state that "satisfaction drops off as members have less opportunity to participate. . . . A group made up of less than five members lacks resources in terms of the number of critical judgments available to analyze the problem and arrive at a decision. On the other hand, adding beyond ten members often does not increase group accuracy. . . ." (Delbecq, Van de Ven, and Gustafson 70). Although NGT has been used successfully with larger groups in community meeting situations, the closer the groups come to the ideal size, the easier the procedure is.

"One of Delbecq's secondary findings that I have found particularly helpful is this: the level of productivity of a group is measurably higher when, at the beginning of their process, they are greeted with warmth. The principle is straightforward. It seems obvious to some, but it is often not practiced."

—Len Silvey (183)

The criteria you use to divide the audience into groups can be linked to your issue. In a school issue, for example, you might have groups of parents, students, teachers, administrators, and neighbors. Or the groups could be geographical, organized by police districts, particular target neighborhoods, or apartment complexes. An easy way to handle the process of putting people into their groups is to color-code sign-up sheets and name tags by group. Then the master of ceremonies can say, "If you have a blue name tag, please go with Officer Richards."

NGT in action. The facilitator plays a key role in each small group. If you are the facilitator, begin by welcoming and warming up the group. Set a conversational tone. If you are new to the area, this is a chance to let them get to know you. Tell them a little about yourself. Then ask everyone to state their name and the area or group they represent. This gets them talking and breaks the ice a little. After this is done, give them an overview of how the process will proceed.

Display the triggering question written on your easel pad and say it aloud as well. Explain the question clearly so all participants understand. Then lead the group through the six application steps.

1. **Direct the silent generation of ideas.** Participants write down their responses to the triggering question, recording as many responses as time allows. A good rule of thumb is to move to the next phase when you see most participants stop writing.

2. **Record ideas.** One by one, each person in the group shares his or her top issue. The recorder writes all responses where everyone can see them, such as on an easel pad, numbering each item for easy reference. When a page fills, tape it in a visible position. (If you write on something in the room such as a white board, ask someone to copy all ideas for you to take with you. Writing down people's responses and taking them with you affirms that their ideas are important.) Repeat until all responses are recorded.

3. **Clarify any confusing entries.** Once the list is complete, make sure participants understand what each entry means. Combine any closely related issues.

This brief discussion step is purely for clarity. Do not let participants argue the merit of ideas at this point. Preventing partisan discussion can be tricky because your larger goal is to build good relations with the community. If you cut George Barton off when he's all set to orate about panhandlers driving away his customers, you may alienate him (and maybe others) if he feels you are using your power against him. Blame your response on the procedure. "I'm sorry, sir, but the procedure just allows us to give people time to make sure they understand the issues, and then we have to move on. Maybe we can talk together after the forum." This works especially well if the small group must join others at a specified time to share results. (And frequently, people in the group who have had to meet with Barton for years will silently offer profound thanks that you stopped another harangue.)

An equally tricky part of this step is to not comment on ideas yourself. If the first solution is to double the number of officers in District One, and you know this is impossible, don't argue. Put the idea on the list. If you start explaining why ideas won't work, or that the break-in at the copy shop wasn't really a problem because it was a fraternity prank, people will perceive that you don't want to hear from them and are just defending the police. Sometimes, of course, you must give information either because it is asked for directly or because false information is being presented, but be very careful about this. Don't embarrass any participant and don't divert the procedure. "Yes, Mrs. Gustafson, the kids who sprayed the school wall have been apprehended. However, the problem could occur again and is still worth our noting and keeping an eye on."

4. **Take a preliminary vote.** Use written ballots or take an oral vote of the participants' most important issues. Usually the top three to five are selected, but the number depends on the time you have for the NGT meeting. This voting is done on a weighted scale. Typically, first-place vote gets five points, second gets four, and third gets three.

   Written ballots allow group members to cast anonymous votes and are easier to handle. Your written ballot should have space for each answer, and might say:

   > Most pressing problem (5 points): ____________.
   > Second most pressing problem (4 points): __________.
   > Third most pressing problem (3 points): __________.

   If you take an oral vote, go down the list of recorded items. Record a five beside an item each time it receives a first-place vote, a four for each second-place vote, a three for each third-place vote. Items with the most points are considered most significant.

   One immediate benefit of this preliminary vote is that it quickly and openly establishes a sense of how strongly the group as a whole feels about an issue.

POCKET GUIDE

Nominal Group Technique

A systematic way to hear from each person in a group.

Preparation

1. Generate a triggering question about the issue to be discussed.
2. Train a facilitator and a recorder for each group.
3. Bring an easel and easel pads, pens, masking tape.
4. Divide up participants into groups of five to ten.

Application

1. Group members silently generate ideas in writing.
2. Record ideas in a round-robin style, taking one from everyone, then a second, and so on.
3. Clarify any confusing entries.
4. Take a preliminary vote to determine which ideas are most important.
5. Discuss the preliminary vote.
6. Take a final vote.
7. Have each group present top findings to the larger group.
8. Keep all records from the meeting.

5. **Discuss the preliminary vote.** Allow the participants to discuss the merits of the top few issues for a set time limit. Delbecq recommends limiting discussion to twenty minutes, finding that longer discussion seldom changes people's viewpoints.
6. **Take a final vote.** Use the same weighted scale process as the preliminary vote. Delbecq found that voting, followed by a brief discussion and then a second vote, often leads to strong consensus.

If you used the NGT procedure to identify problems, you can repeat the procedure to generate solutions for the problem or problems voted most significant.

NGT breakout group findings. When NGT groups are a part of a larger forum, the final step is to present each group's findings back to the larger meeting. A representative from each group presents the top three (or five or whatever number you select) findings to the larger forum. Gradually a picture emerges of the major issues the community faces.

Keep all the records from the meeting. This will give you a list of every issue the various groups found to be significant and the solutions they found to be useful.

Planning a Community Meeting

Advanced planning is essential for a successful community meeting. Planning helps ensure that the audience and the hosts have the same expectations. For example, if

ACTION CLIP

Nominal Group Technique Meetings

In the spring of 1993, sporting a new chief with a strong community-oriented philosophy, the Sacramento, California, Police Department hosted eleven public community forums to which all city residents were invited by neighborhood. The forums were designed to determine which law enforcement problems the public perceived as most crucial, to uncover any solutions they might suggest for these problems, and to provide input on Sacramento's law enforcement priorities to guide the department in developing a strategic plan for the next ten years. Police Chief Arturo Venegas, Jr. attended all forums along with a rotating assemblage of officers. Estimated attendance was fifteen hundred people. Venegas later described the meetings to the Sacramento City Council as "an excellent exercise in listening to the community."

Although some variation occurred because different area lieutenants ran each forum, the same general plan was followed in each forum. The location for most forums was the multipurpose room of a city high school or library. Meetings ran from 6:30 P.M. to about 9:30 P.M. As the beginning hour approached, police cars dominated the neighborhoods around these locations, becoming advertising vehicles for the forums. At the initial forums, local TV vans were visible as the news media converged on the event.

As community members arrived, they were asked to sign in according to police district—in essence, by neighborhood. For example, residents of the grid between 17th and 30th Streets, and N and X Streets were in one group. They were given agendas for the meeting, color-coded to designate their sector and room, and then invited to help themselves to cookies, punch, or coffee (a step designed to establish a social atmosphere), and to gather in a common area for a general meeting.

Opening events included a welcome from the area captain or lieutenant, a speech by the chief in which he introduced any city council members in attendance, and sometimes short speeches by these council members. Chief Venegas tended to speak for ten or fifteen minutes explaining the purpose of the forums and emphasizing the desire of the Sacramento Police Department to work for and with the community. The chief's style was very conversational, often including personal stories from his past experience that exemplified the power of individuals and the importance of community effort. He stressed the importance of the information from the forums for the department's future efforts. His personal attendance at all forums served as a symbol of SPD's commitment to the forums and of their importance.

The large meeting rooms were invariably lined with uniformed officers. The dark blue dress uniforms carried instant identification and authority, making officers very clearly identifiable. Officer turnout for the forums was generally very large even though attendance was voluntary. Often officers not on duty came to the forums, which Chief Venegas made a point of mentioning in his remarks.

After the general meeting, individuals assembled in rooms by district. Because no preregistration was required, group size varied widely, which was unfortunate. Smaller groups were most successful. Each group was led by an officer; a second officer wrote all ideas on large easel pads. Frequently a third officer was in each room to chat with community members.

The group used nominal group technique to address two questions: (1) What problems involving law enforcement do you have in your area? (2) What solutions do you see for these problems? Each individual wrote down at least three problems. These were recorded on the easel pads by going around the group three times. Any problems needing clarification were explained. At that point group members voted on which problems seemed most significant so that each group narrowed their range to three problems. Group members were then asked to generate solutions for the top three problems.

Group members returned to the full meeting, where a community representative from each group related the sector's three major problems and a sample of solutions, and Chief Venegas made concluding remarks. The lists of all problems and solutions were retained by SPD, converted to a typed format, and formed a base for the department's strategic plan.

These meetings succeeded for several reasons. First, top management attended, including the chief and city council members. Audience participation was equalized, so that all who attended were heard. Officers interacted informally and in pleasant circumstances with community members. And finally, the process was very results oriented, giving participants a sense of accomplishment.

you expect to explain community policing to an attentive audience, and the community expects you to listen while they voice neighborhood concerns, the meeting will be frustrating to all. You need to plan carefully what you want to happen at the meeting, and then advertise it clearly, so people know what to expect. (This section details how to plan a large, formal meeting. Some smaller community meetings, such as Neighborhood Watch, require far less preparation and are more casual and informal.) Your planning starts with a planning team.

Put Together a Planning Team

A **planning team** is essential for organizing a successful and effective community meeting. The team is made up of people who represent the various interests and audiences you want at the meeting, and it should make the kinds of decisions discussed in this chapter. The planning team should begin operating *at least six weeks in advance* of the scheduled community meeting.

One advantage of having a planning team made up of representatives from various clubs, religious groups, and civic organizations is that each person can bring in part of the audience. The more people who help you plan, the larger your audience is likely to be. On the other hand, a work group larger than seven people begins to lose efficiency. One way to handle this discrepancy is to have a nucleus of planners who do the bulk of the actual decision making, then a larger advisory group that meets once or twice to give input to this core group. The larger group should contain representatives of the community affected by the issue under discussion: residents, homeowners, business owners, school officials, church leaders, and ethnic groups. *Be sure to invite a representative from the officers who patrol the area.* They may have valuable information for you, and including them helps build bridges with them.

A second great advantage of a planning team is that committees growing out of the team can perform many of the meeting-planning tasks. Your role thus becomes an administrative one of supporting the committees and ensuring that they move with due speed.

Seek cosponsors. Consider seeking well-respected community organizations to officially cosponsor the event. The organizations' members will then be likely to attend, and as public opinion leaders they will encourage others to attend. This is especially useful if you are worried about low turnout or not attracting the speakers you want. The exact responsibilities of a cosponsor are negotiable. The cosponsors may simply lend their names to the event, they may advertise for you, or they may take a more active role, sending representatives to the planning team, helping to shape the program, and even underwriting any costs.

Set up a communication system. Once you have your planning team, set up a way for everyone to stay in touch. Distribute a list of planners' phone numbers, e-mail addresses, and any other contact numbers people want to give out. Schedule regular meetings for the planners to exchange ideas and information. Check in with your planning team regularly. Put a check mark by each name on the list to verify that you talked with everyone.

Decide the Meeting Purpose

The planning team's first task is to determine the purpose of the meeting. The idea of having a meeting came about for some reason; nobody just decides to have one to see what it's like. Whether you want to enlist residents' help in a campaign to take back the park, alert parents to the growing threats of teen drug use, or learn the community's priorities on where the police should focus limited financial resources, you need to be clear on what your purpose is.

A community meeting can have more than one purpose. For example, the primary purpose might be to get input from community members and a secondary purpose, to build relations with them. Or the primary purpose may be to alert community members to crime patterns in their area, which in turn may raise fear. The secondary purpose might then be to allay that fear and to provide suggestions for actions they can take.

Be very clear about the intended purposes of the meeting you are hosting because these affect the rest of your planning. If the planning team has a common sense of what you want to happen at your public meeting, you are more likely to put together a program that will make that happen.

Identify Your Target Audience

The meeting's purpose often implies your audience. However, careful thought may identify additional audience members. Typically the **target audience** are people affected by the issues to be discussed in the meeting. Sometimes you are not certain who the affected people are. Here is where the large advisory planning committee can come in useful, offering insight about parts of town or groups potentially affected by the issue under discussion.

Holland and Washington, for instance, know that one audience they want to target are people who live around M Street Park. Richards reminds them that increased park use might mean increased business for convenience stores in the area, and store owners would be interested in attending. Pet owners might be looking for a place to walk their dogs, runners would appreciate an open space to exercise, and environmental groups care about any stretch of green, even a small park. The officers add these to their list.

Once you have a sense of who you want to come, take some time to gather intelligence about your potential audience. Find out in advance what they most likely want to know, what issues they have, and who the major players are. Try to get an estimate of probable turnout. Use any information you get to plan a program that will provide needed information.

Select a Time, Date, and Location

The planning committee should determine the time and place for your meeting to generate the best attendance. Typically a community meeting will last no longer than two to two-and-a-half hours, including initial informal chatting. After that, participants get tired and attention wanes. If you need a longer meeting, tell people in advance how long the meeting will be, and schedule breaks during the meetings.

Select a date that does not conflict with other important events for your target audience. Watch for things that are important to a community but not always obvious outside the area, such as the high school homecoming, a parade, soccer league playoffs, grand openings, street fairs, even Monday night football. Find a time that fits your audience's needs. If you want to reach a family audience, remember kids' bedtimes. For the after-work crowd, think about how much time you have before they want to eat.

Choose a location where your audience will feel comfortable. A meeting held in a downtown hotel ballroom draws a very different audience than a meeting held in a neighborhood community center or in a park by the river. Be sure you have enough parking, and check for access for the disabled. Also bear in mind the format and any special events you have selected. Do you want breakout rooms where the larger audience will divide into small groups? Then you need space to do that. Do you want people to circulate and look at displays? That requires a very different space from a format where the audience sits in rows. Visit any locations you are considering to note what a phone call might not reveal. Such revelations can range from paper-thin walls, to faraway parking, to an air-conditioning system less effective than ice hung in front of a fan. After you check the location, reserve the date you want.

Create the Program and Enlist Presenters

Keep your purpose in mind clearly as your planning team makes decisions about what format you will use, whom you will invite to present information, any honored guests you would like to invite, and any special events that might enhance the meeting.

Select a format. Consider the meeting formats discussed earlier as you think about your purpose. Is this meeting purely to inform the community? Then you need an abundance of information, additional written handouts, and knowledgeable speakers. Or is your goal also persuasion, to mobilize the community around a common problem? You need testimony about the problem to arouse their concern. Or do you want to receive information, to learn the community's perceptions about issues or their ideas for solutions? Then consider a series of small meetings rather than a large one. Or perhaps the goal is building trust, getting teens in the local high school to feel more comfortable with officers. Then create a program that is informal, fun, and encourages input from student leaders. Select the appropriate format for your purpose.

Invite presenters. In addition to selecting a format, you will need someone to lead the meeting, officials to represent the department, and presenters to serve on a symposium, panel, or public interview or to facilitate the other formats. Consider the information you want to convey and which people might best answer the audience's questions. You may want representatives of city, county, state, federal, or private groups to be on the program or to attend the gathering. Depending on the meeting's purpose, you might want someone from code enforcement, the mayor's office, the office of immigration, the high school, the office of communicable diseases, an activist organization such as Mothers Against Drunk Driving, and so on. If you select a format that demands a moderator, you also need to select this person.

A community meeting also needs an official host—a master or mistress of ceremonies—to welcome the crowd, explain the evening's procedure, and introduce any special guests. Appoint someone to do this if you don't fill this role yourself.

Stay in touch with those on the program. Call them a couple of weeks before the meeting to see whether they need anything special for their presentations. What you are really saying is, "Hey, don't forget this," but it's more cordial to word it as an offer of help. Confirm with them again a day or two before the meeting. The hectic demands of police work can cause last-minute cancellations and changes.

Consider honorary guests. Decide whether you want department command staff or any city or county officials at the meeting as special guests. Consider people whose presence would enhance your credibility or the department's. Sometimes an appearance by the mayor and the chief signifies you are important enough to have contact with those at the top and in the know (even though they may, in fact, know less about the issues than you). Be careful about politicians; they tend to take over events. If you invite them to give a brief welcome that is not part of the official program, stress to them to keep the welcome short, about five minutes.

Decide on special events. Special events can enhance your meeting, either as a drawing card for attendance or by making your meeting more memorable. Some possible special events include antique police cars parked out front, someone in costume as Officer McGruff the Crime Dog, a talking car, SWAT equipment, police motorcycles, several computers set up to access the department's home page, Police Olympics winners chatting about competitions, a demonstration with the star of the canine unit, viewer-controlled public safety videos, or department public relations tapes. You can ask nearby schools to add to your special event: invite a local high school quartet to play as people arrive and sip coffee, or display the elementary school's artwork (which will draw their parents to your event). Whatever the special event might be, plan carefully. Visualize, for example, where the quartet will stand, how loud their music will be, in what patterns the guests will move around, whether they might spill coffee, trip over electric wires, drop napkins.

Publicize Your Meeting

To maximize the time and effort your planning committee has put into the community meeting, you want to make sure you have a strong turnout. Publicity, strategically placed and effectively written, is essential to getting the word out to your target audience. Be sure the audience knows what kind of meeting to expect. For example, "Come hear Chief Zettl explain the plans for controlling cruising on Jefferson Boulevard" signals a different meeting from "Come tell us the problems you've experienced because of the cruising on Jefferson Boulevard." Any fliers, press releases, or other advertising must be very clear so people come to the meeting prepared.

Advertising can be done in many ways. Keep your target audience in mind. Consider how they are most likely to receive information. Your planning committee might have insights about various channels to reach them. For example, if Washington decides Richards is right about the M Street Park audience, he might send fliers to area vets and pet stores to reach dog owners; to health clubs, shoe stores, and health food markets to reach runners; and he could ask environmental groups to put a note in their newsletters. Sometimes, if you have a long enough lead time, you can get local businesses or religious groups to fold announcements in with their mailings.

Media publicity. Your planning team will also seek media publicity. If your agency has a public information officer, ask for help. If not, follow the advice in Chapter 8. If your publicity efforts are successful, be prepared for some reporters to show up at the community meeting, possibly even a TV camera crew. Appoint someone to be available to the media during the meeting to answer questions.

Word of mouth, fliers, posters, and other ways to get the word out. One of the advantages of getting community groups involved in your planning is that they are stars in the word-of-mouth advertising network. They can personally contact leaders of civic organizations in your community. No flier posted on a bulletin board can equal a respected member of the community putting in a personal word. In addition, if you have time, get planning-team members to go to club meetings and announce your community meeting. Community members can also add announcements to church and club newsletters, post fliers in apartment laundry rooms, and even insert them in office mailboxes. Also ask officers speaking at other public events to drop in a reminder about your upcoming meeting. Posters are also useful. Libraries, coffee shops, schools, churches, bus stations, public markets, and various other public spots may welcome posters of a public event.

Sending out direct mail is a bit more expensive, but can be very valuable for reaching a particularly relevant audience. The most successful direct mail is postcards. If you don't have a list of the community "movers and shakers," begin to compile one. A phone call or a personal reminder is even better. The personal invitation, phone call or handwritten note is time consuming, but much more powerful than a mass-produced flier.

Another secret of having a large turnout is to involve many people in some element of the event, even if it is distributing literature or creating displays. The more people who participate in an event, the larger the attendance. For example, one charity fundraiser brings together local musical talent to stage Broadway musical scenes. Amid the songs and dance numbers by the best talent in the city are two numbers, one in each act, performed by over one hundred kids. The effort to costume and train them pays off in the audience members each child brings—mom, dad, maybe a stepparent or two, siblings, grandparents, aunts, uncles, neighbors. The show is a big success for the charity, and the kids have a great learning experience.

Plan the Logistical Details

Every meeting requires a host of logistical planning. Attention to detail is the difference between a polished final event and an ineffective, unsatisfying one. Smooth arrangements can play a central role in how those who attend feel about the meeting, sometimes carrying more weight than the issues themselves.

Amenities. Amenities include refreshments, child care, parking, handicapped access, foreign language or sign language interpreters, security, and anything else that might be necessary for someone in your target audience. Try to figure out what will make the meeting more successful. For example, refreshments set a friendly tone. Offering coffee, tea, and cookies is a small expense for a large reward. Community markets will often supply this free as a goodwill gesture or for advertising. Refreshments encourage people to mingle and chat casually rather than sit rigidly in rows of chairs waiting for the meeting to begin.

Staff. Arrange for volunteers (often planning-team members and community service officers) to handle such tasks as serving refreshments, reserving and delivering equipment (microphones, overhead projectors, etc.), setting up, cleaning up, and so forth.

Registration. Set up a table with name tags, pens, and a sign-in list with space for name, address, phone number, and e-mail address. Consider getting NCR (no carbon required) forms from a local stationery supply house. These make multiple copies at once, allowing community officers to leave with a copy of the list and the department to keep a master list for future events.

Large, visible signs. The day of the meeting, post large signs outside the building to signal to people they are in the right place. Put up directional signs in the parking lot and on the front door if your meeting room is not immediately in sight.

Display table. Set up a table to display free handouts. People feel they have gotten something out of a meeting when they take away something tangible, even if it's just a brochure or some other kind of handout literature. Departments always have crime prevention information and junior badges. Bring plenty of these. Consider bringing magnets with the department's nonemergency numbers, police trading cards, pencils printed with the department's motto, stickers, buttons, bumper stickers, and bags of goodies donated by a local bakery. You might want to invite neighborhood newspapers to give away recent issues; such papers are often looking for ways to expand circulation, and this builds good relations with them. Perhaps you can create something for the event. These giveaways are as limitless as your imagination.

Emergency kit. Create an emergency kit that contains extra bulbs for projectors, extension cords, three-pronged plug adapters, batteries, pens, masking tape, duct tape, white board markers, chalk, safety pins, scissors, felt pens, blank transparencies, and any other item you might need. (Chocolate is good.)

Conducting the Meeting

All your planning culminates in one short evening. Take advantage of every minute of it. Arrive at least one hour early to make sure everything is set up. Be the amiable host when the audience begins to arrive. Ensure that other officers interact and chat informally with audience members. This helps set a tone of collaboration and may also provide informally gathered information. The audience should feel welcome and comfortable when the meeting begins.

The Master or Mistress of Ceremonies

The tone and enthusiasm of the master or mistress of ceremonies (M.C.) who leads the meeting really sets the mood for the event. Make sure this person has a warm personality and can handle with ease and humor any situation that might arise. You want someone in this role who makes the audience feel welcome and who can build a spirit of community.

The M.C. is also very important to the actual running of the meeting. He or she must set a convivial tone, introduce guests, explain procedures to be followed, and keep things on time and on track. The M.C. begins the community meeting and signals the official start of the event. If you are M.C.:

Planning Chart for a Community Meeting

Planning Team

Team members selected and organized?
Cosponsors invited and organized?
Communication system established?
Regular meetings scheduled?
Committees appointed?

Decisions

Meeting purpose determined?
Target audience identified?
Date and time chosen?
Location checked and reserved?

Program

Format selected?
Presenters invited?
M.C. invited?
Breakout group leaders trained (if needed)?
Special arrangements made as needed?
Honorary guests invited?
Special events organized?

Publicity

Fliers?
Press releases?
Posters?
Other promotion?

Event

Staff selected?
Refreshments planned?
Other amenities addressed?
Registration procedures set up?
Signs made; plans for posting arranged?
Displays arranged?
Emergency kit ready?
Feedback forms ready?
Officers who will attend asked to mingle?

1. **Welcome the group.** Greet everyone warmly and thank them for coming out.
2. **Introduce yourself.** State your name and mention the work you do, stressing your connection to this neighborhood or group. Never assume that everyone knows who you are.

3. **Warm up the audience.** This should be short, but it is a valuable use of time. An "all-business" attitude can be formidable to community members unaccustomed to public meetings. Take time to joke a little or speak of a local team victory or some other common interest. Basically, you want to warm up the audience for the rest of the meeting.
4. **Thank your cosponsors.** Briefly name and thank any cosponsors. Acknowledging someone's support is vital to receiving that support again.
5. **Provide an overview.** Explain in general terms the agenda, format, timeline, and ground rules. For instance, if you are using a public interview format and want questions submitted in writing, explain how to submit questions. If the audience will hear a speech and then break into groups, give time estimates for each segment.
6. **Introduce any honored guests.** If you have any well-known or highly ranked people in the audience, such as local legislators, introduce them by their names and exact titles. Be sure you pronounce their names clearly and correctly. If they are just going to stand and wave, you can introduce them before the overview. If they are going to talk, even briefly, it's good to give the overview first. This establishes the context of the meeting and helps prevent guests from leading the meeting astray.
7. **Explain necessary information.** Let the audience know about any amenities or other details, such as the restroom locations or that it is okay to get up and get more coffee during the meeting.
8. **Introduce all the presenters.** State each presenter's name and title, and give a brief explanation of why he or she was selected to speak. (See Chapter 4 for how to introduce a speaker.) Your goal is to establish the speakers' credibility and to arouse the audience's interest in the topic. Once the specific format begins, the M.C.'s duties vary, depending on the meeting format.
9. **Facilitate the forum.** Turn the meeting over to the presenters. If the M.C. is also the moderator, he or she must fulfill the duties of the chosen format.
10. **Facilitate the question-and-answer period.** After the formal presentation, the M.C. (or in some cases the panel moderator) recognizes audience members who have questions and comments. Generally the M.C. simply calls on questioners and keeps the procedure on track. The speaker, panel members, or agency representatives answer the questions. Emphasize from the outset that questions should be short so all get to participate, and interrupt long questions with that reminder. (See below for what to do when a meeting turns ugly.) Almost every meeting has its share of "questions" that are really speeches, people with issues unrelated to the meeting, and future political hopefuls with a need to impress others. It is the M.C.'s task to stop them without stifling other people. Cogan says that a good M.C. will "maintain a healthy balance between friendliness and firmness" (14).

11. **Close the meeting.** The M.C.'s final job is to end the meeting on a high note. *Don't let the meeting just fade out*. This is the final memory the audience takes with them. Depending on format, you may want to include some highlights of the final group reports. Plan a closing statement that makes the audience feel their participation is meaningful and they are contributing to a safer community.

    Practice your closing out loud. Don't wait for last-minute inspiration and then fall back on some lame "Well, I guess we're done. Thanks for coming" (unless the city's giving out a dull award and you want to be a contender). Instead talk about the importance of community meetings in general and the accomplishments of this one in particular. Some common sentence starters include:

    "Tonight we've taken the first step toward. . ."
    "This has been a very productive exchange. Working together we can. . ."
    "We all want to make our neighborhood safer. With a common effort we. . ."
    "I have a vision of what our community will look like with all of us working together. It can. . ."

    Fill in the blanks with your vision of what can be. End with conviction and enthusiasm that will carry people forward to continue the work after the meeting.

The M.C. is a visible symbol of the meeting. Your role is significant in affecting the mood of the audience. Prepare carefully, adapt to your audience, and leave them with hope for the future of their community.

Provide Feedback Forms

If you or the department plan to hold many community meetings, audience feedback about the format, timing, and staging of the event can help make future meetings even more successful. An evaluation form will help you get such feedback. The form must be quick to fill in, allowing audience members to circle or dot in choices, but also be sure to include an open-ended question for comments. Hand out evaluation forms at the end of the meeting and ask participants to drop them into a waiting box.

After the Meeting

At the conclusion of your meeting you have a network of contacts, including those who planned, spoke, volunteered, and attended the meeting. You must send a thank-you to all the planning-team members, presenters, and anyone else who helped stage the meeting.

A nice gesture is to send a letter to everyone who attended thanking them for their community interest. You need to assure those who attended that their input was valuable. If your meeting was a problem-solving one that generated useful suggestions, send a letter detailing follow-up plans within twenty-four hours. Everyone has received form letters they don't believe, so be careful to include specifics in your letters showing that audience ideas will lead to future action. In a month or so, send a second letter updating them on the progress.

Arrange a Final Planning-Team Meeting

Hold a final meeting of the planning team soon after the community meeting is over. First of all, you want to acknowledge and thank everyone who helped out. Ask for their thoughts about the meeting itself and the planning. Make notes of their suggestions for your next community meeting.

The Hostile Audience

A **hostile audience** is one of the most feared aspects of community policing. No one, not even a professional speaker, enjoys working with a hostile group. The hostile audience ranges from people who are disappointed, disagreeable, and silent to those shouting their anger, who are highly emotional and potentially out of control. Hostile audiences tend to speak in loud voices, interrupt you and one another, and not really hear what is said to them.

Prepare for the hostile audience so you can handle the situation comfortably. As an officer, you train for the negative in the physical aspects of your job. You learn arrest control techniques in the hopes of avoiding injury to yourself and suspects. You go through disaster drills so you are prepared to respond to any crisis, whether a natural disaster such as flood or earthquake, an accident, such as train derailment, downed aircraft, or chemical spill, or civil disobedience such as a riot. *The negative should never be a complete surprise in policing. This includes public meetings.*

Understand the Anger

To prepare for the hostile individual or group, first explore the possible causes for their anger. Most community policing assignments are in areas where police intervention has been necessary for some time. In such neighborhoods police are stereotyped as the enemy. The community members in these areas may have a "we've had enough" attitude. Their frustration with ongoing problems, whether traffic, drug dealing, or property crimes, can lead to anger that is often taken out on the representative assigned to help in the problem-solving process. In most situations this will be you—the community officer.

A second general cause of frustration and anger in the community is the perceived bureaucratic process. Many members of a community are not only fed up with their problems but disillusioned and angry with the slow response from government. They cannot easily see a way to affect the process other than through negative actions and even violence. As the person out front, you can become the focus of their anger.

Sometimes the anger is caused by a specific event. For example, someone has been shot and the audience's anger comes out at the police. The audience is angry because they are frightened. You can't eliminate that fear or the anger it generates, even though you may feel the brunt of it at the time.

> "Another outburst like that and I'm gonna handcuff your lips together."
>
> —Sgt. Wojohowicz, *Barney Miller*

Remember, however, that anger is not entirely bad. As organizational consultant Gordon Shea points out in *Managing a Difficult or Hostile Audience*, "A hostile audience is an interested audience. . . . When people are upset with you or with your position on an issue, you may not like what you are hearing, but at least those people are involved. Signs of resentment or anger show that there is energy, and if you help redirect that energy to positive ends, a net gain may result from your meeting" (92). Such a net gain is your goal in a hostile meeting. To achieve it, you need to plan your strategy.

Plan Your Strategy

Planning ahead can help you deal with anticipated hostile crowds. Adopt a friendly style, prepare the right information to address concerns, and if you anticipate an "audience versus police" encounter, invite an outside moderator to preside.

Build bridges at the start of the meeting. The first step is an easy one: be friendly as people arrive at your meeting. Greet them, shake hands, smile, mingle. The socializing that goes on at the beginning of a community meeting has a purpose: such personal contact can build rapport. Shea says that your goal at this time is to "establish the highest level of good will and trust possible before the meeting starts" and adds, "The payoffs in lessened tension and hostility (toward you, not necessarily toward the issue) can be substantial" (86). An added benefit is that mingling and listening can give you a sense of the audience mood that might help you during the meeting.

> "People who want to affect a hostile audience regard this time [before the meeting begins] as found money and use it to build bridges between themselves and their protagonists."
>
> —Gordon Shea (87)

Come armed with the right information. One way to defuse potential crises is to have facts on hand to counter those community members who are negative about police work. For example, a neighborhood that believes it is not getting adequate police attention could benefit from hearing exactly how many officers are on each shift, where these are deployed, and the comparable crime rates for each district. You might want to have crime statistics for residential areas, copies of departmental reports on the issue under discussion,

ACTION CLIP

A Hostile Crowd

A public housing residents council in Sacramento called an emergency meeting to discuss the neighborhood police officers' harassment of the local kids. Officers Greg Dieckmann and Harold Bickel went to work to find the reason for the meeting. By asking around they learned that the community was angry about what was perceived as random and unwarranted searches of kids in the community. The officers prepared their response.

1. They agreed to let the community members express their anger.
2. Officer Dieckmann would explain the legal requirements associated with stop-and-frisk-type searches.
3. Officer Bickel and an audience member would become role players to simulate a stop-and-frisk search.

The community vented for almost an hour, as years of frustration came to the surface. Then a very vocal community member was selected to play the part of the police officer during the role-play demonstration. The police dispatch call was of a man with a gun described as a "male, white, brown jacket with a gun." Officer Bickel matched this vague description. The community member talked to Bickel and did a brief pat-down search, finding nothing. Dieckmann then explained how the police handle calls like this. As he talked, Bickel removed a small pistol from his boot. A hush fell over the crowd as Bickel pulled a larger pistol from the rear waistband of his pants. Then Bickel reached over his head and behind his back, very slowly removing a cut-down, sawed-off shotgun that had been concealed inside his jacket. A voice from the back of the room broke the silence. "Officer Bickel, we get the point. You can search my kids anytime."

Officers Dieckmann and Bickel prepared for their talk by assessing their audience. They then developed a plan that they felt was appropriate for the community in which they worked. During the meeting they were the target of a tremendous amount of anger. They knew this going in and promised each other that they would remain calm and would demonstrate, both verbally and nonverbally, their understanding and concern for the community.

and visual aids such as pie charts and crime maps that support your agency's position on issues.

Lt. Joel Batesta had met with the Lake Park Community Association on many occasions. The topic of the meetings varied each time. The official agenda for tonight's meeting was to discuss problems with teens cruising on Jefferson Blvd. But this time he knew that there might be an off-agenda item that would dominate the conversation. Lt. Batesta had been in contact with community leaders. They were very concerned about the random shooting of a retired couple while they were walking their dog. The shooting appeared to be unprovoked, and police were denounced for not being there to prevent it.

Sensing trouble, Batesta went to work getting ready for the meeting. He prepared a set of responses to anticipated questions, invited experts to address the specifics of the shooting, and alerted community and civic leaders. And when the questions came rolling in like a tidal wave, he was comprehensive and professional in his responses. The meeting was a success because he had anticipated issues and brought needed data.

Invite a neutral party to host the meeting. When you know a meeting is about a highly controversial issue, invite a neutral party to chair the meeting. The police department should not be in the moderator's role. Select a person who is credible to both your agency and the community to moderate the discussion. This could be a religious leader, a newsperson, a legal figure, or a community leader. The moderator will function almost as a referee. Such a meeting occurred in Ann Arbor, Michigan, when the investigation following a series of rapes stirred up anger. The community was particularly angered when blood samples were taken from about 160 African-American men. After the rapist's trial ended, the police called a town-hall meeting. Police believed much of the anger stemmed from misinformation. Because the meeting potentially would pit police against residents, they invited a criminal justice professor from another city to moderate. This format allowed the community to discuss issues central to all those involved, with someone everyone perceived as objective to control both community and police speakers.

Plan Your Communication Approach

Whether you are the leader or a speaker at a hostile meeting, your interpersonal skills are vital. You must demonstrate understanding and concern through both your verbal and your nonverbal messages. People are more likely to listen to you when you can show you understand their viewpoint. Certain communication techniques can help.

1. **Remain calm and treat audience members with respect.** Cogan says of responding to a hostile audience: "When they shout, be reasonable. When they talk rapidly, speak slowly and deliberately" (102).
2. **Allow people to vent; acknowledge their feelings.** Shea points out, "Sometimes people just have to be heard. Once they have expressed an emotion or a problem and it is recognized by another person, they no longer feel alone" (116). Make notes capturing the essence of each comment to see if a pattern exists.
3. **Demonstrate empathy and understanding.** Paraphrase what they have said and how they seem to feel about it to show you've heard the message. Try to put yourself in the audience's shoes, with the caution that you can never fully understand someone else's life. False empathy can be spotted a mile away and will destroy your credibility. When appropriate, confirm that their emotions are right: "You are wise to be upset. We're upset too. Together we can do something about this problem."

4. **Don't overcontrol the meeting.** You may overcontrol without being aware of it. Some common ways leaders overcontrol are by cutting people off before they get to express their point or ask their question, getting in the last word, or selecting people to speak who will support the leader's point of view rather than calling on a cross section of the audience.
5. **Respond to the whole audience, not just the hostile questioner.** Look at the whole audience as you respond to a hostile question. Turn to them, even walk toward another section of the room casually, making eye contact with various people in the group as though you are having a personal conversation with each of them. As you end the answer to your question, make eye contact with someone other than the hostile questioner and recognize that person's question (Stein).
6. **Rephrase a hostile question in neutral terms to focus audience attention on issues, not argumentative phrases.** You can do this in the process of restating the question to make sure the whole group has heard it. "When are police going to pay attention to safety in our part of town instead of just where the rich people live?" becomes "The question concerns distribution of police resources in this part of town." Look for specifics. If an audience member charges, "It always takes you too long to get to our area when we call," ask for specifics: "Tell me about the incident when this occurred." Answer based on the facts of the case at the time.
7. **Educate the community.** An informed group makes better decisions. Use this time to give the audience information about how police do business. If legal restrictions prohibit some responses, explain that. This means being well prepared. Very calmly present all the facts you can about the situation. Facts show that you are not covering up.
8. **Use problem solving.** Try to turn the meeting into a results-driven process. "Your ideas are essential to finding the best solutions we can to this problem." Then either seek a solution or seek a second community meeting set up in a problem–solution format. By focusing the audience energy on solving the problem, you have taken anger and made it constructive.
9. **Admit when you are wrong.** Sometimes you need to say, "This was a mistake, and we want to change it. What suggestions can we generate to improve the situation so this won't happen again?" This response may not be comfortable, but it can be very effective when it is true.
10. **Remember which communication behaviors tend to generate defensive responses.** You may face a deluge of such behaviors, and automatically become defensive. (Refer to Chapter 2.) You may find yourself growing defensive when audience remarks *evaluate* you or your agency negatively, try to *control* your behavior, when audience members speak as though they are *superior*, when they are *certain* of their position (or certain yours is wrong), when you

feel they are simply *strategically* manipulating you or the rest of the audience, or when they are unconcerned or *neutral* about your feelings or ideas. Forewarned is forearmed. When you realize you are responding to the *way* things are said rather than to legitimate issues, curtail your own defensive reactions.

In your responses, use supportive techniques. Show *empathy*, paraphrase *descriptively*, treat audience members as *equals*, make *provisional* statements, and maintain a *problem orientation*.

> A soft answer turneth away wrath.
>
> —PROVERBS 15:1
>
> A kiss on the nose does much toward turning aside anger.
>
> —SNOOPY

11. **Make allies out of enemies.** Often the people most passionate about an issue are the same people who are willing to help resolve the problem. Recruit these people to assist in the problem-solving process. You may want to meet with them individually after the meeting or invite them to participate in a problem-solving committee.

Above all, when you face hostile comments, remember that the hostility is about a situation, directed at the meeting's host or at someone in a uniform. *Don't take it personally.*

Problem Personalities

Some types of negative responses are so predictable you can prepare in advance to deal with them. Such predictability does not mean the individuals do not have serious concerns; it simply means people have limited styles for dealing with stress. Knowing the common types can help you prepare. Figure 5-2 describes such recurring responses.

Community meetings are central to successful community policing projects. They allow officers and community members to meet in a problem-solving setting, they encourage information exchange, and they invite neighborhoods to unify. Despite the demands associated with staging a community meeting, the rewards make the time and effort well worthwhile.

Personality	Strategy
Cynics	Cynics doubt that anything will come of the community's efforts. Acknowledge the cynic's doubt, but add that this situation is different. Point out steps already underway—someone keeping records, plans for a follow-up meeting, public action scheduled, and so on.
Dominators	Dominators simply talk too much and for too long. Several techniques can help deal with them: ▪ Call attention to the number of items on the agenda or the number of others who might want to speak. ▪ If you can anticipate who the dominator will be, throw the person off-balance by asking him or her to speak first. After that, ask others to respond or offer comments, effectively cutting off the dominator. ▪ Elaine Cogan advises moving physically closer to the dominator. Wait for the speaker to take a breath, and say, "Thank you"—nothing more. Then redirect the discussion to someone else. ▪ If your dominator is the mayor or another VIP, remind him or her tactfully before the meeting that your purpose is to hear from the crowd.
Attackers	Attackers may strike against ideas or against you and others who plan the meeting. Attackers usually talk loudly and rapidly. Don't answer using their hostile tone and accusatory language. Slow down the momentum and answer in a modulated tone. Then use some of the same techniques you use on the dominator to get the attacker out of the speaker's spot.
Stage hogs	These people have a hidden agenda: to be in the community spotlight. Reduce that spotlight as much as possible. Don't return arguments that give them an excuse to respond. Thank them for their comments, then ask for concerns from other people. If one or two people cause an ongoing problem, change your meetings. Meet with subgroups of the larger group. A smaller group automatically operates with a more conversational norm, which cuts down on the stage hog's dramatic orations. In addition, individuals in the smaller audience will very likely be more active than they might be as audience members.

Figure 5-2: Strategies for dealing with problem personalities

Ice Breakers for Community Meetings

Start with a Laugh

Supplies: None

Purpose: Reduces audience tension.

Procedure: Say to the group: "We are going to take a brief survey to assess the type of audience we have here today. This quiz is based on your individual preference for one of four symbols." Draw a circle, triangle, "z," and square, naming each as you draw it. Then say, "These symbols represent basic differences in personality traits. Which one appeals to you the most?" Allow a moment or two for thought, then ask: "How many thought the square best represented you?" Write the number down, then inform the group the square represents intelligence. Proceed with the triangle, stating that it represents leadership; then the "z," which represents creativity. Finally ask how many preferred the circle. Inform the group that the circle represents sex and booze. Follow with some well-chosen comments about what this reveals!

Informal Hello

Supplies: None

Purpose: Relaxes the audience so they interact more easily.

Procedure: Ask people in an audience to turn to the people on either side of them and say hello to get acquainted. Generally people feel comfortable doing this and realize it is appropriate for a community meeting. It can get the audience relaxed and set them up to interact more comfortably.

If your meeting group is smaller than about twenty, ask them to introduce themselves and share one nonthreatening item that tells a little about them. Vary the topic if you meet with the same people regularly. Add elements such as:

- What I like to do in my free time.
- My favorite childhood movie and why.
- My dream vacation.
- If I won the lottery.

Just Like Me

Supplies: None

Purpose: Energizes the group at the beginning of a session or after a break.

Procedure: Explain to the audience that this ice breaker allows people to have fun to relax the meeting. Sometimes a group of adults needs an explanation to motivate them to act silly. Then begin. As leader, you make a statement. The audience members to whom this applies stand, raise their arms in the air, and shout, "Just like me." Plan in advance to have some confederates in the audience willing to participate energetically. After you get going, you can point to various audience members and ask them to make a statement.

Here are some generic examples. Stronger ones are tailored to your own situation.

- I was born in this state.
- I'm a (local sports team) fan.
- I love horses (or motorcycles).
- I've been to Hawaii.
- I can name the seven dwarfs.
- I've been white-water rafting.
- I love giving public speeches. (Expect laughter from this one rather than response.)

Corners

Supplies: Tape, pieces of poster board in sets of four

Purpose: Physically moves people around and lets them congregate with others who share their concerns or interests.

Procedure: List one of four conflicting choices on each poster board in a set. Post one in each corner of the room. When you indicate it is time to do so, each participant moves to the corner of his or her choice. He or she must talk with another participant and share the reason for selecting that corner. The group reconvenes in the center of the room as you post a new set of signs. Participants again move to a corner based on the new options and talk to another participant. Repeat the process for each set of posters.

This activity can be done with fun choices where the purpose is simply to have fun. Or you can use it to introduce people for more serious purposes. Often a neighborhood is made up of small areas. The neighbors may have common concerns and come from what can be called the same neighborhood, yet not know one another. The Corners activity lets them chat informally. The four corners can represent different blocks or subareas of the neighborhood. Or the four corners can represent issues to discuss and people can congregate by the issues of greatest concern for them. After people have introduced themselves to one another, each group can discuss some small issue relevant to the main subject of the evening. A spokesperson can share the group's perspective.

The Easy Sign-In

Supplies: Pens, name tags, a pre-composed sign

Purpose: Gets people circulating and involved with the issue to be discussed.

Procedure: Tack up a large sign people will see as they enter, which directs them to interact. You might write, for example, "Yes! This is the right place! Help yourself to tea or coffee. Get a name tag. Then please find two or three people you don't know and share with them what you hope to accomplish here." If you have people do this, be sure you ask in the general meeting for a sampling of these responses to bring the activity back into the sequence of the evening. People won't always comply, so you need to have some confederates who will start the interaction. Others will then go along.

Name tags can be much bigger than the standard size and can say more than names. Members can include home area, special interests, hobbies, or favorite TV show. These serve as conversation starters for casual interaction.

A variation of this ice breaker uses arrival time to congregate people in one area. Put a large poster board on the wall. As participants arrive, ask them to sign the board with their names, neighborhood area, and any pertinent information, such as group membership if they represent groups, areas of concern, or other items you might want to know about. Although each person signs in alone, the sign visually represents the group immediately and people assemble in the same area, which leads to interaction.

Works Cited

Bongle, Bill. Web page, Michigan State University Center for Criminal Justice. http://www.ssc.msu.edu/~cj/cp/cptoc.html. 22 Oct. 1997.

Brinkworth, Bill. "Rural Justice: The Challenge of Policing an Agricultural Community." *Sheriff Times*. Winter 1998. www.communitypolicing.org/shtimes. 14 Mar. 1998.

Chicago Police Dept. http://www.ci.chi.il.us/CommunityPolicing/Beat Meetings/Tips/. 22 Oct. 1997.

Community News Project. www.mcs.net/~commnews/dnchome.htm. 19 Oct. 1997.

Cogan, Elaine. *Successful Public Meetings*. San Francisco: Jossey-Bass, 1992.

Cohen, Marjorie. "Resolution Is the Solution." *Community Policing Exchange* Jan./Feb. 1998: 8.

Delbecq, Andre L., and Andrew H. Van de Ven. "A Group Process Model for Problem Identification and Program Planning." *Journal of Applied Behavioral Science* 7 (1971): 466–92.

Delbecq, Andre L., Andrew H. Van de Ven, and David H. Gustafson. *Group Techniques for Program Planning: A Guide to Nominal Group and Delphi Processes*. Glenview, Ill.: Scott, Foresman, 1975.

Dewey, John. *How We Think*. Boston: D.C. Heath, 1910.

Shea, Gordon. *Managing a Difficult or Hostile Audience*. Englewood Cliffs, N.J.: Prentice Hall, 1984.

Silvey, Len. "Leading Useful Meetings." *Applied Organizational Communication*. 2nd. ed. Eds. Michael Dues and Michael Burgoon. New York: Primis-McGraw-Hill, 1998.

Stein, Debra. *Making Community Meetings Work*. Washington, D.C.: Urban Land Institute, 1996.

Stephan, Jacqueline. "Prevention Program Makes Youths Integral Contributors to Their Community." *Community Policing Exchange* Jan./Feb. 1998: 4.

Van Gundy, Arthur B. *Techniques of Structured Problem Solving*. 2nd ed. New York: Van Nostrand Reinhold, 1988.

Activities

1 Role Reversal I

Place yourself in the shoes of community members you will encounter at your community meeting. Consider your own neighborhood. Identify five areas of concern to you, *as a community member*. Visualize the conference procedure you are planning and see how it addresses your concerns in each of these areas. What information do you need that the format does not provide? What feelings do you have that the meeting ignores?

Now select one problem and think of a solution you would like to advance for this problem. Imagine a problem-solving format and envision how you would be able to suggest your solution in that format.

An even stronger option is to have a mock run-through with others while you role-play the community member. Either imagining or doing a practice run helps you better understand the community members' position.

Consider this variation for when you are actually holding a community meeting: Prior to the meeting, do the previous exercise on problems in the community you serve. Imagine yourself a resident of that area. Again identify five areas of concern and solutions for each. Then conduct your community meeting. Compare your understanding of the problem and solutions to those of the community.

2 Role Reversal II

Attend a community meeting on something that interests you. For example, if you are a parent, go to PTA open house. Or look in the paper for announcements of any upcoming meeting. After the meeting is over, analyze how you feel. Were you welcomed when you came in? Did you sit with other parents and listen to the principal talk or did you participate? How excited were you? What added to that excitement or took away from it? Even if you are not interested in the subject, you will learn by being an audience member. Note how well you can see and hear, how much interaction occurs, when your mind begins to drift. Experiencing a meeting from the audience's perspective can help you plan your own meeting to avoid negative experiences.

3 Analyzing Models

Record public discussions shown on PBS or cable showings of your local Board of Supervisors or City Council. Analyze these in terms of the strengths and weaknesses of the formats used in the public meetings you record. Also note the style of the leaders of these meetings.

4 NGT Rehearsal

Supplies: easel pads, pens, paper, masking tape

NGT is a complicated process. Having a run-through improves the final implementation. Lead a group of volunteers through an NGT session on *one* of these topics:

- What are the top three problems law enforcement personnel face in maintaining current training?
- What three steps should our agency take to improve media coverage of community policing activities?
- How can we begin in our effort to rebuild neighborhood spirit?
- What approach can we take in the early grades to prevent drug addiction later?

5 A Soft Answer

Role-playing helps hone communication skills. In stressful situations, such as hostile meetings, you need to respond quickly and appropriately. You increase your chances of doing that if the appropriate response is automatic. Role-play calm responses to make them habitual.

Focus on an issue in your district, home neighborhood, or educational environment. Ask your partner to take the role of the cynic. After your partner speaks, respond in a way that would soothe the cynic's doubts. Then ask your partner to assume the role of an attacker. Again, respond appropriately, remaining calm and professional. Move on to the roles of dominator and stage hog.

Chapter Six

Beyond SARA

Creative Problem-Solving Techniques That Work

"There is no success without risk."

ARTURO VENEGAS
CHIEF OF POLICE,
SACRAMENTO

In a daze, Randy Washington stares out the window of the neighborhood apartment the officers use as an office. Diedra Holland seems obsessed with checking the pencils in the Officer McGruff mug to see if they are sharp. Alan Richards reaches for an apple from the table and tosses it from palm to palm. "We have to do something," he says.

"That's a good idea," snaps Holland. "Why don't we do that."

Richards glares. "If you have a better idea, let's hear it."

"Don't fight," sighs Washington, turning back to the room. "That's what our whole problem is—fighting. Stupid, snot-nosed little teeny-boppers who ought to be in school getting into fights."

"School's out when most of the fights break out," remarks Alan Richards, crunching into his apple.

"It's the media coverage that's getting to O'Malley." Washington shakes his head. "If those damn media clowns didn't sit right on our tail these would just be a few more neighborhood fights."

*"But that's the point—*more *fights," Holland argues. "Another and another and another, day after day. It's no wonder the captain wants us to do something proactive to stop the fights from breaking out again. We need a creative idea." She frowns at Richards. "What are you doing with that apple?"*

Richards looks up. "I'm eating it."

"That's not how you eat an apple. You don't take little bites all the way around until you divide the apple in half like that." She glances at Washington for confirmation.

"She's right," he nods. "You hold it at the base and start eating at the stem. Eat in a circle until you get down to the bottom."

Holland's mouth drops open. "No, you don't! I can't believe I'm teamed up with people who don't know how to eat apples! You put your thumb in the stem hole and your middle finger in the bottom hole and eat across!"

They stare at each other until finally Richards shrugs, "Well, at least we're not in an apple-eating rut. I wish we could be as creative about stopping after-school fights."

THIS TEAM IS NOT ALONE IN THEIR NEED for a creative solution. "Creativity and originality are essential in building a successful community policing effort against drugs," declares David Carter of Michigan State University's School of Criminal Justice. That mandate extends well beyond the drug issue. Creativity is one of the hallmarks of any community policing effort. COP literature abounds with examples of the need for creative solutions. Fortunately, the literature also details some creative responses. For example:

- In Eugene, Oregon, a bunch of "counterculture" young people camped out daily on a vacant lot in a business district. The plot of dirt they occupied was owned by the city; once it had been filled with greenery. Their "sit-in" was not illegal, was not in fact even a political statement, but it was very disruptive to area businesses and to their customers who complained of the panhandling. The community officer gathered affected business leaders and city representatives in a meeting. The group hit upon a creative strategy: they spread the land with chicken manure and heavy fertilizer. The "squatters" problem disappeared instantly (and in a short time, so did the aroma) (Saxon).
- The Hispanic Youth Leadership project in southern Minnesota sought "ways to creatively broadcast alcohol and drug prevention messages to the young public." They sponsored Clearing the Air, a program for seventh to twelfth graders to work with media professionals making alcohol and drug prevention messages. Billboards they created were placed prominently in nine counties for a month. A youth focus group rated a radio message created by this program as their favorite. Not only did the team come up with ads that knew how to reach other kids, but they also had the unexpected benefit of a positive effect on the media professionals, which increased their coverage of alcohol-related crimes and accidents. (Ganey)
- The DARE 911 Band is an antidrug rock-and-roll band composed of officers from the Lexington Police Department, the University of Kentucky Police, and the Blackburn Correctional Institution. Since 1993, uniformed officers have performed throughout central and eastern Kentucky for thousands of school-age children. Their unique rock-and-roll message about the negative impact of drugs and violence in the lives of children has been cause for hundreds of letters of praise and appreciation from students and teachers. In May 1995 the DARE 911 Police Band was awarded the Law Day Award for dedicated service (Police Activities League).
- Many communities have a gun buy-back program. In Boston, a youth group working with the organization Hands Without Guns started a *toy gun* buy-back because they were concerned about their siblings being exposed to the gun culture (Horwitz).

These situations had one thing in common: creative solutions.

Creativity

Creativity is not some mysterious talent that blesses only the artistic. Creativity is simply a mental process through which the mind generates ideas. We are all creative every day in small ways we don't even register as creativity—wearing a new combination of clothes, taking a new route to work, inventing that new lunch of teriyaki chicken and pancakes. Sometimes the creativity is more significant—working out a new process for dealing with a work issue or resolving a conflict in a ways others didn't think of. Yet too often people perceive of themselves as noncreative simply because they don't recognize their own day-to-day abilities.

The Creative Process

Back in 1926, psychologist Graham Wallas described the four stages of creative thought:

1. **Preparation.** This first stage is gathering information. You research to find out everything you can about your problem—what difficulties you face, possible causes of the problem, its consequences, and solutions attempted both in your community and in other communities with similar issues.
2. **Incubation.** The second stage is the classic "sleep on it" phenomenon, in which you get away from the problem and let your unconscious mind work on it awhile. In *How to Be More Creative*, David Edwards describes incubation this way:

   > Once you've completely saturated yourself with a problem and have reached an impasse, drop it altogether. Go for a walk, go fishing, go to a movie, forget it. What you're doing, of course, is putting your subconscious mind to work on the problem. There is truth to the cliché "let me sleep on it." The time your subconscious needs to deliver a solution may vary from an hour to weeks. The danger lies in relying too heavily upon this type of inspired solution and skipping all the heavy mental work beforehand. Inspiration favors the prepared mind. (94)

   As hard as this "do-nothing" activity is to justify in a work-oriented culture, researchers increasingly find that engaging in other activities, especially playful ones, can help release good ideas in your mind.
3. **Illumination.** At some point, typically when you are very relaxed or engaged in an entirely different task, you enter the third stage, illumination. You experience an insight, the sudden appearance of a solution to the problem that looks as though it will be successful.
4. **Verification.** The final stage returns you to the work mode as you test your idea by discussing it, assessing potential implications, and ultimately putting it into place.

Once you understand the **creative process**, you realize that you need to research your problem thoroughly and then allow yourself a little time away from it. Pushing too hard, too fast can lock out potentially creative ideas.

Blocks to the Creative Process

The creative process is hampered by **blocks**—beliefs and habits that squelch creativity. *A Whack on the Side of the Head* by Roger von Oechs is an engaging discussion of blocks. The title comes from the notion that sometimes we get so stuck in ruts that we need a good whack on the head to see other options. Like Diedra Holland, we believe only one way exists to eat an apple. Lack of creativity can be equated to a candle that begins to melt, dripping hot wax down one side. As the candle continues to drip, the wax continues to flow down the same path. If a notch is cut on the other side of the candle, the wax flow can change. Likewise, we get stuck in our own ruts, forgetting to look for alternatives.

> "So much of the creative begins with the weird, the zany, and the truly bizarre that a nonthreatening climate must be maintained to give creativity a chance."
>
> —John Tropman (76)

Research shows all children are initially creative. Over time, we learn not to be. Von Oechs says lack of creativity stems from a combination of having been taught what is "right" and a fear of doing what is "wrong," even in areas that need new ideas. Beliefs taught in school almost as survival skills block us. We learn there that we must follow the rules, find the one right answer, make no mistakes, and be logical, practical, and sensible. Consequently, we grow very uncomfortable with ambiguity. We learn that play is frivolous, daydreaming is a waste of time, and we should avoid any hint of appearing foolish. All of these precepts, while useful in running a classroom of ten-year-olds, work against generating new ideas. Profiles of creative people show a tolerance for ambiguity, a tendency toward risk taking, an openness to new approaches, and a spirit of fun.

Getting beyond these blocks is not easy when they are deeply ingrained. Simply recognizing them as blocks, not truth, can help. If you, like Diedra Holland, believe only one way exists to eat an apple or solve panhandling problems or shut down prostitution or catch a thief, you are blocked. Becoming aware of alternatives can help. Getting out of your day-to-day world aids in that process. Expose yourself to new experiences, whether than means touring a museum, watching a NASCAR race, or reading stories to kids at the library. Travel, meet people from other professions (not just drug dealers), learn about ethnic groups outside your background, read widely.

All police work demands some element of problem solving. However, traditional police work is more likely to prescribe what procedures to follow than is community policing. When trying to stop chronic problems, you have to be creative. This will involve coming up with ideas others may consider foolish and impractical. Sharing such ideas inherently demands risk taking.

"But I'm not creative!" you say. That's another block, and one of the worst. Believing yourself to be noncreative creates a self-fulfilling prophesy. Begin now thinking of yourself as creative.

Another block to creativity is the tendency to immediately judge ideas. The creative process demands an openness to possibilities. As soon as you begin to "edit" your thoughts, you close down your capacity. Don't reject an idea while you are generating possible solutions.

One more block worth noting is frustration. In the middle of the creative process, we can get stuck. No matter how hard we try, the idea path looks like the Sahara Desert. This is when it's time to get away from the problem. Stop thinking about it, let it incubate. Relax, physically and mentally. Get a fresh start tomorrow.

By using the creative process and overcoming any blocks you have, you expand your creativity to help you find solutions to problems your community faces. Some structured formats can help you as well. One of the best known of these in police work is the SARA model.

Finding Creative Solutions with SARA

A task force of the Newport News, Virginia, Police Department designed the four-stage problem-solving model known as **SARA**: Scanning, Analysis, Response, Assessment. Although the SARA model provides a broad framework for dealing with a problem, it does not identify creative techniques to help you come up with unique, creative solutions. Such unique solutions are important. The Community Policing Consortium training literature reports, "Problems will likely persist if long-term solutions are not tailored to key causal factors. Creativity should be encouraged. Off-the-shelf solutions are rarely perfect." Creative problem-solving techniques can supplement the SARA model. This chapter first looks at the SARA model, and then describes other creative techniques.

Scanning

Scanning means problem identification. You are looking for chronic problems, not one-time incidents. In the initial phase you recognize that some problems recur repeatedly. Rather than simply responding over and over to individual crime calls, you begin to recognize clusters of problems. Taking both a broad and a close-up view as you scan, you look at various elements such as the time and location of the crimes. You are scanning for patterns, determining whether an individual problem is part of a larger picture or should be dealt with using the normal routine.

> "Problem solving is not new; police officers have always tried to solve problems. . . . But the routine application of problem solving techniques is new."
>
> —Kenneth J. Peak and Ronald W. Glensor (79)

In Lauderhill, Florida, for example, officers frequently responded to calls in a shopping plaza of twelve stores, a third of them vacant. Scanning revealed this was a chronic problem, expressed in gang activity, loitering, disturbances, and public drinking, all spilling over into a nearby park and apartment complexes. Officers and community were especially concerned because the plaza was near an elementary school and a boys and girls club (Lauderhill).

Analysis

Analysis is the heart of problem solving. **Analysis** involves identifying as many characteristics of the problem as possible in an attempt to unearth its causes. It is the preparation phase of the creative process. Here you research the history of the problem, pulling up police records, gathering background information, and researching thoroughly. If you analyze a problem, you are more likely to understand it and to develop a custom-made response to fit it.

Do not minimize the importance of identifying the right problem, as strange as that sounds. Sometimes what seems like the obvious problem is just a symptom. The Community Policing Consortium points out that "analysis is the most difficult step in the SARA model, and the one that officers and citizens tend to skip most in their enthusiasm to develop timely solutions. Without understanding the targeted problem, there is a high risk of developing solutions that don't work in the long run."

> "A problem well-defined is half solved."
>
> —John Dewey

To effectively analyze any problem, you need more than just police data. Collect information from a variety of sources about crime incidents, the people involved, and responses already tried. For example, possible information sources in a housing project might include, in addition to your personal observations, the housing manager, probation and parole officers, post office, welfare office, utilities records, formal or informal surveys of area residents, conversations with fellow officers, interviews with social service and private agencies, community and business association meetings, crime analysis reports, arrest reports, and more. Complete analysis will provide data that reveal the

ACTION CLIP

Scanning and Analysis

New Helvetia and River Oaks are two public housing complexes in Sacramento. Officers had struggled for years to push back the wave of drug dealers and gang members who preyed on the residents and surrounding community. Officers provided increased patrols and enforcement, but the community was still less than enthusiastic. The officers were slightly bewildered that the solution they devised, heavy enforcement, was not what the community wanted.

Results from a survey of residents were even more surprising. The community's highest priority was to be assigned designated parking spots. In retrospect the residents' reaction was reasonable. In an area of great violence the residents wanted the shortest distance from their vehicles to their solid front doors and brick homes.

underlying nature of the problem, which you can use to clarify or redefine the problem as needed.

In Lauderhill, the analysis process uncovered over 2,300 calls to the area in a two-year period, involving, among other things, 300 narcotics arrests. Investigating further, officers found the owner of the plaza showed little concern about the property. The plaza was unsightly, lighting was broken, walls were spray painted, garbage was not picked up. They observed overt drug dealing and truancy. On the positive side for possible options, the plaza was located within 100 feet of a school and within 200 feet of a public park, which put the plaza in a special legal situation. Florida law specified that any narcotic offense committed in such an area carried a mandatory three-year sentence and that if a property is a site of drug activity on more than two occasions within a six-month period, the Nuisance Abatement Board could declare the site a nuisance and close it down.

Response

Response involves finding and implementing long-term, creative solutions, tailoring the response to specific characteristics of the problem. Remember that solutions can go beyond traditional criminal justice system remedies to involve other community agencies or organizations. COP practices suggest you can:

1. Eliminate the problem.
2. Reduce the problem.
3. Reduce the harm created by the problem.
4. Deal with the problem better.
5. Remove the problem from police consideration.

Doing any one of these helps fight the problem, and any or all of them can be done through creative techniques you develop yourself.

Don't get stuck on one idea as your ideal solution and don't wait until you find the perfect solution. Be open to other possibilities and continue to scan the situation to suggest additional possible responses. In Lauderhill, a small task force developed a five-pronged attack on the problem:

1. They strengthened narcotics enforcement, creating a presence dealers could not ignore and involving patrol officers in the arrest procedure.
2. They brought in the department's truancy enforcement team and worked closely with the school resource officer to stop the truancy.
3. They upgraded lighting and installed barricades in the plaza.
4. They filed nuisance abatement complaints.
5. They formed a community support group. (Ultimately they felt the community was less supportive than it might have been due to a combination of apathy and

lack of confidence in the task force's resources. Business owners in the plaza and nearby apartment complex owners provided the most support.)

Next, they were ready to assess their response.

Assessment

In the **assessment** stage, you periodically evaluate your strategy's effectiveness to see if your solutions are working. Consider both positive and negative effects because negative effects can produce major unintended consequences. If the solution is not effective, collect more data or even redefine the problem. Maintain contact with any original complainants to keep abreast of any further problems. Also maintain contact with any agencies helping you.

Lauderhill's assessment of their response is that their approach is successful, although it created a highly adversarial relationship between the plaza owner and the department. The number of calls for service dropped, and community comments have been very positive about the changes in the plaza. However, officers fear the drug activity has simply been displaced rather than conquered. Officers intend to continue monitoring and responding to problems.

The SARA model implies ongoing change. You constantly scan the situation for changes, analyze and respond if needed, and re-assess. The model has generated some excellent results. Creative problem-solving techniques can help generate additional innovative solutions.

Finding Creative Solutions with Creative Problem-Solving Techniques

The degree to which a problem needs a creative solution depends on the kind of problem it is. Some problems are simple enough to be resolved by a rule of thumb or general guideline. Some of these stock solutions to common problems in community policing include evicting residents with a criminal history, condemning vacant housing used for drug activity, and locking off alley access to nonresidents. However, when such tried-and-true techniques don't work or only address a portion of the problem, you need creative solutions. Creative problem-solving techniques can help find custom-made responses for specific problems.

Collecting and Adapting Ideas That Work

One of the easiest ways to find creative solutions is to build on successful efforts that have worked elsewhere. Community policing programs are going on all over the United States and Canada. Officers tell their success stories in conference presentations, on the Internet, in law enforcement publications and popular magazines, and even by that old communication system, word of mouth. When you find out about a successful intervention, save the article, print the screen, jot down notes, call the officers. Ideas that work in Michigan or Florida could be modified to work in your community. Code or file the solutions by problem type so you can access the right type of solution when you need an idea.

Collect creative solutions from fields outside the criminal justice world, too. Creative ideas are often fostered by unexpected connections. Read. Surf the Web. Talk to people in areas you know little about to find out how they deal with problems. Then adapt others' ideas for your situation or use them to spur your own creative solutions.

Brainstorming—The True Way

Brainstorming is a way to generate ideas. The term often is used informally to stand for any quick origination of ideas. However, if this process is not done correctly, it can inhibit ideas. The key to brainstorming the true way is to avoid *any* negative comments.

Advertiser Alex Osborn developed brainstorming in the 1950s to help advertising executives come up with ideas. He writes:

> Until recently it was customary to leave the idea-finding part of creative problem-solving largely to chance. Now it is realized that you can *deliberately* increase production of good ideas by following two basic principles. These are summed up as follows:
>
> 1. **Deferment of Judgment:** You can think up almost twice as many good ideas (in the same length of time) if you defer judgment until after you have created an adequate check-list of possible leads to solution.
> 2. **Quantity Breeds Quality:** The more ideas you think up, the more likely you are to arrive at the potentially best leads to solution. (124)

Osborn repeatedly stresses the importance of deferring judgment—offering no negative comments: "Any of us will put out more and better ideas if our efforts are appreciated. Unfriendliness can make us stop trying. Wisecracks can be poison" (50). He laid out ground rules for brainstorming:

> 1. Criticism is ruled out. Adverse judgment of ideas must be withheld until later.
> 2. "Free-wheeling" is welcomed. The wilder the idea, the better; it is easier to tame down than to think up.
> 3. Quantity is wanted. The greater the number of ideas, the more the likelihood of useful ideas.
> 4. Combination and improvement are sought. In addition to contributing ideas of their own, participants should suggest how ideas of others can be turned into better ideas; or how two or more ideas can be joined into still another idea. (156)

The brainstorming pool. Osborn says the optimal size of the "brainstorming pool" is about a dozen people. One person facilitates or keeps the group focused on the process. One person records ideas. (Mindmapping, discussed later, is one way to record ideas.) Five people are "core members," those directly involved in the problem. The remaining five are guests, people who are aware of the kind of problem facing the group but who are not directly involved in this problem. Too many of the same people meeting over and over fall into predictable role patterns. New idea people add variety, which spurs creativity.

One word of warning from Osborn has particular relevance for police work: people brainstorming should be of "substantially the same rank" because even the nonverbal expressions of higher-ranking officers can inhibit others. There are exceptions, however. In some nonpolice cases, "higher-ups" simply sat in and observed at brainstorming sessions with no negative effects.

> *The group had gathered to discuss problems connected with rampant teenage cruising in River Heights that led first to irritated residents of the area, then to complaints by business owners, and finally to violence between cruising gangs. To start the brainstorming session, the deputy chief asked for ideas. Lt. Stefan Ivancic remarked that the real problem was lack of alternatives for kids. He suggested setting up a computer space for kids to work, associated in part with the high school Regional Occupational Program.*
>
> *The deputy chief exploded. "That has nothing to do with this! I don't want ideas like that!"*
>
> *Ivancic visibly shrank before the group. He offered no more ideas. Across the table from him, Lt. Joel Batesta proved to be a fast learner, and he, too, remained silent for the rest of the meeting. The group produced no useful ideas. The dual force of rank and criticism quashed the brainstorming effort.*

The brainstorming session. About two days before the meeting, the facilitator provides group members with a one-page background memo about the problem. This starts the brainstorming pool thinking and allows incubation to occur. At the meeting, the facilitator explains the four ground rules and presents the problem as simply as possible but in very specific terms. Osborn explains, "Failure to narrow the problem to a single target can seriously mar the success of any brainstorm session" (173).

The brainstorming pool should generate ideas for thirty to forty-five minutes. Do not stop too soon: you'll miss some of your best ideas. Osborn described studies that showed when "the first half of the ideas produced during a sustained effort were compared to those in the second half . . . the second half provided 78 percent more good ideas than did the first half" (Osborn 132).

The purpose of a brainstorming group is to generate ideas. The group can determine the utility of these ideas at the end of the brainstorming session or leave that

POCKET GUIDE

Rules for Brainstorming

1. Set aside a time clearly designated for brainstorming.
2. Put together a brainstorming pool: 5 people involved in the problem, 5 who are aware but not directly involved, 1 facilitator, 1 recorder.
3. Explain the issue to be brainstormed.
4. *Withhold judgment of ideas until later.* The purpose now is to generate ideas, no matter how impractical they may seem.
5. People call out ideas as they think of them, operating in random order. No one should hesitate because an idea seems impractical or repetitious or obvious or outright stupid. The wilder the idea, the better.
6. Build on one another's ideas. One person's ridiculous suggestion is another person's inspiration. Use every idea to help you generate more. Combine ideas, modify ones already suggested, turn them around, add to them.
7. Quantity breeds quality. The more ideas you generate, the greater your chances of having generated the one you need!

Critical comments kill ideas.

analysis to the people who will implement the solutions. This judging phase is completely unrelated to the brainstorming phase.

You can use a variation of brainstorming without a group. Although working alone does not have the benefits of a group, such as stimulation of others' ideas and excitement, it nonetheless helps you come up with ideas. If you are brainstorming alone, set a time limit during which you do nothing but generate ideas. Write down all the ideas you think of and do not evaluate them in any way.

Brainstorming is a very functional technique. Used individually, it is a way to begin coming up with solutions. When done in a group, it allows people to work together to develop a team approach to problem solving. Or you can direct individuals to brainstorm alone, then share results in the process known as nominal group technique (described in Chapter 5). Brainstorming does not work well when you are stuck or when you have thrown out all the ideas you have and none is right. Then you need to go beyond your natural flow of ideas and try another technique.

Brainwriting

Sometimes asking group members to spontaneously generate ideas and report them orally does not work. Shy people may not speak out comfortably in groups, vocal members may dominate, or some members may persist in giving negative comments. In that case, you might generate more ideas with a written version of brainstorming, called **brainwriting**. Give each participant a large index card. Participants write one or two ideas on a large index card and then throw the card into a pile in the middle of the table. Each person selects a second card from the pile, reads the idea on it, and using that to spur a new idea, adds an idea. Continue this until participants run out of ideas. A variation uses sheets of paper with a 21-square grid, 7 down, 3 across.

People write one idea in a square and put the paper back. Then they take another sheet, read the ideas, and add to the list.

Brainwriting allows one person's idea to spark someone else without one group member dominating or negative comments discouraging or inhibiting the idea flow.

Osborn's Checklist and SCAMPER

If you sit down to generate ideas and your mind goes blank, you can use Alex Osborn's checklist to spur your thought processes. Osborn designed this checklist to help participants expand their ideas in brainstorming sessions, but you can also use it alone without a group. The checklist consists of nine words that you can use as questions or idea-starters: *magnify, minify, modify, combine, adapt, substitute, reverse, rearrange,* and *put to other uses.*

Consider a typical after-school program for at-risk kids in a housing project. Currently the program meets two days a week for an hour and a half each day. The kids study for forty-five minutes and then participate in physical activity for forty-five minutes. You'd like to help the kids learn to work on computers, which have been donated, but you have no more time and no other resources. What can you do?

Use the Osborn checklist to generate ideas. Think of your program now and imagine how you can change it based on the nine words on Osborn's list. Ask yourself (or a group), for example, "How can we magnify the program?" Write down all the answers that come to mind. Wait for later to evaluate them. When an idea comes, don't worry about whether it's "magnify" or "modify" or whatever. The goal is to get ideas, not to play by the rules.

Magnify—Make it bigger in size, resources, time, scope or anything else you can think of—Work with high school students, too, on condition that they help the younger kids learn the computers.

Minify—Make it smaller—Cut out the other after-school projects or work with only two kids on a computer at a time, or work on computers only one day a week or get one volunteer to teach two kids on two computers one day a week.

Modify—Change it—Do computers one day, other homework the next until the kids learn the basics. Then do the other homework on the computers whenever possible.

Combine—Put ideas together—See if local soccer leagues will help teach the kids soccer during the activity period, and you help beginners with computers. Or see if a local Radio Shack or Macintosh Users Group or college computer class will send a teacher or let you send kids to them until the kids learn the basics.

Adapt—Fashion other ideas to your project—The ideas don't have to be directly related. One effort to control rush-hour traffic encourages some people to start work at seven, some at eight, some at nine. Adapt that plan, so younger students who get out of school earlier come first, and then leave when the middle graders arrive.

Substitute—Replace one thing with another—Substitute a computer class for your after-school program. Get a local computer store to donate the lessons as a goodwill gesture.

Reverse—Turn your problem around—Let the computer teach them. Get software to do it for you.

Rearrange—Move things around—Offer some of the computers to a local school in return for some training for the kids.

Put to other uses—Use your problem or items in it for other projects—Have the kids write stories, and you or a knowledgeable volunteer type them into the computer. The kids see their product on the computer.

Bob Eberle rearranged this list into the mnemonic SCAMPER. The spur words are not exactly the same, but they tap into the same concepts, and sometimes a group remembers the word *scamper* better than Osborn's list.

S	=	Substitute
C	=	Combine
A	=	Adapt
M	=	Modify, Magnify
P	=	Put to other uses
E	=	Eliminate
R	=	Reverse, rearrange

SCAMPER and Osborn's checklist are but two of many such lists to jump-start your idea-creating process. Any stimulus can be used. Other techniques suggest simply opening the Yellow Pages or a magazine randomly, placing your finger on a page, and then thinking of how the item you touch can be used to solve your problem. The underlying premise of all these techniques is that creativity is in us all, waiting to be released, and ideas can come from anywhere.

Force Field Analysis

Sometimes the easiest way to solve a larger problem is to break it into smaller elements and then change one of the smaller elements. Communication consultant Anne McIntosh uses an analogy of eating a hot dog: "You can't cram a hot dog down someone's throat. They have to bite off what they can chew, digest it, and come back for more. It's the same with problems. You can't handle all of them at once." Instead break your problem into smaller parts and attack the most important.

Force field analysis, developed by social psychologist Kurt Lewin, grows from the premise that any change toward your goal will help solve your problem. This five-step technique helps you define your problem, identify strengths in the situation that might help you solve it, and identify forces working against you that you can potentially weaken:

1. Write an objective statement of your problem, as though it were reported in the newspaper.

2. On the left half of the page, describe the situation as if everything fell apart. Imagine the worst.
3. On the right half of the page, describe the ideal version of the situation—how it could be if everything worked out. Dream the best-case scenario.
4. Draw a line down the center of the page. Imagine a tug of war between the worst-case left side (negative) and the best-case right side (positive). As you look at these, identify the forces pulling in each direction. List these forces on the appropriate positive or negative side.
5. Use one (or all) of these ways to help solve your problem:
   - Strengthen an already present positive force.
   - Weaken an already present negative force.
   - Add a new positive force.

"The primary benefit of the force field," writes William C. Miller in *The Creative Edge,* "is that it identifies strong points in a situation as well as problem areas. These strong points can be the foundation of the most effective solutions, which might have been overlooked otherwise" (73–74).

Attribute Listing

When you have a process, procedure, or product to improve, one method is to write down all the attributes of the item and see how you can better any one of them. Identifying attributes, then changing one or more gives you new ideas immediately. For example, Richards is planning a day to paint over graffiti and clean up the area. After the work is done, he wants a gathering in a park. Typically this would mean eating hot dogs, playing volleyball with the kids, maybe hearing a speech from the chief. He decides to make it more memorable. Changing one element will change the day:

- **Food:** Serve ethnic food from various neighborhood groups or let a high school group have a bake sale as a fund-raiser or ask every family to bring a cake and take a different one home or talk McDonald's or Burger King or Kentucky Fried Chicken into selling meals at cost for the afternoon.
- **Time:** Arrange a sunrise community party, followed by a park cleanup or a midnight madness sing-along to show it's safe to use the park at night.
- **Entertainment:** Instead of a speech, how about getting a band from the local university or community college? Or a have clown give a clown-training session? Or organize a dance lesson?

Small changes can make a new event, which will be novel for the community.

Mindmapping

Sometimes a new way of recording information can help you see problems in a new light. Instead of making lists, try recording a visual image. **Mindmapping** operates on

ACTION CLIP

Force Field Analysis

Although Officers Harold Bickel and Greg Dieckmann did not use force field analysis by name, their approach to their assignment in a low-income housing area clearly illustrates the process. They began by listing both negative and positive forces at work in the area.

The worst-case scenario was that hopeless families would continue to be trapped in the crime-dominated complexes. Forces pushing in that direction were massive. The area had the highest crime rate in the city. Gang activity and drug dealing were blatant, and frequently grew violent, resulting in homicides. Most residents feared leaving their homes. Both complexes had poor and broken lighting. Residents parked on their lawns, inadvertently creating hiding places for those the officers might pursue. Teens often sped through the complexes, endangering children. Residents and gangsters alike were often publicly inebriated. The complexes housed numerous people on parole and probation.

The positive vision was of a stable, safe neighborhood where families, though poor, could live safely and happily. Forces pushing in that direction were those with similar goals, including district police, county probation officers, the state parole office, a multi-agency drug task force, housing property managers, the resident council, and many residents who were deeply concerned about their children's welfare. That the officers were assigned exclusively to this area was also a positive force.

The officers chose the option of weakening two negative forces: drug dealing and poor lighting. Realizing that the open drug dealing caused many of the other problems, they chose to focus on it first. Their larger goal of empowering the residents to stand up to the dealers demanded that the officers reduce the fear of crime. Their first attack involved traditional policing efforts. They made 70 arrests in the first 40 days of the response. They varied their times at work, days off, and consequent arrests to undercut any sense of safety drug dealers might have had. They used a creative technique they called "vehicle decoy": while concentrating on enforcement in one section of the housing units, they parked an extra patrol car in another section to increase the perception that more officers were working in the area. They also arranged to have all lighting repaired and extensive foliage around the lighting standards trimmed. Additional sodium lighting was added. A resident was employed to report burned-out lighting.

At the same time they began working closely with other positive forces, drawing on allies. They contacted the local parole and probation officers and worked closely with them; eventually both offices assigned agents to the area to supervise parolees and probationers. They started a children's after-school program that drew in not only the children but also their parents.

These steps alone did not solve all the problems of this housing area, but breaking the problem down into recognizable dimensions allowed them to attack at various points and to slowly overcome what many had initially perceived as a hopeless case.

the notion that breaking away from a standard linear pattern can help generate ideas, whether in a brainstorming session or alone. In her book on the subject, Joyce Wycoff calls it "one of the most effective skills in the process of creative thinking. Mindmapping is a whole brain, visually interesting version of outlining. It has none of the constraints of outlining—you don't have to follow a strict format of Roman numerals, capital letters, numbers, etc. Because mindmapping is not restrictive, your mind allows information to flow more freely" (39–40).

Mindmapping is a fairly simple process. First, write your problem—or even better, draw an icon or symbol for your problem—in the center of a page. Ideas flow out from this center focus. Write them on lines radiating out from the problem, much as highways lead out in multiple directions from a city. As related ideas occur to you, write them on other lines that connect to related highways. When you complete your map, use colored markers to highlight related ideas. Figure 6-1 shows a sample mindmap.

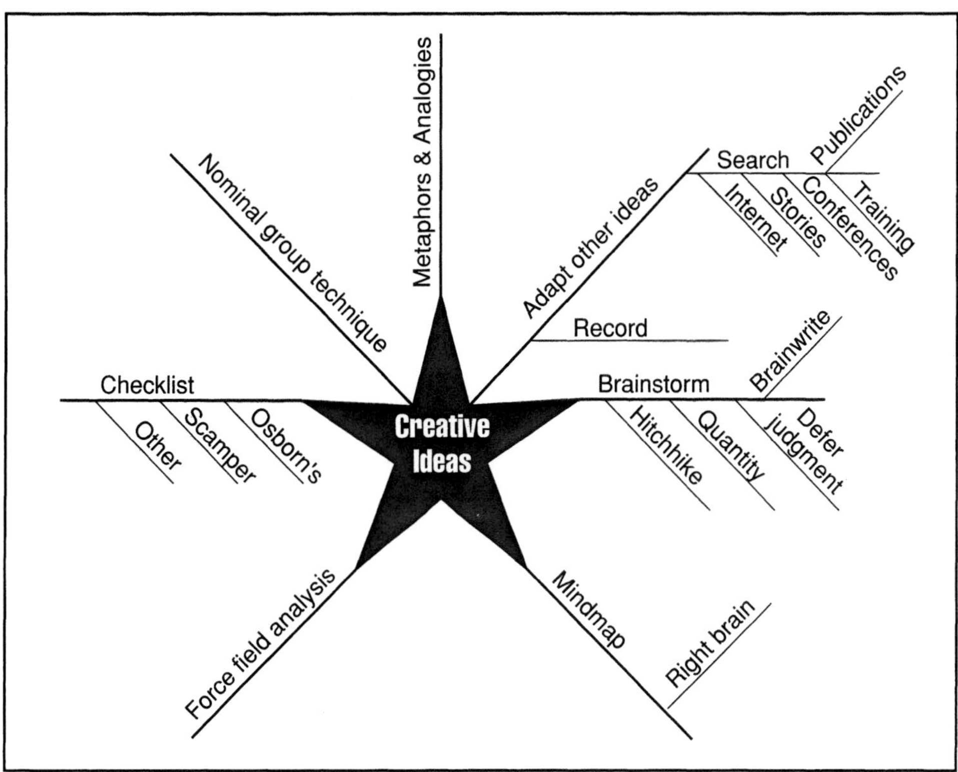

Figure 6-1: Sample mindmap

This visual format often stimulates your brain in ways a verbal listing does not. Brain research on accident victims uncovered very different behavioral patterns depending on which side of the brain was incapacitated. That research confirmed that different centers of the brain control different thought functions. The left side of the brain is very linear. It treats information serially, one piece at a time, and is analytical, rational, and objective. It is the center of language and mathematical ability, handling reading, writing, and arithmetic. The right side of the brain is holistic, visual, and intuitive. Here is the center of spatial ability, touch, music, motor skills, subjective thought, and emotional response.

Making lists about your problem calls on the left side of the brain. Drawing, color, and visual symbols activate the right side of the brain. Using a different format for thinking about your problem, such as mindmapping, can help you come up with different solutions. Drawing your problem can get your brain out of its candle-drip rut. The software Inspiration allows you to mindmap on your computer.

Mindmapping can be used by groups. The recorder of a brainstorming pool can record ideas around an image of the group's problem. Then the brainstorming group can see the relationship between their ideas. And, as a bonus, with mindmapping, the outline for any report you might have to make on your ideas is done! Each major highway is a main topic, and the smaller roads are related points for each topic.

People who use mindmapping regularly advocate even greater uses for the technique, such as to plan meetings, organize your day, even plan speeches. It can also be used to analyze a problem and its full implications before moving on to find solutions.

Using Analogies and Metaphors

Sometimes something completely unlike your problem can give you a solution you might not otherwise have seen. Take communication and cars. How far can you go in your Jeep Cherokee without adding fuel? Would you take it on the road endlessly without changing the oil, checking the tires, or adding antifreeze when the temperature drops? Wouldn't you see that it gets regular maintenance? If your problem is one of communication with residents in your district, you can use the Cherokee for ideas. Good ongoing communication demands regular maintenance, too, in the form of regular conversations, recurring contact, enjoyable moments shared, kind interactions, and productive meetings. And solving problems requires the "fuel" of information.

"Charged with the mission of coming up with a method for reducing the vandalism of telephones, the firm considered a variety of images, including the incredibly durable mesas that dominate the Southwest. From that emerged the idea for a telephone built into the side of a building."

—Denise Shekerjian (42)

Such a comparison is an **analogy**, a statement about how objects, persons, situations, or actions are similar in process or relationship to one another (Van Gundy 82). Analogies are often stated as comparisons. For example when Diedra Holland met with a neighborhood group, community member Olga Skolnikov used an analogy to describe the neighborhood association's goal of keeping the M Street Park clean: "Keeping litter picked up in this park is like doing the dishes; there's always another load to wash." Depressing as that thought is, it can lead to solutions: (1) the notion of getting a dishwasher—pressuring the city to clean the litter; (2) taking turns doing dishes—Week 1 Danny Lopez cleans the park, Week 2 Carl Ellison does, Week 3 is Mary Tanaka's turn; or, (3) one person washes and another dries—having teams charged with clean up—Week 1 is

ACTION CLIP

Creative Ideas at Work

Cape Girardeau, Missouri: "I discovered that many of the residents didn't know to call the parks department to have the neighborhood park mowed, or that the sanitation department will pick up trash left curbside for days, or that it's legitimate to complain to city departments about overgrown weeds and abandoned cars. I developed a resource card that my partner and I now distribute to every new resident we meet. The card lists phone numbers for such resources as shelters, clinics, family support and food distribution centers. It includes a comprehensive list of city departments. . . . The cards have effectively taught citizens how to utilize city service. The message is that city departments are one of the most valuable and overlooked resources available to police departments and citizens; we just need to help spread the word." (Officer Charles Herbst. "Maximizing Community Resources." *Community Policing Exchange* Nov./Dec. 1995.)

Middletown, Connecticut: The Blue Crew is a rap group with a difference: all five rappers are officers. Officer Rick Siena came up with the idea to reach teenage audiences about drug and crime prevention. Sergeant Gregory Sneed wrote lyrics and script for the production titled "Don't Drink and Drive." With the help of community college video students, the Crew made a video, and then won an award that enabled them to give the video to every school in the state. They produced a second video and are planning a third. More than 70 copies of the videos have been distributed to law enforcement agencies. The Blue Crew has performed live for more than 8,000 students since 1989. (http://www.community-policing.org/newslinks-old/artbytop/w1/w1-eldbc.htm. 18 June 1998.

Eugene, Oregon: "Our Latino liaison has initiated drivers license classes for the local Spanish-speaking population and is using that as a vehicle to introduce officers on an individual, non-threatening basis." (Officer Ken Saxon, Eugene, Oregon. Michigan State University Center for Criminal Justice. http://www.ssc.msu.edu/~cj/cp/cptoc.html.)

A Colorado idea was explained to a British audience: An American idea that could be used in the United Kingdom involves training dustmen [garbage collectors] to scan streets for suspicious activity. They then report to their dispatchers, who can call in the police. The "Crimebusters" program, which is entirely voluntary, began in 1990 in Aurora, Colorado, and has already spread to cities in Massachusetts, Utah, and Texas. "People just think we're low-lifes," said Utah garbage man Patrick Shockley. "But we see everything that goes on out there." (Global Ideas Bank. http://www.newciv.org/worldtrans/BOV/diyfut/Diy-89.html. 18 Oct. 1997.)

Seattle, Washington: Judge Joe B. Brown has . . . ordered several burglars to open their homes to former victims. With deputies in tow, they can take what they want, up to a limit set by Brown that approximates the value of what they lost. "The burglar learns what a good citizen feels like, worrying whether he's going to come home and find all his stuff there," said the judge. An administrator at the public defender's office said, "He's being very creative. A lot of things that have been done in the past aren't working, so somebody needs to be creative." (Based on an item by Woody Baird in *The Seattle Times*, 10 April 1992. http://www.newciv.org/worldtrans/BOV/1993/1993-64.html. 18 Oct. 1997.)

the Lions Club, Week 2 the high school seniors, Week 3 the garden club or volunteers from the bank.

Metaphors work in much the same way. A **metaphor** is a figure of speech in which one thing is described as if it were another. For example, Chief Robert Wadman of Aurora, Illinois, uses a medical model to talk about community policing. He feels that too often police must act like a triage unit, responding to the most critical situations, and don't have time to work on wellness as a long-term solution (McLanus). Sometimes expressing your problem in terms of something else can give you a whole new perspective. That can affect your attitude as well as occasionally suggest very practical solutions.

Evaluate Your Ideas

Once you have compiled a list of possible solutions, you can switch back into a critical thinking mode and evaluate the strengths and weaknesses of each idea. Select your best solutions for initial use in the Response phase of SARA. Keep other productive ideas at hand, however. As you continue to assess the situation to which you are responding, you may decide to try new ideas, expand ones that seem to work, or adapt some of the ideas you initially overlooked.

Developing Your Creativity

Creativity is a topic of interest to many, and, as a consequence, an increasing number of books are available that advise you how to break down blocks to creativity and how to generate unique ideas. Research shows that people really can become more creative. This news is as valuable to community police as it is to inventors.

With an understanding of how creativity works, you can watch for ways your habits and thinking blocks your creativity. Then you can supplement the basic SCAN model with creative problem-solving techniques that help you improve your city.

Works Cited

Carter, David. Reported by Tina McLanus. "New Ideas from Around the Country." National Center for Community Policing, Michigan State University. http://www.ssc.msu.edu:80/~cj/cp/newideas.html. 26 July 1998.

Community Policing Consortium. "Using the SARA Model and the Crime Triangle. Training Module Three: Community Policing Problem-Solving." http://www.communitypolicing.org/mod3.html. 8 Nov. 1997.

Edwards, David. *How to Be More Creative*. San Francisco: Occasional Productions, 1980.

Ganey, Anne. "Youths Clarify Mixed Messages." *Community Policing Exchange* Jan./Feb. 1998: 6.

Horwitz, Joshua. "Emphasizing Hands Without Guns." *Community Policing Exchange* Jan./Feb. 1998: 1–2.

Lauderhill Police Department. This information is taken from a case reported on the POP Network, an Internet site sponsored by the Police Executive Research Forum at http://www.policeforum.org/popnet.

McIntosh, Anne. Personal communication. 28 May 1998.

McLanus, Tina. "Creative Tactics: From Visual Disruption to Code Enforcement. New Ideas from Around the Country." http://www.ssc.msu.edu:80/~cj/newideas.html. 4 Aug. 1998.

Miller, William C. *The Creative Edge: Fostering Innovation Where You Work*. Reading, Mass.: Addison-Wesley, 1986.

Osborn, Alex. *Applied Imagination*. 1953. 3rd rev. ed. New York: Charles Scribner's Sons, 1979.

Peak, Kenneth J. and Ronald W. Glensor. *Community Policing & Problem Solving: Strategies and Practices*. Upper Saddle River, N.J.: Prentice Hall, 1996.

Police Activities League. www.lfucg.com//police2.htm. 18 Oct. 1997.

Saxon, Ken. Michigan State University Center for Criminal Justice. http://www.ssc.msu.edu/~cj/cp/cptoc.html. 22 Oct. 1997.

Shekerjian, Denise. *Uncommon Genius*. New York: Penguin, 1990.

Tropman, John. *Making Meetings Work*. Thousand Oaks, Calif.: Sage, 1996.

Venegas, Arturo. Personal interview. 5 Feb. 1996.

Van Gundy, Arthur B. *Techniques of Structured Problem Solving*. 2nd ed. New York: Van Nostrand Reinhold, 1988.

Von Oechs, Roger. *A Whack on the Side of the Head*. Rev. ed. New York: Warner, 1990.

Wallas, Graham. *The Art of Thought*. New York: Harcourt, Brace, 1926.

Wycoff, Joyce. *Mindmapping: Your Personal Guide to Exploring Creativity and Problem-Solving*. New York: Berkeley, 1991.

Activities

1 Enhancing Your Creativity

Falling into ruts is dangerous for creativity. Doing the same thing in the same way over and over leaves people running on autopilot instead of generating new approaches. Encountering new situations and new stimulation gets the creative juices flowing. Expanding your creativity is essentially a process of getting out of ruts and beginning to stretch yourself. Try these ideas.

1. Break one habit or change one pattern. Take a different route to work and back. Eat dinner in a new restaurant. Have ice cream for breakfast (make a

Cheerios sundae). Use your nondominant hand for an hour. Take public transportation. Watch the dawn and write about it.
2. Generate at least twenty-five uses for a paper clip.
3. Write up a police report on the break-in that occurred at the Three Bears House, including a description of the suspect known as Goldilocks. Or take a statement from the giant about the theft of his golden harp by Jack. Or if you aspire to homicide investigations, write the wolf's version of what happened at Red Riding Hood's grandmother's house on that dreadful evening.
4. Write from the viewpoint of a vending machine.
5. Explain ways that 2 + 2 = 7.
6. List twenty things you can do with a collection of two million ping-pong balls.
7. Thomas Edison is said to have known 1,800 ways NOT to make a light bulb. Dr. Seuss' first children's book was rejected twenty-eight times. The point is, creative people try and fail, and learn from their failures for the next try. What big error or failure did you have in the last three years? List some beneficial consequences for you.

2 Collect Good Ideas

Start a file of good ideas that have worked for other people facing similar challenges as you. Keep these organized by problems they solve. Remember to include the originator's name and a contact for more information if you can find them.

3 Random Inspirations

A number of creativity techniques grow from the perspective that a random inspiration can be useful precisely *because* it is random. An unpredictable formulation forces you to look at a problem in a new way.

Select a problem to consider. Open a magazine, a catalog, the Yellow Pages, or some similar source, and randomly place your finger on an image or word. Make a connection between your problem and the image or word, and then use the connection to generate an idea.

4 Mindmapping

In the center of a blank sheet of paper write "Neighborhood Safety" (or a topic of your choice). Create a mindmap of ideas on how to make your neighborhood safer. Write down ideas as they come to you without concern for practicality.

Chapter Seven

Build It and They Will Come

Turning Ideas Into Action

"Nothing in the world can take the place of persistence. Talent will not; nothing is more common than unsuccessful men with talent. Genius will not; unrewarded genius is almost a proverb. Education will not; the world is full of educated derelicts. Persistence and determination alone are omnipotent."

ROGER VON OECHS

"It'll never work." Sgt. Emilio Fritz crosses his plump white arms, leans back in his swivel chair, and devotes his attention to cleaning his teeth with his tongue.

Officer Diedra Holland sighs. She'd predicted Sgt. Fritz would be this way. She can already hear Lt. Batesta bellowing about cost; he always does. What is the point of coming up with new ideas if her team has to run them past big cement roadblocks in human form? Being line officers with no power to order anyone in the department to do anything is hopeless. And it's too bad, because an after-school teen center in the old bakery is a good idea. The center would cut down on the fighting, keep some at-risk kids off the streets, and help unite the community.

Although, actually, Fritz isn't really saying no, just that they'll never bring it off. What can they do now?

HOLLAND'S TEAM FACES THE CHALLENGE of turning an idea into reality. This is the point where good ideas survive only if those who conceive them understand how to influence others both within their organization and outside it. How do you get your great ideas turned into reality if you can't order people to support you, have little or no funding, and the task seems overwhelming? You must develop what business professors Allan R. Cohen and David L. Bradford call "influence without authority." You achieve your goal by relying on your own power, building support, organizing the community, and overcoming opposition.

Relying on Your Own Power

Diedra Holland was wrong when she believed that without rank she had no power. She was confusing power with authority. You have power as a human being to the extent that you can influence other people—sway their emotions, change their opinions, link your cause to theirs, and enlist their support.

Recognize Types of Power

Power comes in many forms. Almost forty years ago, sociologists John R. P. French and Bertram Raven identified five sources of personal power: legitimate, reward, coercive, expert, and referent.

Legitimate power is the power the law or culture gives one person over another. It's the power the police department confers on the captain to make decisions, issue orders, and demand compliance; the power that causes Holland to obey Sgt. Fritz. It's the power teachers have to grade, judges have to preside in court, parents have to control children, and fire marshals have to make you rearrange your perfectly functioning office with the six cardboard boxes of files blocking the back exit. In many situations, you have legitimate power as an officer in the community. You have a legitimate right to demand to see a motorist's license, to search a youth on searchable probation, to order people away from a danger site. Legitimate power is convenient, but it's not the only way you have to get people to do what you want.

Reward power is what it implies: compensating people for their contributions. The compensation does not have to be tangible, such as money or a promotion or even a public award. Some people seek intangible rewards, such as appreciation, recognition, a sense of accomplishment, or team camaraderie. Finding out what people value, and helping them get it, gives you power. Reward power is especially important to keep in mind as you work with community volunteers because they often work for their own reasons—to help their neighborhood, benefit their kids, or save something they treasure. Your help or backing is a reward. That Holland, Richards, and Washington have cut down on the teen gangs congregating in front of the supermarket is a reward for the shoppers and the supermarket owner.

Reward power, by the way, is not just top down. Your superior officers also appreciate such intangible rewards as a word of thanks, an invitation to lunch, or even having someone competent with whom to work.

Coercive power, the other side of reward power, is your ability to withhold rewards or to actively punish people. An officer's coercive power is inextricably linked to legitimate power, and some people's apprehension of police grows from their fear of this coercive power. Coercion is larger than the possibility of arrest, however. If fights break out at a fraternity party, you can close it down. That's coercive power. Note that except when used to stop crime, coercive power generally works against the goals of community building. Use this power sparingly.

Expert power, sometimes called information power, is a person's ability to influence as a result of knowledge or experience. For example, you take your doctor's advice on medical issues over your golf partner's, and you ask for help buying a computer from someone who talks about downloading and operating systems until your eyes glaze over. When you want to know about problems a certain neighborhood faces, some people can tell you in detail with factual references, exact statistics, and specific names and places. Others have only a vague sense of issues. People who can spit out the facts and figures have more power to influence than those who can make only empty assertions.

You can use expert power to achieve your goals by becoming an expert about your project and your neighborhood. If you do your homework and can show your project's specific benefits, present detailed cost estimates rather than guesses, and answer any objections thrown at you, you will have more power to influence community members and fellow officers.

Referent power is the influence a person or group has because he or she is admired or respected or attractive. For instance, if four people give you four different versions of an event, do you automatically believe one person? That's referent power. If community member Kimo Ah Yun asks you for a favor, would you try very hard to do it just because Kimo asked? If so, he has referent power with you. You go out of your way to accommodate some people, and conversely you know people you can influence because of your relationship with them. This is one way you get things done—by talking directly to individuals, developing a relationship based on your integrity, and building referent power with them.

Draw on Your Credibility

Your credibility is how believable and trustworthy you seem. Credibility research has identified three primary areas that influence whether a person appears credible: expertise, character, and dynamism. Displaying these three characteristics increases your chances of influencing others. (This applies for you as a public speaker, too.)

Expertise, or competence, is how well a person performs and what he or she knows. A competent person gets the job done well and on time. A competent person is knowledgeable, organized, and attends to details. He or she anticipates potential reactions to actions taken now. Over time, we get a feel for a person's competence based on performance. In the short run, however, we often judge competence by how "together" people appear—whether they wear professional attire or dirty jeans, whether their papers are neatly organized or flying out of folders, whether responses are direct and to the point or ramble.

Character reflects a person's honor. "I give you my word" has meaning only if you believe the person's word. Trustworthy people are honest; they "don't play politics behind closed doors, are consistently fair with others" (Phillips and Wallace 10). Few things can undermine credibility as much as appearing untrustworthy. A person's behavior over time ultimately determines our judgment about trustworthiness. In the short run, we judge people by their credentials or profession.

Dynamism can be thought of as energy. The personal characteristics of charm, magnetism, and excitement add to a person's credibility. We believe a person who speaks with conviction more than we believe a person who speaks hesitantly. Someone who looks people in the eye, and presents ideas logically and fluently is more likely to influence others than someone who stammers out thoughts haphazardly. People who are skilled presenters, who are organized and articulate, and who speak with confidence and enthusiasm are more likely to influence others than people who seem uncertain, voice their position hesitantly, or can't find their data. This is why learning communication skills is so vital to your position.

Use Your Power Tools

In addition to your credibility and the forms of power you choose to use, you have other sources of power. Sociologist Rosabeth Moss Kanter, after studying power in organizations, identifies three "power tools" you can use: information, resources, and support. Information is knowledge; resources include funds, materials, space, and time; and support is your backing for others' projects. Too often we consider only the category she calls "resources" and forget that our power is larger than that. Anything that others need in some form is valuable.

Community police can use all three power tools to encourage others to join in a project. Information might include data about crime in your area, technical knowledge about laws and procedures, political intelligence, and your personal expertise. Resources include your time and presence, which is often a valued asset. Support, often overlooked as a tool, means your public endorsement, which gives legitimacy to community projects.

To enhance your own power, remember the five types of power, enhance your own credibility, and rely on power tools. Expand your knowledge and expertise in your area, develop your communication skills, and remember that the character you show today influences your success tomorrow. Using your powers, you can approach community leaders and organizations to help you achieve your goal.

Building Support

Any cause is stronger when backed by an organized, committed group. The first way to make an idea become a reality is to find other people whom your idea will affect. Determine how your idea will help individuals, neighborhood groups, and organizations achieve *their* goals. Consultants Dennis Phillips and Les Wallace explain in *Influence in the Workplace,* "Your chances of selling an idea are enhanced the more you relate it to the achievement of shared objectives. . . . Your homework begins in determining what your organization has decided is important and finding ways in which your idea will advance its work" (107). This process involves developing *stakeholders*, people who have a stake in your success. Cohen and Bradford advise you to "see each person . . . as a potential *strategic ally* or *partner*. You increase the number of your potential allies by seeing who has a stake in your area and working at building mutual trust" (17). An organized, committed group of allies makes your project more likely to succeed.

> "One secret to bringing about change is helping people to discover what they want. This is an especially useful truth to those of you who are supporting change in others but who are not in a position to cause them to change."
>
> —Geoffrey M. Bellman (34–35)

What's in It for Them?

You must reach these people and develop them into your supporters. Stanford University business professor Harold Leavitt stresses that "human emotionality is the essence from which change is made" (8). Try to reach people emotionally. Show them how your project offers ways to achieve their goals or fulfill their needs. In *Managing Group Creativity*, communication professor Arthur Van Gundy advises, "Assess the needs of the people to be influenced. . . . Most people will respond favorably to an idea if they believe that it will satisfy one or more of their basic needs. If you can determine what these needs are, you will increase the chances of getting your idea accepted" (216). He suggests that basic needs include power and control, security, affiliation, personal growth and development, helping others, freedom, dominance, being liked, recognition, impressing others, being seen as creative or intelligent, task accomplishment, and avoiding crisis situations. If you can offer a person the chance to fulfill a need, you have a start on developing a supporter. Community members' needs may be directly related to your project or peripheral to the project but still something you can offer. They may, for example, feel a need to bring about greater family safety, which is what your project is about; or they may want to meet new friends or develop leadership skills, which working with your team will accomplish. Whatever the need, if your project helps them fulfill it, they will work with you.

The experience of Officers Harold Bickel and Greg Dieckmann illustrates this. When they began their project in two housing complexes, they faced problems involving multiple ethnic groups and diverse ages. They describe their strategy:

> The most effective way to mobilize the community was through the children. First, the children were more apt to have a favorable relationship with police because they had fewer preconceived notions about law enforcement. Second, the children were more likely to socialize with children of other nationalities, because they had less of a language barrier, and were acquainted with each other from school. Third, both adults and children felt there were no positive activities for the children. . . . Fourth, without positive alternatives, many of the children were unable to fight the peer pressure of the gangs that dominated the community. (Bickel and Dieckmann 4)

The parents "of the ethnically diverse children would be asked to assist with the program, enabling them to begin socializing with people of other races and become more involved in the community" (Bickel and Dieckmann 4). The officers were able to reach the parents by giving them what they needed: safety for their children.

Make a Good Case for Your Project

When you determine how your program benefits people, present your ideas to potential allies person-to-person, in public presentations, and in writing. When you approach them, never start from the perspective of what you need. Instead, explain how your project will benefit them. "This is how cleaning up the neighborhood will help your business" has a better chance of winning support than the altruistic plea "we're looking for volunteers to help clean up the area."

Show the need. In a debate, the burden of proof lies with the side that wants to make change. This is the condition you face. You must do your homework. Have figures at your fingertips. Gather crime data, look at comparable projects in other cities, determine the financial implications, plan administration details—raise or address whatever issues are relevant. Be able to prove that a need exists and that your project or plan will solve the problem. You might give speeches, talk to small groups, call a community meeting, write a formal proposal, seek grant funds, and get the approval of someone like Sgt. Fritz. Have the information you need to do that.

Make it visual. Frequently, people don't really understand what you are trying to do. The more innovative or unusual your idea, the harder it becomes for people to visualize it from your words. Make it easy for them; show them what you plan to do. A demonstration, model, or drawing can show how the project will work more clearly than your words. For example, do you want to acquire sensitive video cameras to tape what's going on in the alleys at night? Borrow a camera and tape one night to demonstrate the camera's potential. Do you have an image of what a neglected plot of city land could be if volunteers took care of it? Get a few volunteers to do one corner. Do you envision a computer room set up in the mall to draw at-risk kids off the streets after school? Get someone to draw a picture or make a small model or set up one computer. A demonstration can be powerfully convincing.

Find Sponsors in High Places

For all our society's lofty ideals about democracy, some people have much more influence in a community (and in a police agency) than others. If such powerful people support your project, you have a greater chance of success. Kanter writes: "Overwhelmingly, studies of innovation show the importance of backers and supporters, sponsors and friends in high places, to the success of innovation" (184). Find opinion leaders in the community at large, in organizations with which you deal, and in your own agency, and enlist their support. Get on a first-name basis with people in agencies you work with regularly. One practical meaning of that is that your phone calls are returned, your ideas are heard, and your project has a chance to be supported. Also seek to influence those who influence others. Van Gundy advises:

> Identify key opinion leaders within the larger organization and convince them to support the change. It is much easier to convince a small number of individuals about the need for a change than it is to convince an entire organization. Once the opinion leaders are convinced of the need for a change, they can help convince others. These opinion leaders need not be in formal positions of authority, however. Change may receive broader support if informal leaders are perceived as supporting the change. (214)

Much change occurs because one person talks to another personally. Take the time to explain your project to people who might help you or who might know someone else who will help you. This is the basic foundation of community support.

Organizing the Community

No matter what you are doing, community backing increases your chance of success. Increased involvement of the community in police work has been referred to as community mobilization, community activation, community collaboration, and community participation. Which term you use is less important than achieving the desired results.

"Is there an existing group that ought to be involved in preventing crime? A home-school organization like PTA; a tenants' group; a fraternity or sorority; a community service club such as Lions, Rotary, or JayCees; a social club; a church; a mental health association; a taxpayers' or homeowners' association—these are just some kinds of groups that can be a base for action."

—National Crime Prevention Council

Affiliate with Established Groups

One quick way to gather support for your idea or project is to collaborate with existing community groups, such as religious organizations, children's clubs (with their sponsors and parents), and non-profit companies, whose purpose is similar to your own. In Etowah County, Alabama, for example, the sheriff wanted to use county prisoners to remove trash from the roadways, but lacked funds to pay a deputy to supervise them. The department allied with the Clean and Beautiful Commission (CBC), an affiliate of Keep America Beautiful. The CBC now provides the funds raised from local donations. The Sheriff's Department supplies the deputy and a van. The county commission supplies a trailer. Between 1994 and spring 1997, the program reduced litter by 82 percent and saved the county $6 million that would have been paid for the service. Sheriff James Hayes offers this advice: "Find an organization like the CBC and form a community partnership" (Smith 1). Established organizations tend to have well-developed structures, know how to attract portions of the community, and generally are very concerned about social issues.

Build a Team

An efficient and productive way to reach a common goal is through teamwork. A **team** is a group of people with a specific objective or goal who coordinate their activity to reach the goal. For a community project, a team generally begins with a nucleus of concerned people willing to work to attack a community problem. The team can be the leaders of a larger group, such as a steering committee; or the team can be the larger group itself. Teams can be short term or long term; they can do problem solving or decision making, and can be interdepartmental, multidisciplinary, or interagency. The business world commonly recognizes that people working together as a team outperform individuals working alone. Picture a football team with the best quarterback in the history of football and the worst offensive line and receivers in the league. Would you be surprised to find the team finishing last in the standings? One superstar cannot make the entire team shine.

You may already be a member, and in some situations a leader, of more teams than you realize. You can be part of a work team that includes your peers, a resource team that includes individuals from agencies, a team referred to as a family, a sports team, and so on. Each one of these teams has an objective or goal that is shared by its members.

> "People acting together as a group can accomplish things which no individual acting alone could ever hope to bring about."
>
> —Franklin Delano Roosevelt

Researchers Carl Larson and Frank LaFasto were developing a system for monitoring team effectiveness and providing feedback to improve performance when they discovered consistent characteristics of effective teams. Their research was not limited to one field, but included a variety of teams such as the Mt. Everest Expedition team, the Presidential Commission on the space shuttle Challenger accident, cardiac surgery teams, and the 1966 Notre Dame championship football team. Ultimately they studied more than seventy-five teams. They found eight common characteristics present in successful teams:

1. **Clear goals.** High-performance teams have both a clear understanding of the goal and a belief that the goal embodies a worthwhile or important result.
2. **Results-driven structure.** The team uses an appropriate structure for achieving its objectives. A structure that focuses on procedures is less likely to be successful than one that focuses on achieving results.
3. **Competent team members.** Team members on strong teams possess the necessary ability to achieve the objectives. They also have the personal characteristics and skills to work well with others.
4. **Unified commitment.** Members have a "team spirit," loyalty and dedication, an unrestrained sense of excitement and enthusiasm, and the willingness to help the team succeed.
5. **Collaborative climate.** Members communicate openly, disclose problems, share information, help each other overcome obstacles, and discover ways of succeeding.
6. **Standards of excellence.** The leader sets achievement levels that are acceptable for the team, and team members seek to excel.
7. **Support and recognition.** The team is given the resources it needs, is supported by those who are capable of contributing, is recognized for its accomplishments, and has incentives tied to achievements.
8. **Principled leadership.** The team has an effective team leader, who establishes a vision of the future and creates change.

You want the community team you develop to have these characteristics. It may not be easy. The membership composition of the team can be as diverse as the

POCKET GUIDE

Benefits of Teams

Improved effectiveness
Increased involvement
Greater feeling of control
Increased satisfaction, commitment, involvement, and motivation
Reduced stress
Strengthened relationships

community. You may work with officers from other agencies, employees from city or county government, or community members in your neighborhood. These community members may be business owners, residents, government employees, mental health professionals, educators, and so on. For them to work as a team, they need a team image or group identity, a sense of themselves as a team. This comes from working together as a group and succeeding. Urge them to take on a small task where they will likely succeed fairly early in the group's history to develop that sense of group identity. Also help your group develop a clear goal. Successful teams have a shared vision of what they can accomplish.

One important characteristic of most community team members is that they are volunteering their time. Most are not paid to work for you. Therefore you need to get them involved, so they are committed to the goal.

Get Volunteers Involved and Invested

"Human beings don't love other people's babies nearly as much as they love their own," Leavitt observes in *Corporate Pathfinders* (30). People who are invested in an idea or project, whether by virtue of time volunteered, ideas contributed, or energy used, become more committed to that idea or project. Or as Leavitt puts it, get people "involved in making the baby, and everybody will love and nurture it" (30). Make your volunteers more committed to the "baby" by giving them necessary and reachable tasks.

People who feel needed and central to the team tend to pitch in more than those who feel their contribution doesn't matter. The more people there are working together on a project, the less each has to do. This helps fight volunteer burnout. Of course, some people are much more reliable and talented than others. Responsibility for a central task might motivate some people but overwhelm others. Some promise to accomplish tasks they do not accomplish. If some have boundless energy but seem unreliable, give them attention, make them feel part of the team, and assign them a less essential job until you see if they will follow through.

Be sure team members know exactly what they are to do and by when. You may ask for volunteers for tasks or you may appoint someone, but either way, use clear and unambiguous directions. Avoid directives such as: "You guys go out and change that." With such instructions, no one has authority to direct anyone else, no deadline is set, no line of responsibility organizes the working process. Instead, make specific assignments and include a deadline. If you need to hold a meeting, ask someone to convene it by a particular time. If you need fliers distributed, seek a volunteer to be in charge of it. If multiple people are needed to accomplish a task, put together a committee with a direct charge of what to do and a deadline, and ask someone to oversee it. *Then, be sure those who volunteer get credit for their work.* Such recognition becomes a motivation for their future contributions.

Set Up Communication Networks

All people involved in your project need to keep in touch. The results-driven structure so important to teamwork demands communication. Contact and information reinforces volunteers and spurs enthusiasm. To ensure quick contact, set up communication networks for several different groups.

- Your core team members, whether these are the board of directors or steering committee or agency representatives, must be able to contact one another quickly. All members should have one another's phone numbers, e-mail and mailing addresses, and pager numbers when applicable.
- Establish a larger network for volunteers. Keep a mailing list, a phone list, and an e-mail list. Set up a phone tree to keep volunteers apprised of events. The phone tree chair can then call ten reliable volunteers who each call ten others to ensure high turnouts at events. Set up an e-mail list as well.
- Your personal network may be larger than the list of volunteers. For instance, stay in touch with relevant officials in your own agency, and city or county leaders who may be able to support your project.

With these networks established, your team can begin to enlarge your support base. Make an effort to tell the community what you are doing as a way of seeking additional community backing.

Start Small Where You Have Guaranteed Success

You want people to respond positively to their early experiences of working in a team to improve the neighborhood. To assure that, help them quickly experience a sense of accomplishment. Start small. Tackle a little project that you know your fledgling team can conquer. Clean up one block, one park, one playground. Handle one aspect of a problem. Later you can take on Goliath. Success builds your team internally, and with each success you draw more volunteers and build more commitment for your cause.

Community support grows with progress. Each time you accomplish some small project, you not only move forward toward your goal, you also attract support. Although it may seem logical to form a strong organization and then attack community problems, in reality the community organizing process operates more like a spiral

ACTION CLIP

Engage the Community

The Decatur, Alabama, Police Department concentrated on stopping the drug activity in a low-income area. At the end of a five-year initiative the department conducted a survey. One of the most significant findings was "one that brought us up short," they report. "Do the police in your neighborhood ask for help in deciding which problems need attention?" the survey asked. Sixty-four percent of respondents said the police had never consulted them about the problems they believed to be serious.

Sgt. Danny Dutton reports: "Even though we did attempt to hold community meetings to get citizen input, we lost our momentum when community participation dropped off. Our mistake was that we simply accepted the residents' lack of interest rather than finding ways to get and keep them involved. . . . Now we concentrate on developing police–community partnerships as well as enforcing the law" (Dutton 8).

than a logical sequence. A small nucleus of leaders accomplish small goals, this accomplishment encourages others to join their team, the larger group tackles larger projects, and so on, ultimately emerging as a strong community force and perhaps a formal organization.

Recruit Supporters

Successes give you something to tell the community when you describe your project. The best way to spread information throughout the community is by personal contact. No handbill announcing a meeting can equal a personal phone call from someone whom you know. When the Citizens Committee for New York City studied successful and unsuccessful block associations, they found that strong associations "recruited new members by personal contact rather than through general announcements or by word-of-mouth" (Citizens Committee 4). The Sierra Club advises that when you are holding a meeting, if you give "everyone a reminder call in addition to the mailing, you are likely to double the attendance at the meeting. *Nothing brings out people to a meeting like a telephone call from a concerned neighbor*" (Pick 35 [italics added]). The call should come two to three days before a public meeting. What you say can be very simple. You can even have a "script" (but don't sound like it!): "We hope you can come to our meeting. We value your input and want to hear your views on this issue. We'll see you Thursday night at 7:00 at the Community Hall."

Personal contact is not the only effective communication channel, however. The Citizens Committee also found that successful associations "used a wider variety of ways to communicate with members (e.g., fliers, newsletters, community newspapers, bulletin boards, etc.)" than did unsuccessful ones (4). (Chapter 8 discusses in detail how to reach the media.)

Wording is important. In your messages about upcoming meetings and when you speak about your team, use words that unite the community and imply that everyone together faces a common threat or seeks a common objective. Words such as *we, our, us, let's, you and I,* and *together* imply a team working together.

Collect contact information at every meeting by putting out sign-in sheets with spaces for names, e-mail addresses, postal mailing addresses, and phone numbers. Ideally, use NCR (no carbon required) forms so that both you and community leaders have lists immediately.

Consider a Structured Organization

If your project is a large one or involves multiple and diverse supporters, you might want to form a structured community organization. A structured organization with a name and officers gives your project the credibility of an established group, and its members help you communicate with the neighborhood and provide a predictable support base. This is the difference between a group of neighbors collecting old books to sell and the Friends of the Library. The Sierra Club, with its successful history in community activation, offers advice on how to proceed if you want to form a structured community organization to back your cause.

First, choose a name. Choosing a name accomplishes more than just giving the group a convenient label. The process of choosing also brings together your group as they make a decision as a team. The Sierra Club advises:

> Ask everyone in your core group for suggestions. . . . The name should be able to grow with the organization. . . . Make sure the name is easy to say and easy to remember. . . . The name should reflect your membership and your purpose. (Pick 27)

Next, the group should select officers and appoint people to committees. This gives you a slate of volunteers to contact when you need support. In addition to the usual steering committee of president, vice president, secretary, and treasurer, be sure you have a communication committee to quickly spread the word about any upcoming meetings and to advertise causes. They should set up a phone tree and e-mail lists. As for postal mailings, Maritza Pick advises, based on Sierra Club experience, "Always make the mail crew sessions fun. Order pizza and drinks. Put on some lively music. Crack jokes. The more tedious the work, the more volunteers deserve rewards" (34). You also might want a newsletter with someone assigned as editor. A newsletter is valuable as a tool to reach and update members and other concerned neighbors and as a public relations document to send city and county leaders.

ACTION CLIP

Kane Street Turnaround

Police Commander Michael J. Nila described the experience of the Aurora, Illinois, Police Department as they cleaned up a challenging city area:

"In late 1992, Chief David L. Stover made a decision to try to end the nightmare of life on Kane Street. He assigned Officers David Jacobs and William Hall. . . to a long-term, problem-oriented policing project. Stover instructed the officers to use a combination of traditional and community policing initiatives to take back Kane Street. Jacobs and Hall were tasked with arresting street-level drug dealers and enlisting the aid of a mistrusting neighborhood.

"In the first phase of the project, the officers introduced themselves, and the community policing concept, to Kane Street residents. Jacobs and Hall administered a survey that asked the residents to identify the issues they perceived as problems. As part of their strategy, the officers went door-to-door and delivered crime bulletins that included a phone number for citizens who wanted to anonymously report criminals and their illegal activities. . . .

"Officers Jacobs and Hall had 20 years of citizen mistrust to overcome and knew they couldn't get discouraged during the slow process of rebuilding the community's confidence. The two officers persevered and were eventually rewarded for their patience when a few residents offered their homes as surveillance locations. Soon after this show of support, neighborhood meetings began.

"Having witnessed positive results and an unprecedented growing trust in the police, Kane Street citizens formed a group called the 'Inner Circle'. With a focused sense of purpose to reclaim their neighborhood, the citizens initiated neighborhood statement marches. The citizens' new partners, Hall and Jacobs, along with other Aurora officers including Chief Stover, accompanied citizens in these marches. The demonstrations had their intended effect. Deterred by the citizens' determination to take back their territory, the gang members eventually packed up and left Kane Street.

"A landlord who owned most of Kane Street's apartment buildings was of tremendous assistance to Hall and Jacobs. The landlord bought and distributed cameras for his tenants to use to film drug deals. Through this mechanism, residents supplied tangible evidence that enabled the officers to make numerous drug arrests. . . .

"The Inner Circle continued to grow and published its first newsletter in May 1994. The publication was an indicator that determination and commitment was replacing fear of retaliation from gang members and drug dealers." (Nila)

Overcoming Opposition

Rarely is a new idea embraced with open arms. Some people oppose change, others are not willing to make the effort change requires, others cite financial, legal, or practical restrictions to change, and some people simply may not like the particular project you support. You must overcome these blocks. Rosabeth Moss Kanter identified a number of tactics that people trying to bring about change or innovation can use to disarm opponents:

> . . . *waiting it out* (when the entrepreneur has no tools with which to directly counter the opposition); *wearing them down* (continuing to repeat the same arguments and not giving ground); *appealing to larger principles* (tying the innovation to an unassailable value or person); *inviting them in* (find ways that the opponents could share the 'spoils' of the innovation); *sending emissaries to smooth the way and plead the case* (picking diplomats on the project team to periodically visit critics and present them with information); *displaying support* (asking sponsors for a visible demonstration of backing); *reducing the stakes* (de-escalating the number of losses or changes implied by the innovation); and *warning the critics* (letting them know they would be challenged at an important meeting. . . for example). Note that many of these are more likely to succeed when the innovation group has a strong coalition backing it. (193–194)

Having the community behind you gives you the power to make change. However, organizing the community to make a change takes persistence. Draw on your own power, build support, affiliate with established groups, get sponsors, build a team to organize and lead the community, find volunteers and get them invested, overcome opposition you face, and persevere.

Building Support Within Your Agency

Community policing cannot succeed without support from within the organization as well as from without. Naysayers will always find reasons not to support

Avoiding the Penalty Flag

As your community organizing succeeds, you may become a major player in the political world. Your involvement with the community creates a level of exposure that politicians, government managers, and police administrators envy. You possess the key to a communication door that others would like to open. This can put you in a ticklish position.

Educate yourself about your job and what your bosses expect. Keep them informed about your project. Educate the community about your role: who you are, where you can be reached, what they can expect, and what they cannot expect from you. Be sure they understand the limits of your decision-making authority. Involve community, business, and government leaders in your projects so they know what's going on and are less likely to be critical. Remain loyal to your agency. Don't say anything you don't want to read in the local paper.

community policing, or worse yet, not to support you. Two major causes for lack of support are a lack of understanding of COP and a lack of involvement in the process. The burden for correcting this falls on your shoulders. Just as you must reach the public, you must reach officers in your agency. Remember that accurate and timely communication becomes vital as you work in an increasingly creative environment. You must proactively use the communication channels available to you to let fellow officers know about your community efforts. If you have an agency newsletter, be sure the editor knows what you are doing. If you have roll-call video, talk to the producer. However, the most powerful communication technique remains interpersonal conversation.

> "There is no limit to what can be accomplished if it doesn't matter who gets credit."
>
> —Anonymous

Get Dirty and Let It Show

Your responsibility is to demonstrate to your peers, many of whom are not involved in your project, that you work just as hard and get just as dirty as they do. One of the first ways to include patrol officers in the problem-solving process is by involving yourself in *their* world. Attend briefings to gather information from your peers and to provide them with information. This is critical to your success. Briefings also provide the social communication necessary to improve overall team communication and performance.

A second way to relate to patrol officers is to bring them into your world. If you have a neighborhood office, give them a key. The key demonstrates trust. Access to creature comforts, such as a desk, phone, restroom, and coffeepot, provide a reason to stop by. These contacts improve patrol officers' understanding of COP, increase the exchange of information related to problem solving in your area, and help to create a partnership between you and them. Invite other officers to assist with the fun and rewarding parts of the job. Include them in serving search warrants, in undercover operations and decoy stings, as well as any special parties, sporting events, and public relations activities. Allowing the patrol officer into your community policing world breaks down any perceptions of isolationism or elitism. It also increases their commitment to your project and the community.

Randy Washington worried about patrol officers feeling uninvolved in the neighborhood assignments given to Richards, Holland, and himself. He knew the officers' continuing presence was vital to the neighborhood, and he realized that the work his team was doing provided him with some contacts that could benefit patrol. The problem was that he did not have the ongoing contact with them that he did in his patrol days when they met intermittently at calls. He decided to resurrect that contact by partnering with various patrol officers for a shift. While riding with them, he described the active criminals in their overlapping areas, even pointed out a couple of them, shared information on strategy, and explained the support he needed to get convictions. He also pitched in and helped the officers he rode with deal with their calls.

Be sure you do your share of the work. You may have suffered through the infamous call dumping where a call, not usually assigned to you, is thrust upon you for a reason that defies all logic. With this in mind, don't dump your least desirable work on others just because COP may make it easy to do so. The one reputation that will last an eternity is not handling your share of the work. Community policing draws a lot of attention to you. How you handle your perceived share of the work will be scrutinized by many. Develop a reputation for handling your assigned calls, volunteering calls, and taking your own reports.

Maximizing your success also requires the support of sections of your organization not frequently associated with COP. The criminologists who process your evidence, the fiscal staff who ensure your purchase requests are handled promptly, the detectives who conduct the follow-up, and the dispatchers all want to be part of

Planning Chart for Building Community Support

Trust Building

How can we build credibility and sufficient trust? What personal credibility do we have? What strengths can we point to that show we are ethical, competent, have expertise in this area, and have a history of commitment to projects we undertake?

Coalition Building

1. Who shares our goals? Who can we enroll as supporters in our program?
2. How will we approach them to explain our shared objectives? Consider how this directly benefits them. How does it help them accomplish their objectives or their agency's objectives?
3. How can our pitch reach them *emotionally?*
4. Who else will benefit from our project? How? (Or how can we find out?) What resources do we have to entice the interests of these potential allies? How can we get them involved in this project so that they become stakeholders?
5. Which established groups might help?
6. How can we demonstrate that this project will work? Would models, mock-ups, or visual presentations help?
7. What special techniques can we think of to promote our ideas?
8. What negative responses can we anticipate? How can we prevent or respond to these?
9. How can we share the credit to nourish others' involvement?

Communication Building

How can we set up a system to stay in touch? How can we include all involved people in advisory discussions?

something rewarding. Including them in the COP process helps to meet this need. The support they provide you will make your job easier and more effective.

The rewards you will experience through working with the community will greatly enhance your assignment as a community officer. Improving the quality of life in a community is not a simple charge. Progress is not easy, but what you accomplish changes lives, very likely in ways that go far beyond the results you can see.

Works Cited

Bellman, Geoffrey M. *Getting Things Done When You Are Not in Charge*. New York: Fireside-Simon and Schuster, 1992.

Bickel, Harold, and Gregory Dieckmann. "New Life in Sacramento Apartment Communities, Part Two." *Problem-Solving Quarterly* 10 (Spring/Summer 1997): 1–7.

Citizens Committee for New York City, Inc. "What Makes a Community Organization Effective." *Community Policing Exchange* Sept./Oct. 1995: 4.

Cohen, Allan R., and David L. Bradford. *Influence Without Authority*. New York: John Wiley, 1991.

Dutton, Danny. "Don't Forget to Ask Your Customers What's Most Important to Them." *Community Policing Exchange* May/June 1998: 8.

French, J. R. P., and B. Raven. "The Bases of Social Power." *Studies in Social Power*. Ed. D. Cartwright. Ann Arbor: University of Michigan, 1959. 150–167.

Kanter, Rosabeth Moss. "When a Thousand Flowers Bloom: Structural, Collective, and Social Conditions for Innovation in Organization." *Research in Organizational Behavior, Vol. 10*. Greenwich, Conn.: JAI Press, 1988. 169–211.

Leavitt, Harold J. *Corporate Pathfinders*. New York: Penguin, 1986.

National Crime Prevention Council. "Neighborhood Action: Neighborhood Organizing. Getting Together to Fight Crime." www.ncpc.org/2gether.htm. 17 June 1998.

Nila, Michael J. "War on Kane Street Ends." *Community Policing Exchange* Nov./Dec. 1995. Article Five.

Phillips, Dennis, and Les Wallace. *Influence in the Workplace: Maximizing Personal Empowerment*. Dubuque, Iowa: Kendall/Hunt, 1992.

Pick, Maritza. *How to Save Your Neighborhood, City, or Town. The Sierra Club Guide to Community Organizing*. San Francisco: Sierra Club Books, 1993.

Smith, Pat. "Influence Program Reduces Litter and Offender Recidivism Rate." *Sheriff Times* 1 (Spring 1997): 1. http://www.communitypolicing.org/shtimes/s4_sp97/s4smith.htm. 12 March 1998.

Van Gundy, Arthur B. *Managing Group Creativity*. New York: American Management Association, 1984.

Von Oechs, Roger. *A Kick in the Seat of the Pants*. New York: Harper and Row, 1986.

Activities

1 Teamwork

Ask five or six volunteers to sit on the floor in a circle back to back with their feet on the floor without crossing their legs. Then, without putting their hands on the floor, the individuals should stand.

This is a good activity to illustrate the value of teamwork. If the group works together, they can rise easily. If they work individually, they are unlikely to succeed. In order to accomplish their goal, the group must negotiate together to help each other. After the group succeeds, discuss the process the individuals went through as they negotiated for teamwork.

2 Teamwork: The Puzzle

This activity was suggested by one developed by Project Adventure in Brattleboro, Vermont, and reported in *Community Links*, Spring 1998.

Make a large (about four foot by five foot) map of your district or community. Cut it into a twelve-piece jigsaw puzzle. Assemble a team of twelve people and give each team member one piece. (You can be one of the team members.) Blindfolded, the group must assemble the puzzle. This activity requires teamwork, but it also helps build a team because it is fun and relies heavily on communication. After the team has assembled the puzzle (or given up), talk about what communication was needed to work together as a team.

3 Your Personal Power

Divide a sheet of paper into two columns. In the left column, list the five dimensions of personal power: legitimate, reward, coercive, expert, and referent. Under these, list the three elements of credibility: expertise, character, and dynamism. In the right column, assess your own personal power in a particular situation. In some cases, such as referent power, your influence varies by individuals. Show your list to someone close to you who knows you well. Ask for their perceptions. Pinpoint the weaknesses on your list and begin working to improve in those areas.

4 What's in It for Others

Select one person whose support you seek or someone who could help you in some project. Focus on one particular act for which you want support. This act can range from appearing before the city council to donating funds to agreeing to accept a report late. List three ways that engaging in the act you want could benefit the other person. Remember, don't try to persuade by showing how the project helps you. Show how the project helps them. Repeat this activity, focusing on an agency whose support you seek.

5 In-House Information

Consider some program in your agency or university that you know little about. What would you like to know about this program? Make a list of what you know and what you don't know. Describe three ways the people involved in the program could effectively communicate information about their program to you. What would work best? What might or might not work?

Now take those ideas and turn them around. Using your list as a model, list the ideas this gives you for communicating your community policing work with fellow officers or others you know.

Chapter Eight

Hello Out There

Communicating Your Success

"Empathy, fortunately for us all, is
not beyond human capacity;
good journalism often is the means
by which empathy is evoked."

MICHAEL SCHUDSON (8)

Nobody could remember who had the idea first. Prubjote Sandhu was the first to wish for cookies, everybody is sure of that. They all agree that calling the teen center The Old Bakery for its original use influenced them. What no one can remember is who first suggested firing up the ovens again to train interested teens in culinary and business skills. However, almost everybody remembers how the cookies got their name. Just as Officer Alan Richards asked what the brand should be, one peanut butter cookie slid off a cookie sheet. Angie Tam giggled and said of the heap on the floor, "That's how the cookie crumbles." Three months later How the Cookie Crumbles cookies sell out as fast as they come out of the oven. They are prized in the neighborhood, both as a symbol of success and as a treat. The downtown bakery that sends a cook to train the teens has hired three students for their main bakery for the summer.

"This project is great," says Randy Washington, dunking his oatmeal-raisin cookie in milk. "Why don't other neighborhood centers do this?"

"We ought to tell them about it," agrees Diedra Holland, rescuing a chocolate chip that has dropped to her napkin. "It's a great story. Why don't the media ever cover stories like this instead of cops' mistakes?"

Alan Richards answers thoughtfully. "I think you just answered that. We don't tell them about it."

Diedra Holland nods. "Who was that reporter in the station yesterday wanting a story?"

"The guy who kept asking for something besides—what did he call it 'the usual boring stuff'?" Washington asks.

Holland nods again. "This is beyond the usual, isn't it? Should we call him?"

"Call him?" Washington glances at Richards. "Call the media?"

A silence falls over them. Finally Richards shrugs. "I guess we could."

Holland shoves the last bite of cookie into her mouth and reaches for the phone.

COMMUNITY POLICING DOES NOT OPERATE in isolation. The whole notion of community involvement demands conveying information through channels of communication that reach the public. This means you must proactively use a variety of mass media techniques to let the world know about your community efforts, especially your successes.

Cultivating the News Media

Many people would characterize the relationship between police and the news media as strained. Whether *media* means television news, radio commentators, or newspaper stories about crime and law enforcement, police perceive that media focus too much on the negative and believe that reporters insert their own opinions into reports. The media complain about the lack of timely information from police and being denied information that the First Amendment protects.

Community officers must put that antipathy aside. Think of the mass media as a free distribution system to reach your community. Providing the news media with story ideas is in your agency's best interest. Don't be afraid to brag about what has been done and what is planned. Seek out reporters who show an interest in your work and keep them informed. If your agency has a public information officer (PIO), work closely with that person.

> "The success of local media organizations hinges on being involved in their communities. So think of yourself as an important resource for the media. The media need your expertise and advice as they seek to help Americans understand the problems of violence and other crime and how people and neighborhoods can work together to solve them."
>
> —National Crime Prevention Council

Like you, reporters have stressful jobs with unrealistic timelines and no margin for failure. Reporters must fill column inches or air time, working under tight deadlines, day after day. They can struggle to get stories or they can rely on easy sources of information. You can be that source, sending news the media need that also publicizes your events and advances your projects. Community policing generates information about community activities, crime statistics, heart-warming human interest dramas, highly visual community actions, and descriptions of nontraditional policing roles.

This does not mean that everything you do should be handed to the media. In some cases you may have strategic reasons for building relations with your community before you get any media exposure. Officers Greg Dieckmann and Harold Bickel

ACTION CLIP

Partnership with the Community

Police in Louisville, Kentucky, believed that "if the department could form a partnership with the media, as it had with other segments of the population, community policing could be stronger." They deliberately courted the media, inviting news directors, assignment editors, and reporters from radio, TV, and newspapers to the station to meet personally with the chief to discuss ways to support one another. As a result of this effort, not only do reporters get better stories, but police get help. A new program, "Partnership with the Community," features an officer interviewing department members about community policing initiatives. One two-minute show that airs two nights a week during the news features an arrest followed by an officer asking for help tracking down wanted criminals. Sixty percent of the suspects have been captured (Riggs).

report that in the first year of their successful project in Sacramento they refused all media requests. They wanted the community to learn of their arrival by meeting them in the neighborhood, not from what the officers called "some well-dressed, nameless television personality" (4).

News people seek information much the same way you do, by talking to people, developing useful contacts with informants in the know, and checking around. If you really want good relations with the press, develop networks. Get to know reporters and stay in touch with them. Put together a mailing list of media contacts and keep it current. Check that you spell names correctly.

Develop your media relations skills. Work with your PIO. For experience, take over when the PIO is out of town. Some agencies provide training in media relations. A local college may offer a useful course. Take advantage of any such opportunities.

Attracting Media Attention

When you want media attention, keep in mind that you are not alone. Major print and broadcast media receive announcements every day from many organizations wanting their stories covered. An announcement or news release about an upcoming public meeting or a successful student project is unlikely to get much attention unless you can frame it in a way and at a time that fits the needs of the news media.

Media stories fall into two categories: news and features. Typical police stories are news stories about something that happened that day that might affect the community. Features are human-interest pieces, stories that don't have an immediate news value but nonetheless interest the news audience. Features often run as the final story

POCKET GUIDE

How to Talk to the Camera

Cameras are sometimes intimidating. Remember that you are not really talking to cameras or camera people. You are not even talking to reporters or to any other officers in the room. Look through the camera to the viewers in their living rooms. Talk to *them*. Avoid police jargon they might not understand. Don't fidget, swivel in your chair, or use any distracting mannerisms. Even on a hot day out in the field, *never wear your dark glasses*.

Before a radio or TV reporter interviews you, think about what you want the story to say. Typically, the reporter will take a tiny portion of your information in the form of a "sound bite." The average TV or radio on-air comment lasts ten to twenty seconds or twenty-five to thirty words. How can you prepare for such short speaking? Practice your sound bite. Write your own headline: put your message into *seven words*. This forces you to be succinct. Drop this headline into your interview two or three times. The reporter will put together a story by selecting a sound bite to show the essence of the piece. Potentially this will be your smooth, succinct phrase. Knowing your key points is vital. If you know them, you can press them home.

on TV news (called "the kicker") and as inside stories in papers. Your success stories will probably be features.

Different Media Needs

Different media cover stories in very different ways. A three-alarm fire in an abandoned warehouse at 8:00 P.M. is the lead story at the top of the hour for late-night television news, with close-up shots of flames roaring, firefighters charging, and walls crumbling. In the newspaper, the fire is a small paragraph on page three of the Metro section. If radio covers it at all, the story will be a comment from the fire chief.

Television. Television feeds on visual images, preferably moving ones. An announcement about crime going down is good news for the community, but it is not photogenic. If you want television coverage, you must give the cameras something to look at. Announce your crime reduction statistics in a park that people were afraid to use a year ago. If you have a community meeting scheduled on school gun control, call a press conference to announce it and spread out all the guns confiscated from lockers in the last six months. If you are sponsoring a day to clean up the neighborhood, invite a Girl Scout troop to clean up one city block the week before, summon the media to see what the Scouts find, and comment on the upcoming event. Remember, too, that uniforms make instant visual statements.

> "The national crime prevention campaign that urges listeners and viewers to "Take a Bite Out of Crime" is one example of how media and interpersonal channels can complement each other. Although many people learn about crime prevention behaviors through the campaign's media spots, listeners put these behaviors into action only after they become involved in neighborhood watch groups."
>
> —CRAIG E. JOHNSON AND MICHAEL Z. HACKMAN (223)

Television also favors celebrities or city dignitaries offering five- to ten-second "sound bites," quick comments that summarize your situation. Try to get a well-known spokesperson to back your cause, then schedule a press conference or event where the spokesperson can offer comments.

Radio. Radio wants sound bites, five- to ten-second remarks about your subject from someone of importance. One advantage of radio is that you or your authorities can offer comments by phone. Radio stories are generally quite short.

Print. Print wants details. Prepare yourself to answer questions in much more depth for print reporters. In advance, prepare written material to give them that includes any relevant statistical details you have, background information, and other sources for the reporter to contact.

All news media work on deadlines. Except for stories that are happening at the moment, you must give reporters information early enough for them to prepare their stories. For example, to obtain early evening television news coverage, schedule your event in the morning. This gives a reporter time to do follow-up interviews and to edit video and audio content.

ACTION CLIP

The small community of Clever, Missouri, wanted to teach teens about drinking and driving. Chief Steven J. Newton reports that the community "had been struggling with teen intoxication and, sadly, had lost two young people in fatal car accidents." The department acquired a pair of eyeglasses that simulate intoxication when worn. "A person wearing the glasses is unable to walk a straight line, touch his or her nose, or catch a ball, just as an intoxicated person is unable to do" (Newton 2). The department contacted schools, religious organizations, and other groups, offering to make a presentation. The chief reports: "We thought we were on our way to making a difference when controversy hit." Some people feared the program might encourage teens to drink. "It took a lot of individual and group presentations before we finally won the community's support."

The program really took off when the media got involved, as the chief describes: "Initially, our demonstration schedule was light, involving just a few churches and civic groups; that is, until the local news media ran a story on the glasses. It seemed overnight that every high school, middle school and other groups of all types and sizes wanted a demonstration."

The department feels good about the results of their effort. Teens had positive comments about what they learned, and "their comments appeared to be validated by the decreased number of car accidents, DWIs and traffic tickets" (Newton).

Some days are known in the news business as "slow news days." These are the days your evening news spotlights the zoo's newborn orangutan and the daily paper features an interview with the oldest person in the community. In short, reporters are desperate for anything. This is one of your best chances. Typically these slow news days result from the usual sources of news not being active: lawmakers are not in session, no sports activities are scheduled, no press conferences are called by the mayor's office. Weekends and holidays lead the list. Give your local media a story to fill space on those days and you have a good shot at getting media coverage. To give the media your story, send media releases.

Media Releases

You need press coverage in two circumstances: (1) when you plan an event and want publicity and (2) when something has already happened that you think the public should know about. Organizations seeking news coverage typically rely on media advisories and news releases. A **media advisory** is a short announcement sent out before a meeting, press conference, or special event to alert the press and pique their interest. The **news release** is a short news story describing your news, usually sent out the day of the event.

Fax media advisories and news releases to the city editor or metro editor of newspapers and the assignment editor of television and radio. Also send a copy to the Associated Press (AP) if you have one in your city. The AP sends the press a "day book" of what's happening each day. Also, many police agencies belong to Business Wire, a statewide service that sends your news release to agencies all over your state. If you want more than local coverage, fax your news release to Business Wire.

Media advisory. As shown in Figure 8-1, the media advisory simply announces the upcoming event and indicates what visual subjects will be available. To give the media planning time, fax the advisory earlier by about three weeks for weekly news, four or five days for daily papers, and three days for TV and radio. Follow up with calls later that day to appropriate editors, the city desk, or reporters whom you know to call attention to your event. The person you call may not remember your advisory, so be prepared to fax another copy. Then fax a news release the morning of the event as a reminder.

RIVER HEIGHTS POLICE DEPARTMENT

916 Grand Avenue
River Heights

Date:

Contacts:
Diedra Holland, Central City community officer 555-7425
Rita Lopez, Old Bakery Volunteer Coordinator 555-2665

MEDIA ADVISORY

Inner-city teens will present the first copies of their new cookbook *How the Cookie Crumbles* to three River Heights cops Saturday at a ceremony at the Old Bakery Teen Center at 10:00 a.m. The three officers started the teen center and its successful cookie project.

Visuals will include the award ceremony, teens showing how they bake the cookies that gave the book its name, and the new scene at the Old Bakery.

Special guests: Mayor Chris Portola, Councilwoman Grace Chan, Police Chief Morgan Zettl. Mystery author Monica Jackson, author of *Deadly Delight*, will serve officers her deadly delight cookies.

Figure 8-1: Sample media advisory

News release. Editors in a large or even mid-sized city receive dozens of news releases every day. They glance at them and make instant decisions about whether to cover that event. Your news release must grab them immediately and convey your message quickly. The basic rule of thumb is the KISS principle: Keep It Simple, Stupid. Keep your information short, usually one typed page, double spaced, written on official letterhead. (Your agency may have special letterhead for news releases.) At the top include contact numbers that reporters can call for more information. The contact can be you, a community member, or both. If you are hard to reach, include an additional number of another contact person.

Start your news release with anything that you think will really grab attention. What makes this event interesting? Start with that. Then include the basic demands of journalism: who, what, where, when, why, and how. For additional interest, throw in a catchy quote from an authority. Figure 8-2 shows a sample news release.

To increase media interest, whenever possible, also enclose a note from the mayor, the chief, or some VIP involved in the event with the news release. If the number of media is not too large, follow up with a personal call.

Distribute copies of the news release at the event, and fax it to all media who don't show up.

RIVER HEIGHTS POLICE DEPARTMENT

916 Grand Avenue
River Heights

FOR IMMEDIATE RELEASE Date:

Contacts:
Diedra Holland, Central City community officer 555-7425
Rita Lopez, Old Bakery Volunteer Coordinator 555-2665

Inner-city teens presented the first three copies of their new cookbook *How the Cookie Crumbles* to three River Heights officers Saturday at a ceremony at the Old Bakery Teen Center. The community police officers started the teen center and the cooking project that gave the book its name.

Officers Diedra Holland, Alan Richards, and Randy Washington came up with the idea of turning the bakery into an after-school center over a year ago. "If it weren't for them we would be like we were before, out on the street corner," said Willie Perlroth, a frequent guest at the center.

All three officers have been working in community policing for two years. Since they began working in the Four Oaks area, official FBI reports show a 28% overall drop in crime in the area.

The book is named for the popular cookies produced at the teen center. Recipes come from Mayor Chris Portola, local basketball players, Fire Chief Antony Nicoletti, and Police Chief Morgan Zettl. Local mystery author Monica C. Jackson shares her recipe for deadly delight cookies. Jackson is the author of *Deadly Delight*.

All proceeds from cookie sales support the teen center.

###

Figure 8-2: Sample news release

Media packet. If you are holding a press conference or event, bring copies of your news release. One way to get better coverage is to help the reporters by giving them a **media packet**, a folder that includes your news release, photographs, background information, statistics, and possibly a statement from the chief or a community leader. Reporters on large staffs will use this only as a place to begin gathering their own information, but staffs that do not have time to find their own material will rely on yours. This allows you to tell them what you want them to know.

Public Service Announcements

Public service announcements (PSAs) are short radio and TV announcements about your project. Essentially, they are free commercials. Their advantage is that you do not have to tie your information to a news event to have the information aired. The disadvantage is that getting them on air is difficult. Radio and television stations are no longer legally required to air PSAs. These announcements take up air time a station could use for money-making commercials. The few PSAs that do air generally are simple announcements in some sort of verbal Community Calendar. On TV, the audience sees a calendar or the station logo. A public service announcement should last thirty seconds for TV. More variance is allowed for radio, although never more than sixty seconds. Write what will be said. Indicate PSA length at the top. Figure 8-3 shows a sample PSA.

RIVER HEIGHTS POLICE DEPARTMENT

916 Grand Avenue
River Heights

Date:
Contact: Diedra Holland, Central City community officer
Phone: 555-7425

PUBLIC SERVICE ANNOUNCEMENT
:30

Want the best cookie recipe in town? Check out *How the Cookie Crumbles.* It's a new cookbook that benefits The Old Bakery Teen Center. Get favorite cookie recipes from the mayor, Police Chief Zettl, Dragons Coach Marvin Jensen, even some local deejays. Look for the books in all Tower bookstores or call 555-COOK.

Figure 8-3: Sample public service announcement

Using Specialized Media Channels

The larger news media, such as television news and the big daily newspapers, reach large audiences. Sometimes that is not your goal. You may simply want to reach your neighborhood group, a small segment of the city, or a particular target audience. When that happens, turn to the specialized media such as small community newspapers, community calendars, student presses, community access cable, and in-house business media. You need to change the slant of your news release to reach a particular market. If you send a release to the high school paper, for example, stress the issues relevant to the high school. If you send one to senior citizens, highlight issues about senior safety.

Small Community Newspapers

Community newspapers need stories more than do the large dailies with their many on-staff reporters. The smaller newspapers will publicize your community meeting or event and tell your success story if you relate it to their neighborhood. Sometimes they will even send reporters to interview you. Compile a mailing list of these small community newspapers to use whenever you need publicity. (Remember that some larger apartment complexes have their own newsletter.) Send them information. Follow up with a phone call to the editors. This can result in excellent free publicity.

> "Every police department is the child of its city. Before attempting to gain any insight into one, it helps to know a little about the other."
>
> —James McClure (9)

Some bigger daily papers include neighborhood supplements, which have different editors than the main paper. Put these neighborhood supplement editors on your mailing list. Also consider papers and newsletters designed for special groups: senior citizens, businesspeople, particular professions, and religious organizations. You don't have to reach everyone each time, just those who might care about your project.

Bulletin Board Columns

Bulletin Board Columns or Community Calendars are short announcements, essentially listing just "what, when, where" in one short paragraph. Both large dailies and small community papers have such columns, as do city magazines; some television stations announce upcoming events orally. Calendar offices are often separate from the regular editorial department, so you need to send them a news release directly. These columns often need a longer lead time than regular stories. How to submit announcements is usually described at the bottom of the column in each publication. Mail or fax an announcement worded in the form they use directed to the Bulletin Board or Community Calendar editor.

Student Presses

Sometimes high school newspapers are good ways to get your message out; these reach students and often make it home to parents. Be sure to send announcements to these publications if you want their readers to attend your meeting or participate in your special event. More and more, some high schools and especially community colleges and universities offer broadcast news courses, often creating programs that run on community access cable or are broadcast to small in-house audiences. The opportunity to interview an officer on air or to come to your neighborhood and do a story can be a special treat for students. Sometimes the audiences for student press stories are friends of the students, doting families, or simply people interested in the shows. Although the audience is not large, the opportunity is great for building community support.

Community Access Cable Programs

More and more agencies are turning to community access cable to let the community know about crime in their area and to pass on safety tips. If your agency does any sort of community access cable program, volunteer to be on the show to talk about your community program. Or ask cable officials about nonagency programs. Often such shows are hungry for guests and eager for local stories. These programs do not necessarily attract large audiences, but they reach people you may miss other ways. If you have the option, try to appear on programs that air near the city council meeting broadcasts, when community leaders may be tuned in.

In-House Business Media

Large businesses, government offices, hospitals, and universities usually send out newsletters and sometimes air in-house news videos to various branch offices. If your program affects their business or their employees' safety, they may have an interest in telling your story. This can both inform their employees and build you additional support.

Alan Richards winced the first time he watched himself answer questions on the evening news. He gave good information, but that back and forth rocking—when had he done that? Suddenly he became aware of what he was doing as he watched—twisting in his swivel chair. That's what he had done in the interview! He replayed the tape. This time he noticed his crossed leg with his foot lying on his knee—he looked like a kid at camp. The reporter sat that way too, but his leg didn't show. Richards learned a lesson watching his own interview.

The next time the news called, he was ready. He knew details about the incident the reporter had called about. As the camera operator set up, he chatted with the reporter, giving her information to direct her questions in a way he hoped she'd follow. He was friendly, even joked a little, but when the tape rolled, he was professional and succinct. He sat behind his desk so his feet didn't show and he laid his hands on the desk to prevent any fidgeting. Behind him, symbols of the police department hung on the wall. He gave a very effective interview.

ACTION CLIP

Cable TV

In 1985, the Oxnard, California, Police Department began airing its highly successful cable TV program *StreetBeat*. Today that program is the cable channel's most watched program. Estimates put the number of viewers at 5,000 to 8,000 weekly.

Community affairs manager David Keith credits the show's popularity to two elements: "A telephone line in the studio allows viewers at home to call in and talk to police officials live over the air and both the question and response are broadcast for the viewing audience to hear. The second element is the display of a large city map highlighting crime patterns in city limits . . . during the previous two weeks."

After a rape that drew strong public response, the program hosted a special ninety-minute program about the incident, with crime prevention and personal security information included. Subsequently, "Calls reporting suspicious activity in the area increased. Officers patrolling the area saw a corresponding decrease in crime. Disturbances, burglaries, auto theft, and car break-ins all declined. Assaults and rapes dropped as well. In fact, for the three months following the televised meeting, crime dropped nearly 90 percent in the neighborhood" (5).

Now the department regularly features one neighborhood a month. They invite viewers to attend a follow-up meeting two days later to discuss neighborhood watch programs. One hundred to 250 people turn out, and crime rates drop in the highlighted neighborhoods.

StreetBeat was honored by the National League of Cities and the International Association of Chiefs of Police, and featured on ABC News and CNN (Keith).

Setting Up a Web Home Page

Setting up a Web site is a contemporary way to let both fellow officers and community members know about your program and to receive their input. Decide what purposes you want the page to serve. Do you want to post crime prevention tips? Share crime statistics for various neighborhoods? Explain the progress of projects? Do you want to receive input from the community? Do you want make a spot available for kids to link to other sites to learn about law enforcement? Just as you do when planning a speech, determine your purpose and intended audience, and use these to guide your design.

Before you start, use resources on the Web for help. Some Web sites offer advice on page design. Look at other police sites to get ideas and see what content and designs you like. Especially check out the Blue Lightning Web Site (http://pw2.netcom.com/~bluline/blulite.html) for their list of award-winning law enforcement sites. Use these for models to help you create your Web page.

Generally, advice about Web page design contains these recurring directions:

- **Keep your design simple.** Many home computers cannot receive the fancy programs that run video or display moving graphical images. Others receive them so slowly the viewer loses interest. On the Web, speed matters. A simple design loads quickly.
- **Put key information at the top.** Place the most important information on the small section of the screen a viewer sees when the page opens. On a typical 14- to 17-inch computer monitor, this is four inches.
- **Pique the viewer's interest immediately.** Web page consultant Hal Pawluk reports that 35 to 45 percent of viewers go no farther than the first page: "If nothing useful shows in ten or twenty or even sixty seconds or more, they just go away, never to return." To avoid that, include a "headline," something that makes the viewer want to scroll down the page and even link to inner pages.
- **Use dark type on a light background.** A monitor is already 25 percent harder to read than print; don't add to the problem. Light print on a dark background is hard to read and does not print well. A pale off-white shade is best for your background because it shows print better. If you want your information circulated, you want people to print copies to share with others. Also be aware that color changes from monitor to monitor.
- **Include the basics.** Be sure to include the standard features: the latest date you updated the site, an e-mail address where you receive messages, and a link to your department's home page.

Web Sites That Offer Web Page Design Help

Blue Lightning Web Site Award for Excellence in a Law Enforcement Web Site—
http://pw2.netcom.com/~bluline/blulite.html

Hart, Lt. Fran. (Burlington, Massachusetts, Police Dept.) "How—and Why—to Implement the World-Wide Web for Community Policing." International Association of Chiefs of Police—
http://www.iacptechnology.org/TechTalk1296.htm

Pawluk, Hal. Web Site Design—http://www.pawluk.com/pages/sitedesignj.htm

Yale C/AIM Web Style Guide—
http://info.med.yale.edu/caim/manual/pages/graphic_design100.html

Police Graphics Library by Det. Sgt. Tom Bolling—
http://www.murlin.com/~webfx/cops/library2.html

Public Safety Clipart—http://www.ecnet.net/users/bomaf/art/clipart.htm.

- **Include some visual images.** Check out Detective Sgt. Tom Bolling's Police Graphics Library at http://www.murlin.com/~webfx/cops/library2.html. Also see Public Safety Clipart at http://www.ecnet.net/users/bomaf/art/clipart.htm. Both of these offer a wide array of standard police images, from badges to light bars to line drawings, that you can download for free with no copyright restrictions.
- **Change your page regularly.** People will not come back if your site does not provide updated information. Also, regularly check your links to other sites to be sure these sites are still available. Lt. Fran Hart of the Burlington, Massachusetts, Police Department, writes about law enforcement Web sites on the International Association of Chiefs of Police Web pages. Hart says, "To be effective, a site needs to be updated and modified constantly," and warns departments to plan administratively for Web changes:

> Is there someone available to do this updating? Are there funds to pay him to work on the site, or will time be allotted from the regular workday? If so, will it interfere with other duties, and how will that be reconciled? After the initial satisfaction of creating the site wears off, will there be sufficient interest to keep it going? These are all concerns that need to be addressed before committing to the project. (3)

As you look at other pages, you will get ideas for what to put on your pages. Hart suggests some initial possibilities:

- **A virtual tour of the station.** Each page tells about what happens in one room. For example, one page might show "the breath test machine. The text could explain what happens when someone is arrested for driving under the influence. The visitor not only learns about the process, but gets to see where it takes place."
- **An officer photo gallery.** "By clicking on an officer's thumbnail photograph . . . a visitor would be taken to a secondary page highlighting that particular officer" with information such as educational background, hobbies, and accomplishments.
- **A library.** Visitors could read and download safety tips.

Good sites also link to other relevant sites, including even the daily news, government offices, and nearby policing departments. If you have a site just for your community, be sure to link to your department's home page.

Internet Sites Useful for Community Policing

Community Resources

Alliance for Redesigning Government—
http://www.alliance.napawash.org/alliance/index.html
Community Policing Links—http://www.communitypolicing.org/links.html
Community Renewal Resource Listings—http://www.ncl.org/anr/crrl6.htm
Global Ideas Bank—Crime and the Law—http://www.newciv.org
Neighborhoods Online—http://www.libertynet.org/nol/natl.html
National Crime Prevention Council—http://www.ncpc.org/about.htm
National Crime Prevention Council, Canada—
http://www.crime-prevention.org/ncpc/what_is/

Law Enforcement Resources

Coalition of Hispanic American Police Associations—
http://claraweb.co.santa-clara.ca.us/sheriff/chapa.htm
Community Policing Consortium—http://www.communitypolicing.org/
Complete Directory of Law Enforcement Agencies—
http://www.officer.com/feds.htm
COPNet and Police Resource List—http://www.cop.net
International Association of Chiefs of Police (IACP)—
http://www.iacptechnology.org/iacp.htm
International Association of Women Police—http://www.iawp.org/contitut.htm
Law Enforcement Information Management Resource Center—
http://www.iacptechnology.org/menu.htm
Law Enforcement Sites on the Web—http://www.ih2000.net/ira/htm
National Center for Community Policing, Michigan State University—
http://www.ssc.msu.edu/~cj/cp/cptoc.html
National Sheriffs' Association (NSA)—http://www.sheriffs.org/
National Organization of Black Law Enforcement Executives (NOBLE)—
http://www.noblenatl.org/index.htm
Police Executive Research Forum—http://www.policeforum.org (Check Pop Net)
POP Network, an Internet bulletin board restricted to police officers, sponsored by the Police Executive Research Forum at http://www.policeforum.org/popnet.
Regional Community Policing Institutes—http://rcpi.ilj.org/index.htm
U.S. Dept. of Justice Office of Community Oriented Policing Services—
http://www.usdoj.gov/cops

Publications

Community Policing Exchange—http://www.communitypolicing.org/exchange/
Community Links—http://www.communitypolicing.org/comlinks/
Sheriff Times—http://www.communitypolicing.org/shtimes/
All three are publications of the Community Policing Consortium, 1726 M St., NW, Suite 801, Washington, DC 20036, phone 202-833-3305; fax 202-833-9295
Problem Solving Quarterly. Publication of the Police Executive Research Forum. 1120 Conn. Ave. NW, Suite 930, Washington, DC 20036, 202-466-7820; fax 202-466-7826 (not yet online).

Have Fun Out There

In 1936, August Vollmer, considered by many to be the father of modern policing, wrote:

> Policemen should realize their own limitations, and learn to lean heavily upon community leaders and the character-building forces in the city. There is so much these instrumentalities can do that is not done today. Policemen who give talks to school children, sponsor athletic clubs and events, become leaders of boys' and girls' groups, cultivate the friendship of children, and in other ways act like big brothers, are valuable to any police force. (197)

More than sixty years later, Vollmer's admonitions have moved to center stage in the form of community policing. As law enforcement professionals, you are in a service business that is more than just enforcing the laws. You are asked to be marriage and family counselors, serve as chaplains in times of crisis, remain emotionless in times of pain and discomfort, find housing for the homeless and food for the hungry, and throughout all the chaos maintain a smile and a friendly demeanor. You represent your agency and your community. You are on the front line of societal change, a change driven by community leaders who have announced, "We've had enough and we don't have to take it anymore. Our communities belong to us and not the drug dealers and other criminals."

Community policing has ushered in an exciting time for everyone in law enforcement. Increased communication with community members, business, and government provides rewarding interactions and the freedom to meet problems head on, rather than just cleaning up after them. However, increased communication does not automatically mean better communication. Good intentions are not enough. Not only must you communicate, you must communicate well.

Good communication takes practice. It is a skill, just as firing a weapon is a skill. Practice improves your aim and your execution. Practice in communication, coupled with information about communication, will improve your communication skills. Gradually you will master and grow more comfortable in various communication settings. Keep practicing, keep learning, and be as creative as possible.

As you advance in your profession, take advantage of opportunities to learn more about communication and community policing. Find out what is happening in other cities. Ideally, attend conferences that enable you to talk with other officers. If that is not possible, keep up with the latest information in print and on the Internet. A number of police Web sites have online chat rooms reserved exclusively for law enforcement personnel. Take advantage of this new way to stay current.

One more thing—don't forget to have *fun*!

Works Cited

Bickel, Harold, and Gregory Dieckmann. "New Life in Sacramento Apartment Communities: Part Two." *Problem-Solving Quarterly* 10 (Spring/Summer 1997): 1–7.

Hart, Fran. "How—and Why—to Implement the World-Wide Web for Community Policing." International Association of Chiefs of Police. http://www.iacptechnology.org/TechTalk1296.htm. 9 July 1998.

Johnson, Craig E., and Michael Z. Hackman. *Creative Communication: Principles and Applications*. Prospect Heights, Ill.: Waveland Press, 1995.

Keith, David. "Cable Television: A Medium Too Important to Ignore." *Community Policing Exchange*. July/Aug. 1998: 5.

McClure, James. *Cop World*. New York: Pantheon, 1984.

National Crime Prevention Council. "Training and Tools: Partnering with the Media." http://www.ncpc.org/4work2dc.htm. 17 June 1998.

Newton, Steven J. "Special Glasses Simulate Intoxication, Dissuade Alcohol Abuse." *Community Policing Exchange*. Jan./Feb. 1998: 2.

Pawluk, Hal. Web Site Design. http://www.pawluk.com/pages/sitedesignj.htm. 21 June 1998.

Riggs, Troy. "Media Outlets Broadcast Fugitive Profiles, Capture Criminals." *Community Policing Exchange*. July/Aug. 1998: 4.

Michael Schudson. *The Power of News*. Cambridge: Harvard Press, 1995.

Vollmer, August. *The Police and Modern Society.* 1936. Montclair, N.J.: Patterson Smith, 1971.

Activities

1 Practice Speaking Succinctly

Read several news stories that involve police in your local paper. Prepare to be interviewed on each topic. Reduce what you have to say to about seven words. Do this for at least five different stories.

2 Media Advisory

A bunco scheme is working in a nearby city. You fear it will come to your community and you want the media to help expose it. Plan a press conference to get out the word. What will you offer TV for video? Who can provide radio sound bites? What additional information will the press want? Write a media advisory to announce the press conference. Then write a press release to hand out at the press conference.

3 Visual Coverage

The neighborhood you work in has focused its attention on making the neighborhood park safe again for the senior citizens who live in an apartment complex across the street from it. The community has worked together to clean up litter, plant flowers, and keep loitering teens and bums away. Saturday evening, the neighborhood will gather for cookies and soda and general festivities. Think of three different ways you could make this event unique and visual to draw television coverage.

4 The Reporter's Task

Consider a successful project in another community that you have heard mentioned. You want to tell your fellow officers about this program. Make a list of questions you have about what else you would like to know to pass on. This is the role of the reporter. Using this as a guide, make a list of what you could tell local reporters about your program.

5 Organization Newsletters

Select three major organizations in your city or community. Call each, ask for the information office, and request a copy of their newsletter. Read these. Write three safety tips you could provide the employees of these organizations. Send these to them.

6 Web Surfing

Visit six different city police department Web sites. Look for Community Policing pages. E-mail the Webmasters to ask for advice on creating your own home page.

Glossary

active listening – the listener takes in the speaker's words, subtle tones, facial expressions, timing, and other nonverbal elements, then feeds back to the speaker what he or she has heard.

agenda – a schedule of items to be discussed at a work group meeting, listed in the order they are to be discussed, the meeting location, starting and ending times, and a contact number to reach you.

analogy – a statement about how objects, persons, situations, or actions are similar in process or relationship to one another; can be used as a stimulus for creative ideas.

analysis – the fourth step in the SARA model of problem solving that involves identifying as many elements of a problem as possible in an attempt to unearth causes.

artifacts – objects that convey messages.

assessment – the second step in the SARA model of problem solving that involves evaluating a strategy's effectiveness to see if a solution is working.

attackers – people in meetings who attack ideas or the people staging the meeting.

attribute listing – a creativity technique based on identifying various attributes of an item or action, then changing one or more attributes as a way to improve the item or action.

attribution – the tendency people have to attribute specific motivations to others' behavior.

avoiding – a conflict resolution technique in which people repress their own views or withdraw from interaction.

beat meetings – meetings of a small group of neighbors in one police beat, frequently led by an officer, for the purposes of informing one another about crime in their area.

blocks – beliefs and habits that squelch creativity.

brainstorming – a technique for generating ideas involving withholding judgment, throwing out ideas in random order, building on one another's ideas, and seeking quantity.

brainwriting – a technique for generating ideas involving a group writing ideas down and using others' written ideas as spurs for more ideas.

breakout groups – smaller meetings designed for discussion or presentation of ideas; they usually follow a larger group meeting, which is subdivided into breakout groups.

buzz group – a discussion format that divides an audience into smaller groups who discuss a specific issue for a limited time.

channel – a medium used to convey messages.

character – a dimension of credibility; character reflects a person's honor.

coercive power – an individual's ability to withhold rewards or to actively punish people.

cohesiveness – an esprit de corps or group loyalty, the degree of liking members have for each other, and their commitment to the group.

collaborating – a conflict resolution technique in which people seek solutions that will satisfy all sides in a conflict.

collaboratives – work groups in which a variety of social agencies work together to solve problems as a condition of receiving funds.

collectivist cultures – cultures in which members will repress their personal desires in order that the group may succeed or have unity.

community fair – a community meeting format in which people visit tables or booths scattered about a room seeking the information they want and sharing their opinions; also known as an open house.

community meeting – meetings that are open to the public and revolve around discussion of public issues for the purpose of information exchange or problem solving; alternately known as a forum, town-hall meeting, public hearing, public meeting, or advisory meeting.

community oriented government (COG) – a philosophy that mirrors community oriented policing by promoting government–community partnerships that focus on community-identified quality-of-life issues.

community oriented policing (COP) – a philosophy that promotes police–community partnerships; a way of doing business that focuses on the community's identified quality-of-life issues.

compromise – a conflict resolution technique in which people seek ways each side can give up something to get something.

confederate – someone from another culture who will explain to you how the culture communicates.

confirming response – a response to a person or message in which the respondent shows regard for the speaker by acknowledging his or her views, attitudes, and feelings.

conflict (phase in groups) – the third phase of group evolution in which group members express differences of opinion about the decision a group should make or the direction in which the group should go.

connotative meaning – the definitions people assign a word based on the emotional implications of the word.

content component – the topic or subject of a message, what a speaker talks about.

context – prescribes what is appropriate for one person to say to another given the positions they hold and the situation they are in, and thus heavily influences what meaning a listener will give the message.

creative process – the process through which creativity seems to progress, including the four stages of preparation, incubation, illumination, and verification.

cynics – people who doubt community efforts will come to fruition.

decoding – taking a message and translating it into meaning.

defensive climate – a condition in which people feel threatened and under attack, and consequently become cautious, unwilling to share, alienated, closed, and may withdraw.

delivery – how the speaker talks, stands, and gestures, as opposed to the actual content of the talk.

denotative meaning – the dictionary meaning of a word.

deserters – people who gradually abandon a work group.

direct statements – statements that overtly express what a person means to say.

disconfirming response – a response to a person or message that implies that the person responding does not value or confirm the speaker.

discounting – a response to a message that denies the importance of the problem and attributes other causes to the speaker's remarks.

dominators – people in meetings who talk more than a reasonable amount.

dynamism – a dimension of credibility; dynamism can be thought of as personal characteristics of charm, magnetism, and energy.

emergence – the third phase of a work group's progress in which dissent lessens and a decision is reached.

empathy – the process of seeing and feeling things as another does.

empty promisers – people who respond to ideas with excitement and energy and make promises for contributions, and who then do nothing about them.

encoding – translating thoughts into verbal and nonverbal codes.

expert power – a person's ability to influence as a result of knowledge or experience.

expertise – a dimension of credibility, expertise is how well a person performs and what he or she knows.

eye contact – a speaker and a listener looking directly at one another.

facilitator – a person skilled in interpersonal relations and conflict resolution who can moderate a meeting between two historically hostile groups.

feedback – information that is fed back to the source from the receiver; the receiver's responses to the messages of the source.

flight taking – group members' tendency to ignore issue conflict in the name of harmony, pretending nothing is wrong and suppressing their ideas and opinions to retain a superficial group unity.

force field analysis – a creativity technique based on identifying forces working toward success in a problem, which you can potentially strengthen, and forces working against success, which you can potentially weaken.

forcing – a conflict resolution technique in which people attempt to force others to accept their ideas or opinions by arguing, providing evidence, shouting, power plays, manipulation, or threats.

format – the particular arrangement of information and presenters by which a community meeting is conducted.

gatekeeper – a person who receives a message from a source and determines the distribution to others.

groupthink – a condition of blind conformity that occurs when group members strive for excessive unanimity at the expense of clear thinking.

hidden agenda – people's secret goals or private purposes at a meeting.

high-context cultures – cultures in which the situation and the roles of the individuals involved carry much of the message.

hostile audience – an audience that is angry, emotional, and potentially out of control.

I-speaking – verbally taking responsibility for your positions, opinions, and values, rather than generalizing, rendering judgments or blaming others; also known as personalizing.

ice breakers – techniques to use at the beginning of group gatherings to relax the group members or audience and help them feel comfortable working together.

illumination – a point in the creative process in which an insight into the problem, or a solution to it, suddenly appears.

incongruous response – a response to a message that occurs when a person says one thing and does another.

incubation – the time period in the creative process in which a person gets away from a problem and allows the unconscious mind to work on it.

individualistic cultures – cultures that value self-development, unique traits, critical thinking, and individual achievement.

intercultural communication – the communication between members of different cultures.

interpersonal communication – communication in which the message would change if the participants changed; the relationship dimension is at the fore.

intimate distance – how close one person stands to another when talking intimately; in mainstream United States, zero to eighteen inches.

introduction – the beginning of a talk, in which the speaker seeks to develop rapport with the audience, establish credibility, and arouse audience interest in the topic.

irrelevant response – a reply that does not relate in any way to the message to which it responds.

legitimate power – the power the law or culture gives one person over another.

long-winded monopolizers – people in groups and community meetings who talk at length.

low-context cultures – cultures in which meaning depends primarily on spoken language rather than context.

media advisory – a short announcement sent out before a meeting, press conference, or special event to alert the press and pique their interest.

media packet – a folder of information about an event; usually includes a news release, photographs, background information, statistics, and possibly a statement from the police chief or a community leader.

media releases – information sent to newspapers, television, and radio announcing events.

message cues – sounds, symbols, and behavior a listener recognizes as words or meaningful action, and assigns meaning.

metaphors – a figure of speech in which one thing is described as if it were another.

mindmapping – a technique for recording and organizing ideas in a visual format by placing a word or symbol for your problem in the center of a page, then writing solutions and elements that occur to you on lines radiating out from the problem.

mini open house – after an informational presentation at a community meeting, presenters move to selected spots around the room and audience members circulate, asking questions or offering comments to the speakers one-on-one.

Monroe's Motivated Sequence – a way to organizing a persuasive speech involving five steps: getting attention, establishing a need, showing how a solution will satisfy that need, visualizing the situation once the preferred solution is in effect, and making a final call to action.

multimedia presentation – a presentation involving film, video, slide shows, or audio.

Neighborhood Watch – a gathering of ten to twenty neighbors from a one- or two-block area who are devoted to stopping crime in their area.

news release – a short news story describing a news event; sometimes called a press release.

noise – anything that interferes with a listener's attention to a message.

nominal group technique (NGT) – a problem-solving format for discussion and decision making in which participants in small groups proceed through a tightly structured process that produces a ranked list of ideas.

nonverbal codes – communication exchanges in a form other than speech.

nonverbal feedback – behavioral cues that indicate how a listener is responding to a message.

norms – appropriate or normal behavior for a group of people.

one-way communication – a message format when the speaker sends a message, and the listener has no avenue to respond.

open dialogue – a meeting between two groups called to address the specific problem of lack of trust between them in the hopes of building a bridge between the groups.

open forum – a community meeting format that allows any audience member to speak on an issue.

open house – see *community fair*.

opposed audience – an audience that believes a different position than the speaker.

orientation – the first phase of a work group meeting, in which group members get to know one another and explore the range of their task.

Osborn's checklist – a technique to stimulate creative ideas by focusing on ways to augment or change a basic situation through the use of nine base terms: magnify, minify, modify, rearrange, reverse, combine, substitute, adapt, and put to other uses.

panel discussion – a community meeting format in which a number of speakers discuss a common issue with the guidance of a moderator.

paraphrasing – a listener restating in his or her own words the speaker's words and feelings.

personal distance – how close people stand when conversing with friends and acquaintances; in the mainstream United States, eighteen inches to four feet.

personal interest – a person with a cause to support who loses focus on the group's overall goal.

personal space – the distance a person must maintain between himself or herself and another to feel comfortable when conversing.

personalize messages – verbally taking responsibility for your positions, opinions, and values, rather than generalizing, rendering judgments, or blaming others; also known as I speaking.

phatic communication – simple relational messages designed to maintain human contact without much content, generally conveyed in phrases such as "Hi," "How are you?" "Nice day."

Phillips 66 – a technique that divides an audience into six-person groups to discuss a topic for six minutes and come to some conclusion to share with a larger assembly.

physical noise – external elements that interfere with receiving a message.

physiological noise – internal elements, such as your physical condition, that interfere with receiving a message.

planning team – people who represent the various interests and audiences you want at a community meeting.

power struggles – people vying for unspoken positions of influence or status in groups.

powwow – a technique that helps people working on a project get to know one another.

preparation – the first stage of the creative process, involving researching a problem and gathering information about it.

preview statement – an overview of what a speaker intends to accomplish in a talk.

primary tension – a state of mild anxiety at the beginning of a group meeting that comes from not knowing what to expect socially.

psychological noise – a distraction that interferes with receiving a message caused by your own thoughts.

public distance – the personal distance at which interaction turns from personal to public; in mainstream United States, twelve feet and beyond.

public interview – a community meeting format in which an interviewer asks questions that one or more speakers answer.

public service announcement (PSA) – short radio and TV announcements to promote public service projects.

receiver – the person to whom a message is sent.

recognition seekers – people in groups and community meetings who tell entertaining, but irrelevant, accounts of personal adventures at great length, diverting attention away from the task in unproductive ways.

redundancy – repeating your message in a number of ways.

referent power – the influence a person or group has because he or she is admired or respected or attractive.

reflective feedback – paraphrasing that consists of three parts: acknowledging whose problem you are discussing, reflecting the emotions of the speaker, and summarizing the facts under discussion.

reflective thinking – an agenda format for problem-solving discussion involving a systematic, five-step procedure: (1) define and analyze the problem; (2) list possible solutions; (3) weigh alternative solutions; (4) select the best solution; and (5) implement the solution.

reinforcement – the final phase of a work group in which people develop unity and become committed to a decision.

relational component – the part of a message that conveys the relationship between the speaker and the listener.

response – the third step in the SARA model of problem solving that involves finding and implementing long-term, creative solutions to problems.

revolving speakers – a format for community meetings in which those who attend form small audiences, and speakers rotate from group to group presenting and receiving information.

reward power – the ability to compensate people through money, awards, appreciation, friendship, position, and so on.

ridicule – a response to a message that discounts or makes fun of either a speaker's position or the speaker's level of concern about it.

SARA – a process for dealing with chronic crime problems; the process involves four steps: scanning, analysis, response, and assessment.

SCAMPER – a mnemonic created from Alex Osborn's checklist of terms to generate creative ideas. SCAMPER stands for substitute, combine, adapt, modify or magnify, put to other uses, eliminate, and reverse or rearrange.

scanning – the first step in the SARA model of problem solving that involves examining a problem situation in order to identify recurring patterns such as time or location.

smoothing – a conflict resolution technique in which people try to minimize the impact of conflict by pretending it is less severe than it is and giving in for the sake of interpersonal relationships.

social dimension – how people in groups relate to one another; sometimes referred to as the socio-emotional component or the climate.

social distance – how close people stand when conversing in business and social gatherings; in mainstream United States, four to twelve feet.

source – the person who creates a message to send.

stage fright – anxiety about presenting information in public.

stage hogs – people in meetings whose personal agenda is to get attention.

supportive climate – a communication environment in which individuals feel comfortable speaking out, tolerate differences, and are likely to engage in honest dialogue.

symposium – a series of sequential speeches around one topic from a number of speakers.

synergy – a positive result of group work, where the combined efforts of all the group members are greater than the sum total of individual efforts of members.

target audience – the primary audience you want to reach with a program or message, typically people affected by the issues to be discussed.

task dimension – the actual content or business of a group meeting; the task to be accomplished.

team – a group of people with a specific objective or goal who coordinate their activity to reach a goal.

tension relief – ways a group releases the tension arising from differences of opinion and conflict, including joking, telling stories, asking with concern about each other's problems, getting off the subject, and so forth.

territoriality – the use of physical space to convey relational messages such as power, friendship, and so on.

two-way communication – a message format when the speaker and listener interact about a message.

verbal codes – communication exchanges in the form of words.

verbal feedback – formal or informal, spoken or written statements or questions that indicate how a listener perceives your message.

verification – the final stage of the creative process, in which a solution is tested by discussion, considering implications, and putting it into place.

visual aid – visual demonstrations that support a verbal presentation.

work group – a small number of people meeting for a specific purpose such as to make a decision about an issue; also known as a task-oriented small group, decision-making small group, or committee; and depending on the task may be called a task force, board of directors, multi-agency team, crew, jury, strategy-planning session, or departmental staff meeting.

Index

A

B

C

D

E

N

O

P

Q

R

S

T

U

V

W

CPSIA information can be obtained at www.ICGtesting.com
Printed in the USA
BVOW06s0928270813

329568BV00003B/10/P

9 780965 502931